Praise for *jQuery, jQuery UI, and jQuery Mobile*

"de Jonge and Dutson's cookbook approach to jQuery, jQuery UI, and jQuery Mobile teaches how to create sophisticated projects quickly, removing all the guesswork. They really make jQuery seem effortless!"

—*Joseph Annuzzi, Jr., Web architect, PeerDynamic.com*

"This book is great for all aspects of jQuery development; it has it all, from a great UI section down to the most current tech, which is mobile. I found myself referencing this book numerous times for projects I am currently working on.

"This book will be excellent for anyone who is eager to learn more about jQuery and what the capabilities are. The authors put the learning in terms that anyone can understand and build from."

—*Erik Levanger, UI UX engineer*

"I have often said that when it comes to jQuery, half the battle is just being familiar with the types of things it is capable of doing. Having a good foundation can easily help you bridge the gap between 'This is going to be complicated' and 'I can do that with jQuery!' Like any good recipe book, this book includes ready-to-use code samples that demonstrate basic to advanced techniques. In addition to the major areas noted in the book title, there are references on how to customize the jQuery UI features to meet your needs and bonus sections about creating and using plugins. I also really appreciate the authors' insights regarding performance issues and best practices. Lastly, speaking as someone with no previous jQuery Mobile experience, this book provides solid examples to get you up and running fast. Overall, this book will help to greatly expand the skills in your jQuery arsenal."

—*Ryan Minnick, software developer, Verizon Wireless*

"The ultimate cookbook for anyone using jQuery, jQuery UI, or jQuery Mobile."

—*Stretch Nate, Web applications developer, HealthPlan Services*

"Through easy-to-understand recipes, de Jonge and Dutson give the reader a practical introduction to all things jQuery, from the most basic selectors to advanced topics, such as plugin authoring and jQuery Mobile. A great starting point for anyone interested in one of the most powerful JavaScript libraries."

—*Jacob Seidelin, Web developer, Nihilogic*

jQuery, jQuery UI, and jQuery Mobile

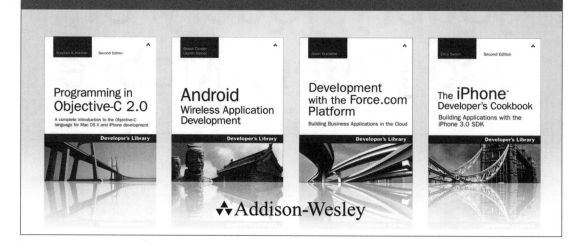

jQuery, jQuery UI, and jQuery Mobile

Recipes and Examples

Adriaan de Jonge

Phil Dutson

✦✦Addison-Wesley

Upper Saddle River, NJ • Boston • Indianapolis • San Francisco
New York • Toronto • Montreal • London • Munich • Paris • Madrid
Capetown • Sydney • Tokyo • Singapore • Mexico City

The publisher offers excellent discounts on this book when ordered in quantity for bulk purchases or special sales, which may include electronic versions and/or custom covers and content particular to your business, training goals, marketing focus, and branding interests. For more information, please contact

U.S. Corporate and Government Sales
(800) 382-3419
corpsales@pearsontechgroup.com

For sales outside the United States, please contact

International Sales
international@pearsoned.com

Visit us on the Web: informit.com/aw

Cataloging-in-Publication Data is on file with the Library of Congress.

ISBN-13: 978-0-321-82208-6
ISBN-10:   0-321-82208-0
Text printed in the United States on recycled paper at RR Donnelley in Crawfordsville, Indiana.
First printing, November 2012

Editor-in-Chief
Mark Taub

Acquisitions Editor
Laura Lewin

Development Editor
Sheri Cain

Managing Editor
John Fuller

Full-Service Production Manager
Julie B. Nahil

Copy Editor
Octal Publishing, Inc.

Indexer
Ted Laux

Proofreader
Diana Coe

Technical Reviewers
Joseph Annuzzi
Jacob Seidelin

Editorial Assistant
Olivia Basegio

Cover Designer
Chuti Prasertsith

Compositor
LaurelTech

❖

To my loving and supportive girlfriend, Christine Kam.
—Adriaan

To my mom, who taught me to love books; my dad, who taught me to love technology; and my family, who supports my indulgence of both.
—Phil

❖

Contents at a Glance

Contents

III: Mobile   183

8 Changing the Look and Feel   185

Preface

When JavaScript first hit the Internet scene, it was quickly disregarded by experts as a toy suitable for diversion and useless for user interaction. Today, it is the driving force that helps create rich user interfaces, seamless data integration, and client-side support.

Although everything is possible using plain JavaScript, many have discovered the use of various libraries and frameworks to help them do more. jQuery is the perfect library to fill the need for JavaScript integration. The motto of jQuery is *write less, do more*. This is something the jQuery team takes very seriously. Whether you are working on a standard desktop site that needs a little DOM modification, or you're adding your own custom set of controls, or even if you're handling mobile devices, the jQuery team has a library that has been handcrafted and tested on as many platforms, browsers, and devices as possible to ensure the very best experience for both the developer and the user.

Why a Recipe and Example Book on jQuery?

Some have been quick to say that if you know CSS, you know how to use jQuery, but this isn't entirely true. Although having this knowledge certainly helps one to understand the selector engine in jQuery, there are so many extra functions to help manipulate, calculate, and add interaction to your site that a book is simply a must-have to ensure that you are aware of the amazing things that jQuery can do. A recipe and example book is essential because it not only informs you about the functions that you can use, but it also gives you self-contained examples that work with quick explanations to point out the tricky parts or confusing areas.

The inclusion of the jQuery UI and jQuery Mobile libraries makes this book a superior reference guide; now you can easily learn about the other libraries that the jQuery team has made and see how they can fit together to make your next project a seamless, crowd-pleasing success.

Who This Book Is For

Those who have a working knowledge of HTML, CSS, and basic JavaScript should feel at home picking this book up and starting to work through the examples. Those not familiar with Web development might need a little extra time to get up to speed with what is presented here. That having been said, those who learn well by seeing the full HTML page layout with the required script to make the example run will learn quickly and efficiently.

How to Use This Book

Each recipe and example is a set of self-contained scripts that can be loaded onto your favorite Web server and accessed from your browser. Although it is possible to run some of the examples by dropping or loading the example code directly in your browser, any examples that use AJAX will fail, so using a Web server is highly recommended.

When finished reading this book, you should

- Be comfortable adding jQuery to your Web projects
- Understand the differences among jQuery core, jQuery UI, and jQuery Mobile
- Be familiar with the basic functionality and functions of jQuery core
- Be proficient adding styles and widgets, and interacting with the user through jQuery core and jQuery UI
- Be able to create a mobile site by using the jQuery Mobile library
- Be comfortable creating your own plugin and incorporating it into your site
- Be able to add third-party plugins such as those from the Twitter Bootstrap framework

Book Structure

Chapters 1 through 5 cover the jQuery core library. Chapter 1 gives an introduction to the basic usage and how to include jQuery along with setting up arrays, using data attributes, and testing browser feature support. Chapter 2 covers how to fine-tune your element selection from the DOM. Chapter 3 teaches how jQuery can help manipulate the DOM structure of your site. Chapter 4 takes a tour of event handling with jQuery and covers the difference between binding in jQuery versions 1.6 and 1.7. Chapter 5 shows you how to communicate with a Web server, including working with AJAX, page errors, page redirects, and XML.

Chapters 6 through 8 cover the usage of the jQuery UI library. Chapter 6 demonstrates the additional functionality that jQuery UI brings, such as draggable, droppable, and sortable objects. Chapter 7 covers using the widgets, including accordions, auto-complete, buttons, date pickers, dialogs, progress bars, sliders, and tab components. Chapter 8 takes on the styles and theme of the jQuery UI along with effects and transitions.

Chapters 9 and 10 give a course on using the jQuery Mobile library. Chapter 9 starts with the basics of setting up a mobile site and covers page structure, page loading, and page transition and animation. Chapter 10 covers the additional widgets and styles that jQuery Mobile provides, including navigation bars, sliders, flip switches, and form elements.

Chapters 11 and 12 cover the use of plugins. Chapter 11 provides a comprehensive overview of what a plugin consists of and how to create your own with method handling and function chaining. Chapter 12 gives examples of using trusted third-party plugins from the Twitter Bootstrap framework to add extra functionality and style to your project.

Additional Resources

There are many places that you can learn more about jQuery, jQuery UI, and jQuery Mobile. The official sites themselves offer excellent documentation and explain the choices behind deprecating code and give hints and warnings about upcoming features.

Here are some helpful sites that you should visit:

- jQuery API docs: http://api.jquery.com/
- jQuery UI docs: http://jqueryui.com/demos/
- jQuery Mobile docs: http://jquerymobile.com/demos/
- Twitter Bootstrap JavaScript docs: http://twitter.github.com/bootstrap/javascript.html
- Zurb Foundation docs: http://foundation.zurb.com/docs/
- jQuery Tools: http://jquerytools.org/
- Stack Overflow forums: http://stackoverflow.com/

Acknowledgments

First of all, I would like to thank Phil Dutson for joining this book project and helping to finish it before the deadline. In addition to Laura Lewin, Olivia Basegio, Sheri Cain, Jacob Seidelin, and Joseph Annuzzi—as mentioned by Phil—I would also like to thank Trina MacDonald, who started this book project at Pearson.

I would like to say thanks to my colleagues, both at my former employer, ANWB, and my new employer, Xebia, for giving me inspiration and great ideas. I love working with people who share the same interest in new technologies!

I am thankful for my family and friends who encourage me wherever I go. And in particular, I am happy and blessed with my girlfriend, Christine Kam. Thank you for your unconditional support!

—Adriaan

I'd like to thank Adriaan de Jonge who started this project and was gracious enough to allow me to help him finish it. I also want to recognize all of the hard work and countless hours put into this project by the amazing team at Pearson. Thanks go to Laura Lewin who brought me onto the project; Olivia Basegio for coordinating everything; Sheri Cain for correcting the flow and helping structure the visual representation of the material; my absolutely brilliant tech editors Joseph Annuzzi and Jacob Seidelin, who not only made sure that the code runs properly, but that the explanations about why it runs were clear and accurate. Thanks also go to Bob Russell of Octal Publishing, Inc., for his commendable copyediting prowess and Julie Nahil at Pearson for all of the coordination during the production process.

I also want to thank my designer friends from UltraCube (Alan Lawrence, Jake Stuart, Candis Sorenson, Kaylee White, and Jen Lewis) who constantly remind me that life is whatever you make of it, and my current e-commerce team (Tracy Cox, Brett Wood, Ryan Jensen, Remo Galli, Eric Barnett, and Chris Lewis) who remind me to always make sure you are doing the things you love.

—Phil

About the Authors

Adriaan de Jonge works as a Consultant for Xebia IT Architects in The Netherlands. Adriaan specializes in Internet, content management, and Java. He is interested in new technologies such as MongoDB, Node.js, HTML5, and various cloud-computing platforms. Adriaan is also the author of *Essential App Engine* (Addison-Wesley, 2012) and several articles for IBM developerWorks on Java, XML, and Internet technologies. He has experience as a conference speaker at JFall 2011 and the Scandinavian Developer Conference in 2012.

Phil Dutson is the lead front-end developer for ICON Health and Fitness. He has worked on projects and solutions for NordicTrack, ProForm, Freemotion, Sears, Costco, Sam's Club, and others. He was an original team member of the iFit team that integrated Google Maps into personalized workout creation and playback. Phil co-founded and currently manages *The E-Com DevBlog*, a development blog focused on Web development and solutions. To learn more visit http://dev.tonic1394.com. He is also the author of *Sams Teach Yourself jQuery Mobile in 24 Hours* (Sams, 2013).

PART I

Core

Chapter 1

Getting Started with jQuery

The motto of jQuery is *write less, do more.* And by using the jQuery library, you can get started doing exactly that with nothing more than your favorite text editor.

This chapter starts with a *hello world*–like recipe to cover the basics, it discusses the fundamentals of the $ function and how to prevent conflicts with other libraries.

To ensure that your own code is just as concise as that of jQuery, the library offers a set of helper functions. This chapter covers the most important functions, which are designed to help you to eliminate useless boilerplate code or perform common tasks efficiently. You will see many of these functions being used in the following chapters.

Recipe: Introducing the Basic Usage of jQuery

jQuery helps you to clearly separate HTML and JavaScript. Instead of mixing the HTML with a large number of `onclick` attributes, jQuery selects all the elements that need to respond to a `click` event and binds a handler function. Listing 1.1 covers the basics of accessing HTML elements from JavaScript code and binding event handlers.

Listing 1.1 **Introducing the Basic Usage of jQuery**

```
00 <!DOCTYPE html>
01
02 <html lang="en">
03 <head>
04   <title>Introduction</title>
05   <style>
06   /*
07     CSS Style sheets are only inline to keep the
08     code examples together for readability. When
09     using this code in production, please
10     externalize all style sheets.
11   */
12   .myclass {
13     background-color: black;
```

(Continues)

Listing 1.1   **Introducing the Basic Usage of jQuery (Continued)**

```
14      color: white;
15    }
16    </style>
17 </head>
18 <body>
19
20 <h1>Introduction</h1>
21
22 <p>The HTML in the examples is kept as simple as
23   possible.</p>
24
25 <p class="myclass">This is a placeholder for content</p>
26
27 <p id="myid">You can click on this paragraph</p>
28
29 <script src="http://code.jquery.com/jquery-1.7.2.min.js"></script>
30
31 <script>
32 // JavaScripts are only inline to keep the code
33 // examples together for readability. When using
34 // this code in production, please externalize
35 // all JavaScript code.
36
37 $(document).ready(function() {
38
39   $('p').css('font-weight', 'bold');
40
41   $('.myclass').html('Different <em>content</em>');
42
43   $('#myid').click(function() {
44     alert('Hello world!');
45   });
46
47 });
48 </script>
49 </body>
50 </html>
```

Caution

As a rule, you should avoid having any CSS and JavaScript within the HTML. This book breaks that rule for the sake of readability, in an effort to keep all the code of one example together. However, normally you should put your scripts in external JavaScript files and refer to them in the same way as line 29 refers to the jQuery library.

Except for the `script` element, the HTML is clean from JavaScript. The HTML contains a few pointers that make the elements easier to find for jQuery. These are the `class` and the `id`.

jQuery can be loaded from a Content Delivery Network (CDN) and included so as to always point to the latest version of jQuery. This can be done by loading the script from http://code.jquery.com/jquery-latest.min.js. You can find a list of CDN providers at http://docs.jquery.com/Downloading_jQuery. By always including the latest version of jQuery, you ensure that your site upgrades to the latest versions of jQuery automatically. For minor versions, this is advantageous because bugs and security risks are quickly eliminated. For major upgrades, you should ensure that you remove calls to deprecated APIs before a new version removes them. Some developers prefer to defer upgrading to new major versions of software until a first bug fix update is released.

Notice that scripts are loaded at the bottom of the page. This allows the browser to render all HTML before loading the script elements. The scripts would still work if they were placed on top of the page; however, the perceived loading time would be longer. This is generally due to request blocking, wherein the browser is unable to fetch more than a few files at a time, and thus it will actually stop page rendering until the download of the requested files is complete.

Even though the code is positioned at the bottom of the page, it is a good practice to bind the basic JavaScript calls to the `ready` event of the `document`, as you can see in line 37. This way, you can ensure that the page is done rendering before executing the code.

The Introduction stated that jQuery is used to separate HTML and JavaScript in a friendly way. Without jQuery, it would take more code to achieve the same result. HTML that is free of JavaScript also loads faster. If the HTML contains many `onclick` attributes, each time the browser reads an `onclick`, it will pause rendering and interpret the JavaScript. If your web application grows, rendering all of the HTML at once—without interruption and binding the events later—is faster.

The HTML adopts some parts of HTML5 but does not yet use all of the new element names to avoid compatibility problems on older browsers. For that same reason, this book uses HTML rather than XHTML.

Line 39 works on all paragraph elements in the document and changes a CSS property. Changing CSS properties this way is not recommended. This book uses the `css()` function mostly to indicate which elements are selected. Line 41 selects a paragraph of class `myclass` and changes its HTML by means of the `.html()` function. This allows you to either get or change the contents of the selector. Finally, line 43 selects a paragraph with id `myid` and binds a click handler that displays an alert box with *Hello World*.

The selectors in lines 39, 41, and 43 are CSS selectors. jQuery supports the majority of CSS3 selectors and adds its own extensions. The simpler and more standard the selections are, the faster they can perform. Selectors are covered in greater detail in Chapter 2, "Selecting Elements."

Recipe: Using jQuery with Other Libraries

jQuery's use of the $ function name might seem odd if you are used to other programming languages. In many languages, $ is reserved and cannot be used as a variable name on its own. As a result, it seems like the $ is part of a language rather than a library.

JavaScript allows $ as a variable name or as a function name, or as a variable name that points to a function, or to an object. As a result, many JavaScript libraries use the $ as a shorthand notation for important functions.

jQuery uses the $ as an alias for jQuery. This means that you can use the longer variable name jQuery when you call jQuery functions. Listing 1.2 demonstrates how jQuery helps you to avoid naming clashes with other libraries.

Listing 1.2 **Assigning the $ to a Different Function**

```
00 <!DOCTYPE html>
01
02 <html lang="en">
03 <head>
04   <title>$.noConflict()</title>
05 </head>
06 <body>
07
08 <p>This example shows how to mix jQuery with non-jQuery code
09    that uses the $ as a function name. Click on this paragraph
10    to test it.</p>
11
12 <script src="http://code.jquery.com/jquery-1.7.2.min.js"></script>
13
14 <script>
15 // please externalize this code to an external .js file
16 $(document).ready(function() {
17
18   $.noConflict();
19
20   $ = function(name) {
21     alert('Hello, ' + name);
22   };
23
24   var clickHandler = function() {
25     $('Reader');
26   };
27
28   (function($) {
29     $('p').click(clickHandler);
30   })(jQuery);
```

Listing 1.2   Assigning the $ to a Different Function (Continued)

```
31
32 });
33 </script>
34 </body>
33 </html>
```

After line 18, the $ is no longer bound to jQuery and can be used for different purposes again. Lines 20–26 show how you can use the $ for your own functions if you insist. It might as well be a different library that uses the $, instead.

Even after calling noConflict, there is a clean way to access jQuery code with the $ without naming clashes. Lines 28–30 demonstrate how to pass the jQuery object to a function, ensuring that the $ only is in scope inside that function. This function is executed directly after it is loaded.

Recipe: Determining the jQuery Version

You can ask jQuery to return its current version. This could be useful when you are upgrading and have multiple versions of jQuery running at the same time, and you want to ensure that you are working with the correct version. Listing 1.3 shows a different use of the jquery property. In case you are in doubt as to whether you are dealing with a jQuery object or a different kind of object, you can use the jquery property to help you to determine this.

Listing 1.3   Testing Whether an Object is a jQuery Object

```
00 <!DOCTYPE html>
01
02 <html lang="en">
03 <head>
04   <title>jQuery Version</title>
05 </head>
06 <body>
07
08 <p>The jQuery version is: <span id="placeholder"></span></p>
09
10
11 <script src="http://code.jquery.com/jquery-1.7.2.min.js"></script>
12
13 <script>
14 // please externalize this code to an external .js file
15 $(document).ready(function() {
```

(Continues)

Listing 1.3   **Testing Whether an Object is a jQuery Object (Continued)**

```
16
17   var a = {b: 1, c: 2};
18   var b = $('#placeholder');
19   var jqVersion = $.fn.jquery;
20
21   if(a.jquery) {
22     a.html(jqVersion + (' (a)'));
23   }
24
25   if(b.jquery) {
26     b.html(jqVersion + (' (b)'));
27   }
28
29 });
30 </script>
31 </body>
32 </html>
```

The a variable on line 17 is clearly not a jQuery object; the b variable on line 18 clearly is one. Line 19 retrieves the jQuery version, regardless of any variable. The code will never execute line 22. Instead, line 26 displays the jQuery version and confirms that b is a jQuery object, as expected.

Recipe: Iterating Arrays with each()

One of the reasons why you can do more with less code with jQuery is because JavaScript can be used as a functional language. Listing 1.4 demonstrates how you can use the each() function instead of creating a for loop.

Listing 1.4   **Numbering Each Value in a List**

```
00 <!DOCTYPE html>
01
02 <html lang="en">
03 <head>
04   <title>The each() function</title>
05 </head>
06 <body>
07
08 <h2>This example demonstrates the each() function by
09   prepending a letter before each paragraph below</h2>
10
11 <p>First</p>
12 <p>Second</p>
13 <p>Third</p>
```

Listing 1.4   **Numbering Each Value in a List (Continued)**

```
14
15 <script src="http://code.jquery.com/jquery-1.7.2.min.js"></script>
16
17 <script>
18 // please externalize this code to an external .js file
19 $(document).ready(function() {
20
21   var values = ['a', 'b', 'c', 'd'];
22
23   $.each(values, function(index, value) {
24     values[index] = value.toUpperCase();
25   });
26
27   $('p').each(function(index, el) {
28     $(el).prepend(' - ');
29   });
30
31   $('p').each(function(index) {
32     $(this).prepend(values[index]);
33   });
34
35 });
36 </script>
37 </body>
38 </html>
```

On lines 21–25, the each() function is used to iterate over a regular array. It calls a function that changes all characters within the array to uppercase.

Lines 27–29 use the each() function to iterate over a set of elements selected by jQuery. Keep in mind that jQuery offers many shorthand notations for its own functions that work without the each function. It is preferable to avoid each() when jQuery provides a better method.

For readability, you might prefer each() over a for loop. For performance, a for loop might be faster in some cases. This is a matter of preference. This book favors each() over for loops.

Recipe: Manipulating Arrays by Using map()

Although each() seems cleaner than a for loop, there is a cleaner way to manipulate arrays. Listing 1.5 illustrates how to use map() for a similar purpose as Listing 1.4. As it turns out, each() is more appropriate for making function calls based on array elements. The map() function is specifically meant to change array elements by processing them into a new array. In map(), the variable assignment is replaced by a simple return.

Listing 1.5   **Modifying All Elements in an Array**

```
00 <!DOCTYPE html>
01
02 <html lang="en">
03 <head>
04   <title>The map() function</title>
05 </head>
06 <body>
07
08 <h2>This example shows the basic usage of a map.</h2>
09
10 <p id="before">Before map(): </p>
11
12 <p id="after">After map(): </p>
13
14 <script src="http://code.jquery.com/jquery-1.7.2.min.js"></script>
15 <script>
16 // please externalize this code to an external .js file
17
18 $(document).ready(function() {
19
20   var arr = [1, 2, 3, 4, 5];
21
22   $('#before').append(JSON.stringify(arr));
23
24   arr = $.map(arr, function(value, index) {
25     return 'done something with ' + value;
26   });
27
28   $('#after').append(JSON.stringify(arr));
29
30 });
31 </script>
32 </body>
33 </html>
```

The change that line 25 makes to the array elements might not be useful in practice; however, it shows that you can easily change an array of integers into an array of strings. JavaScript is weakly typed, after all.

Recipe: Working with Arrays of Elements

So far, you have seen arrays of integers, arrays of strings, and jQuery objects implicitly containing a list of HTML elements. Listing 1.6 displays how you can access the HTML elements within the jQuery object and transform the list into a regular jQuery-free array.

Listing 1.6   **Retrieving Arrays and Elements in Multiple Ways**

```
00 <!DOCTYPE html>
01
02 <html lang="en">
03 <head>
04   <title>The get() function and alternatives</title>
05 </head>
06 <body>
07
08 <h2>Various ways to get an array or a specific element</h2>
09
10 <p>First</p>
11 <p>Second</p>
12 <p>Third</p>
13
14 <button id="get">Get</button><br>
15 <button id="to-array">To array</button><br>
16 <button id="make-array">Make array</button><br>
17 <button id="first">First</button><br>
18 <button id="get-first">Get first</button><br>
19 <button id="get-last">Get last</button>
20
21 <script src="http://code.jquery.com/jquery-1.7.2.min.js"></script>
22
23 <script>
24 // please externalize this code to an external .js file
25 $(document).ready(function() {
26
27   // same as next
28   $('#get').click(function() {
29     alert('Get p = ' + $('p').get());
30   });
31
32   // same as previous, better readability
33   $('#to-array').click(function() {
34     alert('Get p = ' + $('p').toArray());
35   });
36
37   // yet another alternative with the same functionality
38   $('#make-array').click(function() {
39     alert('Get p = ' + $.makeArray($('p')));
40   });
41
42   // same as next
43   $('#first').click(function() {
```

(Continues)

Listing 1.6   Retrieving Arrays and Elements in Multiple Ways (Continued)

```
44     alert('First p = ' + $('p')[0].innerHTML);
45   });
46   // same as previous
47   $('#get-first').click(function() {
48     alert('Get first p = ' + $('p').get(0).innerHTML);
49   });
50
51   // ease of use: get the last element
52   $('#get-last').click(function() {
53     alert('Get last p = ' + $('p').get(-1).innerHTML);
54   });
55
56 });
57 </script>
58 </body>
59 </html>
```

Lines 29, 34, and 39 perform the same function: transform a jQuery object containing a selection into an array of HTML elements. The `get()` method works well but is not the most readable one for this purpose. The `getArray()` and `makeArray()` functions are mostly different in the way they are called and can both be used, depending on preference.

Using `get()` to obtain specific elements from the current selection is similar to accessing the jQuery object by using brackets `[]`. One advantage is the possibility to get the last element by asking for position `-1`.

Recipe: Getting the Position of an Element by Using index()

The last recipe showed how to convert jQuery selections into arrays of regular HTML elements. All HTML elements have a position, not only within the jQuery selection, but in the complete HTML document. Listing 1.7 displays how to ascertain this position.

Listing 1.7   Determining the Index of Paragraphs

```
00 <!DOCTYPE html>
01
02 <html lang="en">
03 <head>
04   <title>The index() function</title>
05 </head>
06 <body>
07
```

Listing 1.7   **Determining the Index of Paragraphs (Continued)**

```
08 <h1>Click on the paragraphs to see their index</h1>
09
10 <p>First</p>
11 <span>Not a paragraph so it does not respond to your clicks</span>
12 <p>Second</p>
13 <p>Third</p>
14 <p>Some nested paragraphs:
15    <p>Nested 1</p>
16    <p>Nested 2</p>
17 </p>
18 <p>And a final non-nested paragraph</p>
19
20 <script src="http://code.jquery.com/jquery-1.7.2.min.js"></script>
21
22 <script>
23 // please externalize this code to an external .js file
24 $(document).ready(function() {
25
26   $('p').click(function() {
27     alert('Index of clicked item is: ' + $(this).index())
28   });
29
30 });
31 </script>
32 </body>
33 </html>
```

By selecting only paragraph elements from a document that mixes multiple element types, it becomes apparent that the returned value of the index() function is independent of the jQuery selection.

Recipe: Finding Elements in an Array by Using grep()

To find an element inside an array, you can use a grep() function (like the Unix command to find text in files), which shares similarities with map() and each(). Listing 1.8 shows how to use grep() to select the months that have the character "r" in their name.

Listing 1.8   **Selecting the Months in a Year That Have an "r" in Their Name**

```
00 <!DOCTYPE html>
01
02 <html lang="en">
03 <head>
```

(Continues)

Listing 1.8   **Selecting the Months in a Year That Have an "r" in Their Name (Continued)**

```
04   <title>The grep() function</title>
05 </head>
06 <body>
07
08 <h2>All months</h2>
09 <p id="all-months"></p>
10
11 <h2>Months when you should take extra vitamin</h2>
12 <p id="vitamin"></p>
13 <script src="http://code.jquery.com/jquery-1.7.2.min.js"></script>
14
15 <script>
16 // please externalize this code to an external .js file
17 $(document).ready(function() {
18
19   var arr = ['January', 'February', 'March', 'April', 'May',
20     'June', 'July', 'August', 'September', 'October',
21       'November', 'December'];
22
23   var rInMonth = $.grep(arr, function(value, index) {
24    return value.indexOf('r') >= 0;
25   });
26
27   $('#all-months').html(arr.join('<br> '));
28   $('#vitamin').html(rInMonth.join('<br> '));
29
30 });
31 </script>
32 </body>
33 </html>
```

Where each() is useful for calling other functions for each array element and map() is useful for changing all values in an array, grep() is useful for selecting a subset of an array. All function calls expect either true or false, depending on whether the current element should be in the result set.

Recipe: Determining the Size of an Element Set by Using length()

In case you need to know how many items are selected by jQuery, the length() function comes in handy. Also note that it will return the same value as the size() function. Listing 1.9 shows how to use this function.

Listing 1.9   **Determining the Number of Paragraphs**

```
00 <!DOCTYPE html>
01
02 <html lang="en">
03 <head>
04   <title>The length() function</title>
05 </head>
06 <body>
07
08 <h2>By clicking on the button below, you can see
09   the length of the selected element set.</p>
10
11 <p>First</p>
12 <p>Second</p>
13 <p>Third</p>
14
15 <button id="get-length">Get length</button>
16
17 <script src="http://code.jquery.com/jquery-1.7.2.min.js"></script>
18
19 <script>
20 // please externalize this code to an external .js file
21 $(document).ready(function() {
22
23   // same as next
24   $('#get-length').click(function() {
25     alert('Length = ' + $('p').length);
26   });
27
28 });
29 </script>
30 </body>
31 </html>
```

The use of length() is straightforward. Line 25 returns the number of paragraph elements selected.

Recipe: Retrieving HTML5 data- Attributes

With HTML5, you can add your own attributes to HTML elements when they start with data-. This can be useful for web applications that need to transfer many small pieces of data connected to the DOM tree that should remain hidden to the web site visitor. Listing 1.10 demonstrates how jQuery helps you to read the contents of these data- attributes.

Listing 1.10   **Reading Hidden Text from data-myattribute**

```
00 <!DOCTYPE html>
01
02 <html lang="en">
03 <head>
04   <title>Using data() for HTML5 data- attributes</title>
05 </head>
06 <body>
07
08 <p data-myattribute="just some random content"
09 id="test-data">If you press the button, you can reveal
10 the text hidden as an attribute inside the paragraph
11 element as an HTML5 data attribute.</p>
12
13 <button>Get data attribute</button>
14
15 <script src="http://code.jquery.com/jquery-1.7.2.min.js"></script>
16
17 <script>
18 // please externalize this code to an external .js file
19 $(document).ready(function() {
20
21   $('button').click(function() {
22     alert('The data is: ' + $('#test-data').data('myattribute'));
23   });
24
25 });
26 </script>
27 </body>
28 </html>
```

If your attribute is called `data-myattribute`, you can fetch the data with the `data()` function, specifying `myattribute` as an argument. In this case, you can consider `data()` as a convenience function. The `data()` function has more uses as you can see in the next recipe.

Recipe: Storing Element Data by Using data()

Manipulating the HTML document is relatively slow. Some web applications abuse the HTML document to store hidden data that is associated with specific HTML elements. An application might use attributes like `data-myattribute` to achieve that.

Previously, storing data inside the HTML document was considered a bad practice. This was due to web developers haphazardly jamming in custom elements that would cause validation errors and could cause potential problems with the page rendering. HTML5 has added support for `data-*` attributes and jQuery provides a means in the form of the data() function to use the data stored in them. In the last recipe, you saw how this function helps you fetch data- attributes. That is not the main function. Listing 1.11 demonstrates how to use data() to store element specific data in a central storage, outside the document.

Listing 1.11   **Storing Element Data without Affecting Other Elements**

```
00 <!DOCTYPE html>
01
02 <html lang="en">
03 <head>
04   <title>The data() function: storing</title>
05 </head>
06 <body>
07
08 <button id="store">Store some data in the paragraph
09    below</button><br>
10
11 <button id="show-data">Show the data in the paragraph
12   below</button>
13
14 <p id="store-data">Even if you look in Firebug, you
15   cannot see any data that is stored related to this
16   element after storing it.</p>
17
18 <button id="show-empty">Show that the next paragraph
19   does not contain the data</button>
20
21 <p id="empty-data">To show you that the data belongs
22   to the other paragraph, this paragraph is intentionally
23   left without any data.</p>
24
25 <script src="http://code.jquery.com/jquery-latest.min.js"></script>
26
27 <script>
28 // please externalize this code to an external .js file
29 $(document).ready(function() {
30
31
32   $('#store').click(function() {
33      $('#store-data').data('myattribute', 'some data');
34   });
35
36   $('#show-data').click(function() {
37    alert('The data is: ' + $('#store-data').data('myattribute'));
38   });
```

(Continues)

```
39
40   $('#show-empty').click(function() {
41     alert('The data is: ' + $('#empty-data').data('myattribute'));
42   });
43 });
44 </script>
45 </body>
46 </html>
```

Open the example in your browser and use developer tools to see what happens with the generated HTML tree; or better, what does not happen to it. The data is stored outside the document. Nevertheless, the data is still associated with specific elements.

Recipe: Removing Element Data by Using removeData()

If your application processes a lot of data, it is wise to think about memory usage. When you no longer need data associated with certain elements, you should remove it. Listing 1.12 shows the use of `removeData()` for this purpose.

Listing 1.12   **Demonstrating Data Removal and the Storage of Objects**

```
00 <!DOCTYPE html>
01
02 <html lang="en">
03 <head>
04   <title>The data() function: removing</title>
05 </head>
06 <body>
07
08 <button id="store-data">Store data</button><br>
09
10 <button id="show-data">Show the data</button><br>
11
12 <button id="remove-data">Remove the data</button>
13
14 <p id="store-data">This paragraph element is the placeholder
15    for the data to be stored. Showing the data will reveal
16    a little bit of the jQuery internals for storing data.
17    You can ignore the technical details.</p>
18
19
20 <script src="http://code.jquery.com/jquery-1.7.2.min.js"></script>
21
```

Listing 1.12   Demonstrating Data Removal and the Storage of Objects (Continued)

```
22 <script>
23 // please externalize this code to an external .js file
24 $(document).ready(function() {
25
26
27   $('#store-data').click(function() {
28     $('#store-data').data('myattribute',
29       {a: 'first', b: 'second'});
30   });
31
32   $('#show-data').click(function() {
33     alert('The data is: ' +
34       JSON.stringify($('#store-data').data()));
35   });
36
37   $('#remove-data').click(function() {
38     $('#store-data').removeData();
39   });
40 });
41 </script>
42 </body>
43 </html>
```

Line 28 shows the data() function being used to store data. Line 29 shows the data that will be saved. This data is in JavaScript Object Notation (JSON) format. Using JSON, you can store data in key-value pairs. You can learn more about JSON by visiting www.json.org/. Line 38 removes all data associated to the button with id show-data. If you only want to remove myattribute, you can pass this as an argument to the removeData() function. This code example contains more than just the removeData(). Line 29 and 34 demonstrate that you can store complete objects by using the data() function and remove them with one call.

Recipe: Testing and Manipulating Variables

JavaScript is a weakly typed language. This means you can never be 100 percent sure what kind of data is stored in variables, especially not if multiple developers are involved or when multiple libraries are manipulating data.

Listing 1.13 demonstrates jQuery's helper functions for testing data types.

Listing 1.13   Showing Variable Types and Modifying Arrays

```
00 <!DOCTYPE html>
01
02 <html lang="en">
```

(Continues)

Listing 1.13   Showing Variable Types and Modifying Arrays (Continued)

```
03 <head>
04   <title>Various variable testing functions</title>
05 </head>
06 <body>
07
08 <p>This is a list of variable type tests, followed by
09   a few modification functions:</p>
10 <p id="placeholder"></p>
11
12 <script src="http://code.jquery.com/jquery-1.7.2.min.js"></script>
13
14 <script>
15 // please externalize this code to an external .js file
16 $(document).ready(function() {
17
18   var testObj = {},
19       testVar = 1,
20       testFun = function() {},
21       testArr = [1, 2, 2];
22
23   var results = [];
24
25   results.push('testObj = ' + JSON.stringify(testObj));
26   results.push('testVar = ' + JSON.stringify(testVar));
27   results.push('testFun = ' + JSON.stringify(testFun));
28   results.push('testArr = ' + JSON.stringify(testArr));
29
30   results.push('<br>');
31
32   results.push('type(testObj) = ' + $.type(testObj));
33   results.push('type(testVar) = ' + $.type(testVar));
34   results.push('type(testFun) = ' + $.type(testFun));
35   results.push('type(testArr) = ' + $.type(testArr));
36
37   results.push('<br>');
38
39   results.push('inArray(3, testArr) = '
40                  + $.inArray(3, testArr));
41
42   results.push('isArray(testArr) = '
43                  + $.isArray(testArr));
44
45   results.push('isEmptyObject(testObj) = '
46                  + $.isEmptyObject(testObj));
47
```

Listing 1.13 **Showing Variable Types and Modifying Arrays (Continued)**

```
48    results.push('isPlainObject(testObj) = '
49                  + $.isPlainObject(testObj));
50
51    results.push('isFunction(testFun) = '
52                  + $.isFunction(testFun));
53
54    results.push('<br>');
55
56    results.push('merge(testArr, [3, 3, 4]) = '
57                  + $.merge(testArr, [3, 3, 4]));
58
59    results.push('unique(testArr) = '
60                  + $.unique(testArr));
61
62    results.push('merge(testArr, [5, 6]) = '
63                  + $.merge(testArr, [5, 6]));
64
65    $('#placeholder').append(results.join('<br>'));
66
67 });
68 </script>
69 </body>
70 </html>
```

Although this code won't win any beauty contests, it demonstrates many different functions that are available for testing data types. Lines 32–35 show how the type() function of jQuery works. This function checks for the existence of an internal JavaScript [[Class]]. When type() finds one, it displays it. The main difference between the jQuery type() and the standard JavaScript typeof() function is in the return. The typeof() function returns an "object," whereas the type() returns an "array".

Lines 39–43 deal with array handling. The inArray() function searches through an array for a specific value and returns either the index of the value in the array or a -1. The isArray() function performs what it is name suggests; it checks to see if the object it is testing is an array.

Lines 45–52 demonstrate the use of object detection. The isEmptyObject() function checks an object for the presence of a value or data content, whereas the isPlainObject() is used to determine if the object being tested was created with either {} or new Object. Lines 51 and 52 show the use of the isFunction() function, which as you can probably surmise checks the argument passed to see if it is a function object. Something to keep in mind when using isFunction() is that the official jQuery documentation states that after version 1.3 of jQuery, checking browser functions such as alert() might not work correctly in some browsers (such as Internet Explorer).

Lines 56–63 demonstrate how to merge arrays and filter the unique elements out of it. When you run this code, you discover that these functions have side effects. They change the array that is passed as an argument.

Recipe: Extending Objects by Using extend()

When you are working with objects, sometimes you want to merge two objects into one or extend one object with functions and properties of the other. Listing 1.14 displays how jQuery's `extend()` function helps to combine two objects.

Listing 1.14   **Displaying the Side Effects of Extending Objects**

```
00 <!DOCTYPE html>
01
02 <html lang="en">
03 <head>
04   <title>The extend() function</title>
05 </head>
06 <body>
07
08 <p>First object:</p>
09
10 <p id="object-1"></p>
11
12 <p>Second object:</p>
13
14 <p id="object-2"></p>
15
16 <p>Result object:</p>
17
18 <p id="object-result"></p>
19
20 <button id="extend">Extend</button>
21
22 <button id="extend-new">Extend into empty</button>
23
24 <button id="reset">Reset</button>
25
26 <script src="http://code.jquery.com/jquery-1.7.2.min.js"></script>
27
28 <script>
29 // please externalize this code to an external .js file
30 $(document).ready(function() {
31
32   var reset,
33         object1 = object2 = objectresult = {};
34
```

Listing 1.14   Displaying the Side Effects of Extending Objects (Continued)

```
35    var show = function() {
36      $('#object-1').html(JSON.stringify(object1));
37      $('#object-2').html(JSON.stringify(object2));
38      $('#object-result').html(JSON.stringify(objectresult));
39    };
40
41    (reset = function() {
42      object1 = {
43        a: 'original a',
44        b: 'original b',
45        c: 'original c'
46      };
47      object2 = {
48        c: 'different c',
49        d: 'different d'
50      };
51      objectresult = {};
52      show();
53    })();
54
55    $('#extend').click(function() {
56      // has side effects for object1
57      objectresult = $.extend(object1, object2);
58      show();
59    });
60
61    $('#extend-new').click(function() {
62      // without side effects for object1
63      objectresult = $.extend({}, object1, object2);
64      show();
65    });
66
67    $('#reset').click(function() {
68      reset();
69    });
70
71  });
72  </script>
73  </body>
74  </html>
```

Compare lines 57 and 63. Line 57 merges the second object into the first object, overwriting functions and properties that already existed in the first object. Moreover, the first object is changed by this function.

If you want to have an extended version of `object1` without affecting `object1` itself, line 63 demonstrates how to merge both objects into a new object. The resulting new object has the same functions and properties as the result from line 57. The difference is that now you have three objects instead of two, and `object1` itself is unchanged.

Recipe: Serializing the Data in a Form

If you need the current data of a form before submitting it, you can select all form elements, iterate over them and read the values. There are shorter ways to achieve the same result. Listing 1.15 shows two ways to get the current input that was entered into a form with a single function call.

Listing 1.15   **Serializing the Current Form Input into Two Different Formats**

```
00 <!DOCTYPE html>
01
02 <html lang="en">
03 <head>
04   <title>The serialize() and serializeArray() function</title>
05 </head>
06 <body>
07
08
09 <h2>Press the buttons to see the result of two
10   different serialization functions</h2>
11
12 <form action="" method="post">
13   <label for="first_field">First field</label>
14   <input type="text" name="first_field"
15     value="" id="first_field"><br>
16   <label for="second_field">Second field</label>
17   <input type="text" name="second_field"
18     value="" id="second_field"><br>
19   <label for="third_field">Third field</label>
20   <input type="text" name="third_field"
21     value="" id="third_field"><br>
22   <label for="fourth_field">Fourth field</label>
23   <input type="text" name="fourth_field"
24     value="" id="fourth_field"><br>
25 </form>
26
27 <input type="button" name="serialize"
28   value="Serialize" id="serialize">
29 <input type="button" name="serialize-array"
30   value="SerializeArray" id="serialize-array">
31
32 <div id="placeholder"></div>
```

Listing 1.15   Serializing the Current Form Input into Two Different Formats (Continued)

```
33
34 <script src="http://code.jquery.com/jquery-1.7.2.min.js"></script>
35
36 <script>
37 // please externalize this code to an external .js file
38 $(document).ready(function() {
39
40   $('#serialize').click(function() {
41     $('#placeholder').html($('form').serialize());
42   });
43
44   $('#serialize-array').click(function() {
45     $('#placeholder').html(JSON.stringify(
46       $('form').serializeArray()));
47   });
48
49 });
50 </script>
51 </body>
52 </html>
```

Line 41 shows the `serialize()` method to retrieve form content. The result is an escaped query string that could be directly used in an HTTP call to the server.

Line 46 uses `serializeArray()` for the same purpose. This function is an internal helper that is called during `serialize()`. It returns an object with keys and values. If you want to transform the form content into a different object, the result from `serializeArray()` might be easier to use.

Recipe: Testing Browsers for Feature Support

One of the goals of jQuery is to help you to handle browser incompatibilities. Many small differences between browser vendors and browser versions are covered by jQuery itself. Still, some differences remain with which jQuery cannot help you. Listing 1.16 shows how jQuery provides properties that indicate whether the current browser supports certain features and characteristics.

Listing 1.16   Listing All Support Testing Properties

```
00 <!DOCTYPE html>
01
02 <html lang="en">
03 <head>
04   <title>The support property</title>
05 </head>
```

(Continues)

Listing 1.16   **Listing All Support Testing Properties (Continued)**

```
06 <body>
07
08 <p>The paragraph under this contains the supported
09   properties of this browser:</p>
10
11 <p id="placeholder"></p>
12
13 <script src="http://code.jquery.com/jquery-1.7.2.min.js"></script>
14
15 <script>
16 // please externalize this code to an external .js file
17 $(document).ready(function() {
18
19 var result = [];
20  $.each(
21  ('ajax boxModel changeBubbles checkClone checkOn cors cssFloat ' +
22  'hrefNormalized htmlSerialize leadingWhitespace noCloneChecked ' +
23  'noCloneEvent opacity optDisabled optSelected style ' +
24  'submitBubbles tbody').split(' '), function(index, name) {
25    result.push(name + ' = ' + $.support[name] + '<br>');
26 });
27
28   $('#placeholder').html(result.join('') );
29
30 });
31 </script>
32 </body>
33 </html>
```

The `ajax` property indicates the browser's support for calls to the server, for example. And `opacity` indicates whether you can create a see-through effect between multiple elements.

A complete reference of all these properties is beyond the scope of this book. For more information about them, go to http://api.jquery.com/jQuery.support/. jQuery also contains a `browser` property that should not be used. Although `support` is preferable over `browser`, it is still better to avoid using it as long as you can.

Summary

This chapter introduced the basics of using jQuery. It demonstrated how to use the $ variable for other purposes than jQuery. After that, a long list of support functions was demonstrated. Most of these functions assist in manipulating variables, objects, arrays, and data elements. Using these functions can help you to keep your code concise.

Chapter 2

Selecting Elements

This chapter demonstrates how to select elements by using jQuery. It covers CSS selectors, extensions, and functions to further find and filter elements. After selecting elements, you can use additional methods to traverse the document.

Recipe: Combining Two Element Sets by Using add()

Using the standard jQuery selector, you can make a single CSS query. However, in some cases, you might want to perform an operation on a set of elements beyond a single CSS query. When using the add() function, additional selectors can be added. This creates additional selections instead of only modifying the original selector. Listing 2.1 shows how you can combine the results of two CSS queries for use with a single operation.

Listing 2.1   **Selecting Paragraphs and Spans Together**

```
00 <!DOCTYPE html>
01
02 <html lang="en">
03 <head>
04    <title>Combine two element sets</title>
05 </head>
06 <body>
07
08 <div>This text should be normal.</div>
09
10 <p>This text should become blue</p>
11
12 <span>This text should become blue</span>
13
14 <div>This text should be normal.</div>
15
16 <p>This text should become blue</p>
```

(Continues)

Listing 2.1   **Selecting Paragraphs and Spans Together (Continued)**

```
17
18 <span>This text should become blue</span>
19
20 <script src="http://code.jquery.com/jquery-1.7.2.min.js"></script>
21
22 <script>
23 // please externalize this code to an external .js file
24 $(document).ready(function() {
25
26 $('p').add('span').css('background-color', 'blue');
27
28 });
29 </script>
30 </body>
31 </html>
```

The example is relatively simple. On line 26, the first query asks for all paragraphs in the document. The second query is an argument to the add() function. This asks for all span elements. The background color is changed for the combined set of elements in a single call.

Recipe: Refining the Selection by Using filter()

After making a rough selection, you can further refine the result with the filter() function. This serves two purposes. First, not all CSS selectors and extensions are equally fast. If you select a set of elements with a fast selector first and then further refine that set with a slower selector, the performance will improve compared to selecting from the complete document using the slower selector.

Second, with jQuery, you can chain functions together. If some of the chained functions should only work on a subset of the selection and other chained functions should work on the full set, the filter() and end() functions help out, as Listing 2.2 demonstrates.

Listing 2.2   **Separating Odd and Even Elements**

```
00 <!DOCTYPE html>
01
02 <html lang="en">
03 <head>
04   <title>The filter() and end() function</title>
05 </head>
06 <body>
07
08 <h2>Filter the selection</h2>
```

Listing 2.2   **Separating Odd and Even Elements (Continued)**

```
09
10 <ul>
11 <li>One</li>
12 <li>Two</li>
13 <li>Three</li>
14 <li>Four</li>
15 <li>Five</li>
16 <li>Six</li>
17 <li>Seven</li>
18 <li>Eight</li>
19 <li>Nine</li>
20 <li>Ten</li>
21 </ul>
22
23 <script src="http://code.jquery.com/jquery-1.7.2.min.js"></script>
24
25 <script>
26 // please externalize this code to an external .js file
27 $(document).ready(function() {
28
29   $('li')
30     .filter(':odd').css('background-color', 'blue')
31     .end().css('color', 'red')
32
33 });
34 </script>
35 </body>
36 </html>
```

Any functions that would have been executed before the filter on line 30 would have worked on the complete li selection. However, as shown, the css() function between filter() and end() only works on the filtered odd elements. The end() function indicates to jQuery to finish processing the stack that the filter() function creates and revert back to the last selection for additional processing. Further chained functions will then work on all li elements, such as the css() call on line 31.

Recipe: Selecting Descendants by Using find() and children()

Where filter() further refines the current selection, you might also want to further traverse the document tree, based on the current selection. For example, you might be interested in the descendants of the current selection. Or, as Listing 2.3 shows, perhaps you want just a subset of the descendants of the current selection.

Listing 2.3   **Demonstrating the Difference Between find() and children()**

```
00 <!DOCTYPE html>
01
02 <html lang="en">
03 <head>
04   <title>The find() and children() function</title>
05 </head>
06 <body>
07
08 <h2>This code highlights the 'special' cases using both
09   children() and find() to show the difference</h2>
10
11 <ul id="ul-root">
12   <li>1</li>
13   <li>2
14     <ul>
15       <li>2.1</li>
16       <li class="special">2.2</li>
17       <li>2.3</li>
18       <li>2.4</li>
19     </ul>
20   </li>
21   <li class="special">3</li>
22   <li>4</li>
23 </ul>
24
25 <script src="http://code.jquery.com/jquery-1.7.2.min.js"></script>
26
27 <script>
28 // please externalize this code to an external .js file
29 $(document).ready(function() {
30
31   $('#ul-root').children('.special').css('font-weight', 'bold');
32
33   $('#ul-root').find('.special').css('background-color', 'red');
34
35 });
36 </script>
37 </body>
38 </html>
```

Lines 31 and 33 demonstrate the difference between children() and find(). The functions are almost the same except for the fact that children() works only a single recursion level, where find() works all the way down the hierarchy.

Recipe: Selecting Elements by Using has() and Testing by Using is()

Where `children()` and `find()` select specific elements below the current selection, by using `has()`, you can filter the current selection, depending on whether a certain child element is contained within the current selection.

The `is()` function works on the current selection and tests whether it is equal to the provided argument or whether it meets the criteria of a CSS selector. The equality can be determined through a matching of included selector, element, or jQuery object.

Listing 2.4 demonstrates both `has()` and `is()`.

Listing 2.4 **Showing the Difference Between has() and is()**

```
00 <!DOCTYPE html>
01
02 <html lang="en">
03 <head>
04   <title>The has() and is() function.</title>
05 </head>
06 <body>
07
08 <div>This text should be <span>normal</span>.</div>
09
10 <div>This text should have a <em>background</em> in red</div>
11
12 <div>This text should be <strong id="select">normal</strong>.</div>
13
14
15 <script src="http://code.jquery.com/jquery-1.7.2.min.js"></script>
16
17 <script>
18 // please externalize this code to an external .js file
19 $(document).ready(function() {
20
21   $('div').has('em').css('background-color', 'red');
22
23   var strongEl = $('strong');
24   strongEl.append(', and .is() = ' + strongEl.is('#select'));
25 });
26 </script>
27 </body>
28 </html>
```

Line 21 filters the current selection based on the presence of em descendants. Lines 23 and 24 show how the `is()` function can determine whether two jQuery selections are the same.

Recipe: Selecting Form Elements by Using Pseudo-Selectors

In addition to CSS3 selectors, jQuery allows you to provide selectors that look like CSS3 selectors but are not standardized. Listing 2.5 demonstrates how to use such pseudo-selectors to select specific form elements.

Listing 2.5   **Selecting text, submit, button, radio, and checkbox Input Elements**

```
00 <!DOCTYPE html>
01
02 <html lang="en">
03 <head>
04   <title>Pseudo-selectors for form elements</title>
05 </head>
06 <body>
07
08 <form action="" method="post">
09
10   <input type="text" name="mytext" value="" id="mytext"><br>
11   <input type="submit" name="mysubmit" value="" id="mysubmit"><br>
12   <input type="button" name="mybutton" value="" id="mybutton"><br>
13   <input type="radio" name="myradio" value="" id="myradio"><br>
14   <input type="checkbox" name="mycheckbox" value="" id="mycheckbox">
15
16 </form>
17
18 <script src="http://code.jquery.com/jquery-1.7.2.min.js"></script>
19
20 <script>
21 // please externalize this code to an external .js file
22 $(document).ready(function() {
23
24   $(':text').css('border-color', 'blue');
25   $(':submit').css('border-color', 'blue');
26   $(':button').css('border-color', 'blue');
27   $(':radio').prop('checked', 'true');
28   $(':checkbox').prop('checked', 'true');
29
30 });
31 </script>
32 </body>
33 </html>
```

Lines 24–28 show how clean these pseudo-selectors can look. Be careful using them, however. Underneath, normal CSS selectors are passed to the browser's native `querySelectorAll()` function. This function performs well and, when supported by the browser (including Internet Explorer 8+ and other modern web browsers), might be faster than using the fallback to the jQuery selector engine (see http://jsperf.com/jquery-vs-queryselectorall999 for performance testing). To learn more about the `querySelectorAll()` function, visit http://www.w3.org/TR/selectors-api2/. In a similar fashion, selectors that include an `id` will be converted to using the browser native `document.getElementById()` function.

Pseudo-selectors are handled by jQuery. If a pseudo-selector is not scoped, jQuery might traverse every element in the document and test whether it meets the criteria. There is no query optimization algorithm within jQuery; therefore, it is wise to limit your usage of pseudo-selectors to the `filter()` function.

Recipe: Nesting Selectors

With jQuery, you can use other constructs that are not supported in CSS. For example, you can nest selectors. Listing 2.6 exhibits how to combine a `not()` and a `has()` selector.

Listing 2.6   Selecting Elements That Do Not Contain an <em> Element

```
00 <!DOCTYPE html>
01
02 <html lang="en">
03 <head>
04   <title>Nested selectors</title>
05 </head>
06 <body>
07
08 <div>This text should have a blue <span>background</span>.</div>
09
10 <div>This text should be mostly normal, except for <em>the em
11   part itself</em> or some <strong>strong parts</strong>
12   because those do not have an em inside.</div>
13
14 <div>This text should have a blue <strong>background</strong>.</div>
15
16
17 <script src="http://code.jquery.com/jquery-1.7.2.min.js"></script>
18
19 <script>
20 // please externalize this code to an external .js file
21 $(document).ready(function() {
22
23   $(':not(:has(em))').css('background-color', 'blue');
24
25 });
26 </script>
27 </body>
28 </html>
```

The result of this selection might be surprising. Not only are the first and third div elements selected, but so are the em and strong elements that are contained within the second div. Remember, the selector is not scoped at div elements. Although the em element is an em itself, strictly speaking, it does not contain another em.

Recipe: Emulating a CSS Hover Selector

Not all CSS3 selectors work in jQuery. For example, the pseudo-elements ::first-letter and ::first-line cannot work in jQuery, because it can only work on actual elements. jQuery cannot change the document element tree without side effects. Also, some selectors that are not used regularly are left out of jQuery.

Selectors with dynamic behavior, such as hover, cannot work in jQuery, because a selection is only made when the code is executed. JavaScript is not declarative like CSS.

Although this particular recipe deals more with an event, it shows how jQuery solves the issue of not being able to directly use some selectors.

Listing 2.7 shows how jQuery emulates the behavior of hover with a shorthand notation that works on mouse events.

Listing 2.7   Changing the Background Color when the Mouse Hovers Over an Element

```
00 <!DOCTYPE html>
01
02 <html lang="en">
03 <head>
04   <title>Simulating hover</title>
05 </head>
06 <body>
07
08 <div>This text should be normal.</div>
09
10 <div><div>This text should be get a red background when the mouse
11   goes over it, and a blue background when the mouse
12   leaves</div></div>
13
14 <div>This text should NEVER get a red background</div>
15
16
17 <script src="http://code.jquery.com/jquery-latest.min.js"></script>
18
19 <script>
20 // please externalize this code to an external .js file
21 $(document).ready(function() {
22
23   $('div > div:contains("red")').hover(
24     function() {$(this).css('background-color', 'red')},
25     function() {$(this).css('background-color', 'blue')});
26
```

Listing 2.7   Changing the Background Color when the Mouse Hovers an Element (Continued)

```
27 });
28 </script>
29 </body>
30 </html>
```

Before the mouse goes over the div that is contained within a div, the background is white. When the mouse goes over the div, it turns blue. When the mouse leaves, the background will be blue. Pointing at the div again makes the background red. The resulting behavior is just like a CSS hover. In actuality, for this specific example, a CSS hover is preferable because this is styling. In case you need to call JavaScript based on such behavior, consider using this hover() utility function.

Recipe: Selecting on Text by Using contains()

Regular CSS3 selectors can test an HTML attribute for its content by looking at the whole value, what it starts with, or what it ends with. Making CSS selections based on the contents of the HTML elements themselves is impossible in CSS3.

Listing 2.8 demonstrates jQuery's extension function contains() for selecting elements based on their content.

Listing 2.8   Selecting Elements That Contain the Word "blue"

```
00 <!DOCTYPE html>
01
02 <html lang="en">
03 <head>
04   <title>The contains() selector</title>
05 </head>
06 <body>
07
08 <div>This text should be normal.</div>
09
10 <div>This text should be colored in blue</div>
11
12 <div>This text should NOT be colored</div>
13
14
15 <script src="http://code.jquery.com/jquery-1.7.2.min.js"></script>
16
17 <script>
18 // please externalize this code to an external .js file
19 $(document).ready(function() {
20
```

(Continues)

Listing 2.8   Selecting Elements That Contain the Word "blue" (Continued)

```
21   $('div:contains("blue")').css('background-color', 'blue');
22
23 });
24 </script>
25 </body>
26 </html>
```

Line 21 displays all `div` elements that contain the word "blue" with a blue background. Keep in mind that extensive use of this function adversely affects the performance of your page.

Example: Highlighting a Single Word

The last recipe only highlights the complete element containing the word "blue." A more desired use case is to highlight the word itself. Consider using such a function to highlight the words that the visitor was searching for recently. Listing 2.9 demonstrates how this could work.

Listing 2.9   Highlighting the Word "blue" Within an Element

```
00 <!DOCTYPE html>
01
02 <html lang="en">
03 <head>
04   <title>Highlight a single word</title>
05 </head>
06 <body>
07
08 <div>This text should be normal.</div>
09
10 <div>This text contain <i>one blue word</i> instead
11   of a full blue sentence</div>
12
13 <div>This text should NOT be colored</div>
14
15 <script src="http://code.jquery.com/jquery-1.7.2.min.js"></script>
16
17 <script>
18 // please externalize this code to an external .js file
19 $(document).ready(function() {
20
21   var selected = $('div:contains("blue")');
22
23   selected.html($.map(selected.html().split(' '), function(n) {
24     return '<span>' + n + '</span> ';
```

Listing 2.9   **Highlighting the Word "blue" Within an Element (Continued)**

```
25   }).join(''));
26
27   $('span:contains("blue")').css('background', 'blue');
28
29 });
30 </script>
31 </body>
32 </html>
```

Line 21 selects the div that contains the word "blue," similar to the way Listing 2.8 does. The contents of the selected div are then split over multiple spans and stored into an array. This is done by use of the map() function for the array creation, the html() function for the data, and the split() function to parse the data. After this replacement, line 27 shows the span that contains the word "blue" is selected and the blue color is applied to it through the use the css() function.

Recipe: Creating Custom Selectors

You can add your own selectors similar to the form pseudo selectors and contains(). Writing your own selector helps you to understand their performance issues working on large data sets. And if you know how to work around these performance issues by preselecting elements, you can still take advantage of their elegant notation. Listing 2.10 shows how to create your own selector.

Listing 2.10   **Creating a Custom Selector for Every Third Element**

```
00 <!DOCTYPE html>
01
02 <html lang="en">
03 <head>
04   <title>Custom selector</title>
05 </head>
06 <body>
07
08 <h2>Every third line gets a blue background color</h2>
09
10 <ul>
11   <li>One</li>
12   <li>Two</li>
13   <li>Three</li>
14   <li>Four</li>
15   <li>Five</li>
16   <li>Six</li>
```

(Continues)

Listing 2.10   **Creating a Custom Selector for Every Third Element (Continued)**

```
17    <li>Seven</li>
18    <li>Eight</li>
19    <li>Nine</li>
20    <li>Ten</li>
21 </ul>
22
23
24 <script src="http://code.jquery.com/jquery-1.7.2.min.js"></script>
25
26 <script>
27 // please externalize this code to an external .js file
28 $(document).ready(function() {
29
30    $.expr[':'].third = function(obj, index, meta, stack) {
31
32      // obj contains the current element
33
34      // index contains the 0 - n, depending on the current
35      //      element and the number of elements
36
37      // meta contains an array with the following values:
38      //      [":third('bla')", "third", "'", "bla"]
39
40      // stack contains a NodeList, which can be transformed into
41      //      an array using $.makeArray(stack)
42
43      return (index + 1) % 3 == 0;
44    };
45
46    $('li:third(\'bla\')').css('background-color', 'blue');
47
48    // li:nth-child(3n) would do the same of course
49    // this example is to show how to implement a custom
50    // selector
51
52 });
53
54 </script>
55 </body>
56 </html>
```

At the core of jQuery is the sizzle selector engine. This is what gives jQuery the ability to transverse the DOM and select what you want. You can use the sizzle selector in jQuery to create your own selectors. Line 30 shows how this is done. By using

`$.expr[':']`, you are informing jQuery that you are going to build a selector. Adding `.third` instructs jQuery how the selector will be accessed. The four variables in the anonymous function are standard in creating a custom selector. Each variable has been explained in the comments to help you understand what each one holds.

This example does not use all possibilities that are available for a custom selector. The `bla` argument passed to it does not have a function. Using the pointers inside the code comments, you can elaborate on the possibilities.

Recipe: Scoping the Selection Context

In addition to `filter()` and `find()`, you can also limit the scope of a jQuery selection from the very first selection query. If you have a regular HTML element, you can use a construction similar to Listing 2.11 to restrict the selection to working only on descendants of that element.

Listing 2.11   **Setting and Reading the context Property**

```
00 <!DOCTYPE html>
01
02 <html lang="en">
03 <head>
04   <title>Select elements within a context</title>
05 </head>
06 <body>
07
08 <div id="not-the-context">
09   <h2>This container is outside the context.</h2>
10   <p>So this text will remain unchanged</p>
11 </div>
12
13 <div id="the-context">
14   <h2>This is the container context.</h2>
15   <p>So this text should get a blue background</p>
16 </div>
17
18 <script src="http://code.jquery.com/jquery-1.7.2.min.js"></script>
19
20 <script>
21 // please externalize this code to an external .js file
22 $(document).ready(function() {
23
24   var selectContext = $('p', $('#the-context')[0]);
25   var selectOther = $('#not-the-context p');
26
27   selectContext
```

(Continues)

Listing 2.11   **Setting and Reading the context Property (Continued)**

```
28      .css('background-color', 'blue')
29      .append('<p>Context element is ' +
30        selectContext.context.nodeName + '</p>');
31
32    selectOther
33      .append('<p>Not the element is ' +
34        selectOther.context.nodeName + '</p>');
35
36  });
37  </script>
38  </body>
39  </html>
```

Line 30 and 34 show how the `context` property can indicate what the original selection context was after the selection has been made.

Summary

This chapter covered CSS element selectors and jQuery's extensions to these selectors. In addition to CSS selectors, the jQuery functions for further selection refinement and tree traversal were demonstrated. The last recipe focused on custom selectors.

Chapter 3

Modifying the Page

This chapter covers jQuery's methods for manipulating the HTML tree. This includes classes, attributes, properties, and elements. This chapter also shows the difference between methods with similar names and discusses potential performance issues.

Recipe: Adding Classes

Without jQuery, browsers restrict you to setting all classes in a single call. You cannot add or remove classes without taking into account other classes on the element. This adds extra complexity and overhead when you want to want to add another class to an element. Fortunately, jQuery offers the `addClass()` function, which overcomes this hurdle by providing the ability to easily add one or more classes to a selector.

Listing 3.1 shows how you can add a class in a single `addClass()` call.

Listing 3.1 **Adding Multiple Classes to a Single Element**

```
00 <!DOCTYPE html>
01
02 <html lang="en">
03 <head>
04   <title>The addClass() function</title>
05   <style>
06   /* please externalize this code to an external
07     .css file */
08
09   p.initial {
10     background-color: blue;
11   }
12
13   p.change {
14     font-weight: bold;
15   }
16
17   p.big {
```

(Continues)

Listing 3.1   **Adding Multiple Classes to a Single Element (Continued)**

```
18    font-size: 72px;
19   }
20   </style>
21 </head>
22 <body>
23
24 <p>This text will have a different appearance after
25   the class change. Click on the text to make it a
26   bit larger.</p>
27
28 <script src="http://code.jquery.com/jquery-1.7.2.min.js"></script>
29
30 <script>
31 // please externalize this code to an external .js file
32 $(document).ready(function() {
33
34   $('p').addClass('initial');
35
36   $('p').click(function() {
37     $(this).addClass('change big');
38   });
39
40 });
41 </script>
42 </body>
43 </html>
```

Line 34 adds one class, while line 37 adds two classes in a single call.

Example: Removing Classes

The removeClass() function works the same manner as addClass(). A common use case is to hide HTML elements that are only used when JavaScript is available. Listing 3.2 shows how to remove the no-js class right after the document is loaded.

Listing 3.2   **Hiding HTML Content When JavaScript Is Not Available**

```
00 <!DOCTYPE html>
01
02 <html lang="en">
03 <head>
04   <title>The removeClass() function</title>
05   <style>
06     .no-js {
```

Listing 3.2   **Hiding HTML Content When JavaScript Is Not Available (Continued)**

```
07    display: none;
08  }
09  </style>
10 </head>
11 <body>
12
13 <p>This page contains both text that is always
14   available and text that is only visible when
15   JavaScript is available</p>
16
17 <p class="no-js">This could be a part of the site that
18   is JavaScript dependent and is better hidden when
19   JavaScript is unavailable.</p>
20
21 <script src="http://code.jquery.com/jquery-latest.min.js"></script>
22
23 <script>
24 // please externalize this code to an external .js file
25 $(document).ready(function() {
26
27   $('.no-js').removeClass('no-js');
28
29   // removeClass() also works without parameter; risk
30   // removing other classes
31   //
32   //$('.no-js').removeClass();
33
34 });
35 </script>
36 </body>
37 </html>
```

The other way around, you can use `noscript` elements to show things that only should be visible when JavaScript is unavailable.

Recipe: Generating Class Names

The `addClass()` function can take more than just static strings as an argument. You can also pass a function, as is demonstrated in Listing 3.3. Especially in dynamic web applications, this can come in handy. Be careful, though; you do not want to make your CSS styling more complex than necessary. With the proper selectors, you can do many things without difficult class names.

Listing 3.3   **Passing a Function to addClass()**

```
00 <!DOCTYPE html>
01
02 <html lang="en">
03 <head>
04   <title>A function as argument to addClass()</title>
05   <style>
06   /* please externalize this code to an external
07      .css file */
08
09   p.changed-0 {
10     background-color: green;
11   }
12
13   p.differentchanged-1 {
14     background-color: blue;
15   }
16
17   p.twochanged-2 {
18     background-color: red;
19   }
20
21   </style>
22 </head>
23 <body>
24
25 <p>This text will have a different appearance
26   after the class change</p>
27 <p class="different">This text will have a different
28   appearance after the class change</p>
29 <p class="one two">This text will have a different
30   appearance after the class change</p>
31 <div>This text will not change</div>
32
33 <script src="http://code.jquery.com/jquery-1.7.2.min.js"></script>
34
35 <script>
36 // please externalize this code to an external .js file
37 $(document).ready(function() {
38
39   $('p').addClass(function(index, className) {
40       $(this).removeClass();
41       return className + 'changed-' + index;
42     });
43
44 });
```

Listing 3.3   **Passing a Function to addClass() (Continued)**

```
45 </script>
46 </body>
47 </html>
```

On line 39, the function works on the index of each returned element from the selector and the current class name of the selected element. Line 41 combines the current class name and the index into a new name to demonstrate the function's possibilities. This example would not be useful in practice, though.

Recipe: Changing Properties and Attributes

Using `attr()`, you can change an HTML element's attributes, such as `rel`, `lang`, or a custom attribute. With `prop()`, you can change an HTML element's properties. Listing 3.4 demonstrates where it becomes difficult. In some cases, something that looks like an attribute from an HTML perspective might be a property from a JavaScript perspective. (There were changes in the 1.6 release of jQuery that caused the `prop()` function to be used exclusively for property values and the `attr()` function to be used for attribute values. You can read about the current and any future changes at http://api.jquery.com/prop/ and http://api.jquery.com/attr/.)

Listing 3.4   **Demonstrating the Difference Between a Property and an Attribute**

```
00 <!DOCTYPE html>
01
02 <html lang="en">
03 <head>
04   <title>Difference between prop() and attr()</title>
05   <style>
06   /* please externalize this code to an external
07      .css file */
08
09   label[other="anything"] {
10     background-color: blue;
11   }
12
13   </style>
14 </head>
15 <body>
16
17 <h2>Convert the radio buttons into check boxes and
18   change properties on the HTML</h2>
19
```

(Continues)

Listing 3.4   **Demonstrating the Difference Between a Property
and an Attribute (Continued)**

```
20 <input type="radio" name="test" id="first">
21 <label for=first>First</label>
22
23 <input type="radio" name="test" id="second">
24 <label for=second>Second</label>
25
26 <input type="radio" name="test" id="third">
27 <label for=third>Third</label>
28
29 <button id="switch">Switch</button>
30
31 <script src="http://code.jquery.com/jquery-1.7.2.min.js"></script>
32
33 <script>
34 // please externalize this code to an external .js file
35 $(document).ready(function() {
36
37   $('#switch').click(function(){
38
39     $('input').prop('type', 'checkbox');
40
41     $('label').attr('other', 'anything');
42
43   });
44
45 });
46 </script>
47 </body>
48 </html>
```

Line 39 uses the prop() function to transform a radio button into a checkbox. In older versions of jQuery, you might have achieved the same result by using attr(). In the current versions of jQuery, the two are clearly separated.

Line 41 sets a custom attribute. If your browser is sufficiently modern, the CSS styles on lines 9–11 will visually display the change of the attribute.

Recipe: Changing the HTML Contained within an Element

jQuery provides a convenient method, html(), for manipulating an HTML element's innerHTML attributes. Listing 3.5 demonstrates its use.

Listing 3.5   **Selecting a Paragraph and Replacing the HTML**

```
00 <!DOCTYPE html>
01
02 <html lang="en">
03 <head>
04   <title>The html() function</title>
05 </head>
06 <body>
07
08 <h2>Press the button to see the old HTML in the
09   paragraph and replace it with new HTML</h2>
10
11 <p>This <strong>contains</strong> some <a
12   href="http://www.w3.org/TR/html5/">HTML</a>
13   of its <em>own</em>.</p>
14
15 <button>Change</button>
16
17 <script src="http://code.jquery.com/jquery-1.7.2.min.js"></script>
18
19 <script>
20 // please externalize this code to an external .js file
21 $(document).ready(function() {
22
23   $('button').click(function() {
24
25     var p = $('p');
26
27     alert('The old HTML was:\n' + p.html());
28
29     p.html('<p>And that can be replaced with ' +
30            '<em>simple</em> new HTML.</p>');
31
32   });
33
34 });
35 </script>
36 </body>
37 </html>
```

You can directly pass HTML strings to html(), or passing a jQuery object that contains HTML also works. The main advantage of html() over innerHTML is that it works directly on a jQuery selection without first transforming it into an array.

Recipe: Adding Content by Using append() and appendTo()

Whereas `html()` replaces the current content—and thus you are responsible for preserving the current content yourself—Listing 3.6 demonstrates how to use `append()` and `appendTo()` to add elements without affecting the current content.

Listing 3.6   Showing the Difference Between append() and appendTo()

```
00 <!DOCTYPE html>
01
02 <html lang="en">
03 <head>
04   <title>Difference between append() and appendTo()</title>
05 </head>
06 <body>
07
08 <div id="append-placeholder">
09 </div>
10
11 <button id="append">append()</button><br>
12
13 <div id="append-to-placeholder">
14 </div>
15
16 <button id="append-to">appendTo()</button><br>
17
18
19
20 <script src="http://code.jquery.com/jquery-1.7.2.min.js"></script>
21
22 <script>
23 // please externalize this code to an external .js file
24 $(document).ready(function() {
25
26   $('#append').click(function() {
27     $('#append-placeholder').append('<p>Test append</p>');
28   });
29
30   $('#append-to').click(function() {
31     $('<p>Test appendTo()</p>').appendTo('#append-to-placeholder');
32   });
33
34 </script>
35 </body>
36 </html>
```

The main difference between `append()` and `appendTo()` is whether it works on the *target* with the HTML as an argument or whether it works on the *HTML* with the target as an argument. The `append()` function attaches the content to the selector from which it is called, as is shown on line 27, whereas the `appendTo()` function works in the reverse, as is shown on line 31 where the content that will be inserted is used as the selector. This tends to make a little more visual sense when appending a jQuery object. For arguments, the `append()` and `appendTo()` functions are capable of taking DOM elements, HTML strings, jQuery objects, and a function.

> **Caution**
>
> If you need to append many HTML elements, it is better to first combine the HTML into a larger `string` and append it in a single function call. The `append()` and `appendTo()` functions work on the HTML document tree, and that makes manipulations relatively slow.

Example: Appending the Outcome of a Function

Instead of passing a static string to `append()`, you can also pass a function. Listing 3.7 shows the use of a function that first determines whether there is enough space to add another element.

Listing 3.7   **Determining Whether There Is Space to Append More Items**

```
00 <!DOCTYPE html>
01
02 <html lang="en">
03 <head>
04   <title>A function as argument for append()</title>
05   <style>
06   /* please externalize this code to an external
07      .css file */
08   div#template {
09     display: none;
10   }
11   </style>
12 </head>
13 <body>
14
15 <div id="append-placeholder">
16   <p>Test!</p>
17 </div>
18
19 <button id="append">Add more. . .</button><br>
20
```

(Continues)

Listing 3.7   Determining Whether There Is Space to Append More Items (Continued)

```
21 <script src="http://code.jquery.com/jquery-1.7.2.min.js"></script>
22
23 <script>
24 // please externalize this code to an external .js file
25 $(document).ready(function() {
26
27   $('#append').click(function() {
28     $('#append-placeholder').append(function(index, html) {
29       var more = "<p>There is room for more</p>",
30         last = "<p>This is the last one</p>",
31         spaceLeft = 160 - $.trim(html).length - last.length;
32
33       if(more.length < spaceLeft)
34         return more;
35       else if(spaceLeft > 0)
36         return last;
37     });
38   });
39
40 });
41 </script>
42 </body>
43 </html>
```

This example adds lines that contain the text "There is room for more" until it establishes that there is not enough room. Before it stops adding lines, the last line displays the text "This is the last one."

Recipe: Adding Content by Using prepend() and prependTo()

The prepend() and prependTo() functions work almost exactly like the append() and appendTo() functions. Whereas appending content places the new content to the bottom of the selected element, prepending places the content at the top. Listing 3.8 demonstrates the use of the prepend() and prependTo() functions.

Listing 3.8   Showing the Difference Between prepend() and prependTo()

```
00 <!DOCTYPE html>
01
02 <html lang="en">
03 <head>
04   <title>Difference between prepend() and prependTo()</title>
05 </head>
```

Listing 3.8   **Showing the Difference Between prepend() and prependTo() (Continued)**

```
06 <body>
07
08 <div id="prepend-placeholder">
09   <p>This content is for reference</p>
10 </div>
11
12 <button id="prepend">append()</button><br>
13
14 <div id="prepend-to-placeholder">
15   <p>This content is for reference</p>
16 </div>
17
18 <button id="prepend-to">prependTo()</button><br>
19
20 <script src="http://code.jquery.com/jquery-latest.min.js"></script>
21
22 <script>
23 // please externalize this code to an external .js file
24 $(document).ready(function() {
25
26   $('#prepend').click(function() {
27     $('#prepend-placeholder').prepend('<p>Test prepend</p>');
28   });
29
30   $('#prepend-to').click(function() {
31     $('<p>Test prependTo()</p>').appendTo('#prepend-to-placeholder');
32   });
33
34 });
35 </script>
36 </body>
37 </html>
```

Lines 9 and 15 both contain content that helps to identify prepended text and visualize how you add content above any existing elements. Just like the append() and appendTo() functions, prepend() and prependTo() are capable of taking DOM elements, HTML strings, jQuery objects, and a function as arguments.

Recipe: Generating HTML Dynamically by Using jQuery

In previous examples, HTML was mostly generated directly as text strings. You can also generate HTML by using jQuery. You can pass attributes as property maps and nest

HTML elements for the child elements within that map. Listing 3.9 exhibits this way of generating HTML.

Listing 3.9   **Building an Unordered List by Using jQuery**

```
00 <!DOCTYPE html>
01
02 <html lang="en">
03 <head>
04   <title>Generate HTML using jQuery</title>
05   <style>
06   /* please externalize this code to an external
07     .css file */
08     .test {
09       background-color: yellow;
10     }
11   </style>
12 </head>
13 <body>
14
15 <p>Under this paragraph, you should see a yellow bulleted list</p>
16
17 <div id="append-to-placeholder">
18 </div>
19
20 <script src="http://code.jquery.com/jquery-1.7.2.min.js"></script>
21
22 <script>
23 // please externalize this code to an external .js file
24 $(document).ready(function() {
25
26   var htmlGen = function() {
27     return '<li>1</li><li>2</li>';
28   }
29
30   $('<p/>', {
31       class: 'test',
32       html: $('<ul/>', {html: htmlGen})33  }).appendTo('#append-to-placeholder');
34
35 });
36 </script>
37 </body>
38 </html>
```

In this example, lines 26–28 "generate" HTML. Line 31 adds a reference to this function, which is executed automatically. The way lines 30 and 31 are nested yields a more dynamic way of building HTML. Line 31 could have been a variable that could have been replaced on certain conditions.

Recipe: Attaching and Detaching Elements

You can detach an element from the HTML tree and reattach it at a different location. Listing 3.10 shows how to do this.

Listing 3.10 **Moving Elements Around the DOM Tree by Using appendTo() and detach()**

```
00 <!DOCTYPE html>
01
02 <html lang="en">
03 <head>
04   <title>The attach() and detach() function</title>
05   <style>
06   /* please externalize this code to an external
07      .css file */
08   .detaching button.attach {
09     display: none;
10   }
11   .attaching button.detach {
12   display: none;
13   }
14   </style>
15 </head>
16 <body class="detaching">
17
18 <div>
19   <button class="attach">Attach</button>
20   <button class="detach">Detach</button>
21   <span>First element</span>
22 </div>
23 <div>
24   <button class="attach">Attach</button>
25   <button class="detach">Detach</button>
26   <span>Second element</span>
27 </div>
28 <div>
29   <button class="attach">Attach</button>
30   <button class="detach">Detach</button>
31   <span>Third element</span>
32 </div>
33 <div>
34   <button class="attach">Attach</button>
```

(Continues)

Listing 3.10   **Moving Elements Around the DOM Tree by Using appendTo() and detach()
(Continued)**

```
35    <button class="detach">Detach</button>
36    <span>Fourth element</span>
37 </div>
38 <div>
39    <button class="attach">Attach</button>
40    <button class="detach">Detach</button>
41    <span>Fifth element</span>
42 </div>
43
44
45 <script src="http://code.jquery.com/jquery-1.7.2.min.js"></script>
46
47 <script>
48 // please externalize this code to an external .js file
49 $(document).ready(function() {
50    var el;
51
52    $('.detach').click(function() {
53      el = $(this).parent().children('span:first').detach();
54      $('body').removeClass('detaching').addClass('attaching');
55    });
56    $('.attach').click(function() {
57      el.appendTo($(this).parent());
58      $('body').removeClass('attaching').addClass('detaching');
59    });
60
61 });
62 </script>
63 </body>
64 </html>
```

Besides moving HTML elements to different locations, an important use case of
detaching elements is heavy manipulation of the HTML tree. When an element is
detached, it requires fewer system resources to manipulate it. You should also be aware
that the detach() function will keep all associated jQuery data (including functions
and objects) with the elements that are detached. This is helpful when appending
the data back into the DOM and is how this recipe is able to remove and reattach
content.

Recipe: Copying Elements by Using clone()

If detaching and reattaching elements only moves them around, how do you copy
elements in an efficient way? To address this, jQuery provides the clone() function.

Listing 3.11 demonstrates how to use the clone() function to emulate a form with repeating elements. The set of repeating elements is copied from a hidden template div.

Listing 3.11   Emulating Repetitive Elements in a Form by Using clone()

```
00 <!DOCTYPE html>
01
02 <html lang="en">
03 <head>
04   <title>The clone() function</title>
05   <style>
06   /* please externalize this code to an external
07      .css file */
08   div#template {
09     display: none;
10   }
11   </style>
12 </head>
13 <body>
14
15 <h2>Add rows under the repeating fields header using the
16   button below</h2>
17
18 <form action="" method="post">
19
20   <h2>Single fields</h2>
21
22   <label for="first">First</label>
23   <input type="text" name="first"><br>
24
25   <label for="second">Second</label>
26   <input type="text" name="second"><br>
27
28   <h2>Repeating fields</h2>
29
30   <button id="add-row">Add row</button><br>
31
32   <div id="repeat"></div>
33
34 </form>
35
36 <div id="template">
37   <label for="third">Third</label>
38   <input type="text" name="third" ></br>
39
40   <label for="fourth">Fourth</label>
```

(Continues)

Listing 3.11   Emulating Repetitive Elements in a Form by Using clone() (Continued)

```
41    <input type="checkbox" name="fourth"></br>
42 </div>
43
44 <script src="http://code.jquery.com/jquery-1.7.2.min.js"></script>
45
46 <script>
47 // please externalize this code to an external .js file
48 $(document).ready(function() {
49   var rowCount = 0;
50
51   $('#add-row').click(function() {
52     $('#template *')
53       .clone()
54       .filter('input')
55         .attr('name', function(index, name) {
56           return name +'[' + rowCount + ']';
57         })
58         .end()
59       .appendTo('#repeat');
60     rowCount++;
61
62     // if the click handler is on a <button> element and the button
63     // is within a <form> element, return false to stop the page
64     // from reloading and inadvertently undoing the clone action
65     return false;
66   });
67
68 });
69 </script>
70 </body>
71 </html>
```

Up until the `clone()` call on line 53, the code is straightforward. On lines 54–58, the code filters out the input elements and changes their name attribute to ensure that each is unique within the form. When you submit this form, the result seems like an array of repetitive elements. The `clone()` function can also take two extra arguments that enable the cloned elements to also contain copies of any element data and event bindings. Although both arguments are Boolean, the first argument refers to just the data and event bindings of the parent, whereas the second argument refers to any child elements.

Recipe: Inserting Elements at Specific Positions

The `append()`, `appendTo()`, `prepend()`, and `prependTo()` functions insert new elements into a selection of existing elements. In some cases, you want to create new sibling elements instead of new children. Listing 3.12 demonstrates the options for doing this.

Listing 3.12   Inserting Elements Before and After a Set of Buttons

```
00 <!DOCTYPE html>
01
02 <html lang="en">
03 <head>
04   <title>The after(), before(), insertAfter()
05     and insertBefore() function</title>
06 </head>
07 <body>
08
09 <h2>Click on the buttons to see the result of each
10   function</h2>
11
12 <div id="target">
13
14 <button id="before">before()</button><br>
15 <button id="after">after()</button><br>
16 <button id="insert-before">insertBefore()</button><br>
17 <button id="insert-after">insertAfter()</button>
18
19 </div>
20
21 <script src="http://code.jquery.com/jquery-1.7.2.min.js"></script>
22
23 <script>
24 // please externalize this code to an external .js file
25 $(document).ready(function() {
26
27   $('#before').click(function() {
28     $('#target').before('<p>Before</p>');
29   });
30   $('#after').click(function() {
31     $('#target').after('<p>After</p>');
32   });
33   $('#insert-before').click(function() {
34     $('<p>Insert Before</p>').insertBefore('#target');
35   });
36   $('#insert-after').click(function() {
37     $('<p>Insert After</p>').insertAfter('#target');
38   });
39
40 });
```

(Continues)

Listing 3.12   **Inserting Elements Before and After a Set of Buttons (Continued)**

```
41 </script>
42 </body>
43 </html>
```

The difference between `after()` and `insertAfter()` is similar to the difference between `append()` and `appendTo()`. If you click the buttons, you will see that with this code example, the resulting behavior is the same. As expected, `before()` inserts elements before the existing selection. Be aware that these functions take the same parameters as the `append()` and `prepend()` functions, meaning that you can pass DOM elements, HTML strings, jQuery objects, and a function as arguments.

Example: Moving Items Up and Down the List

You can use `insertBefore()` and `insertAfter()` to move existing elements up and down a list. Listing 3.13 reveals how you can move a list of `div` elements around via *up* and *down* buttons.

Listing 3.13   **Changing the Order of a <div> List by Using Up and Down Buttons**

```
00 <!DOCTYPE html>
01
02 <html lang="en">
03 <head>
04   <title>Pushing elements up and down</title>
05   <style>
06   /* please externalize this code to an external
07      .css file */
08   div:first-of-type button.up {
09     visibility: hidden;
10   }
11   div:last-of-type button.down {
12     visibility: hidden;
13   }
14   </style>
15 </head>
16 <body>
17
18 <h2>Click on the up and down buttons to move the rows</h2>
19
20 <div>
21   <button class="up">Up</button>
22   <button class="down">Down</button>
23   This was initially the first element.
24 </div>
```

Listing 3.13   Changing the Order of a <div> List by Using Up and Down Buttons (Continued)

```
25 <div>
26    <button class="up">Up</button>
27    <button class="down">Down</button>
28    This was initially the second element.
29 </div>
30 <div>
31    <button class="up">Up</button>
32    <button class="down">Down</button>
33    This was initially the third element.
34 </div>
35 <div>
36    <button class="up">Up</button>
37    <button class="down">Down</button>
38    This was initially the fourth element.
39 </div>
40 <div>
41    <button class="up">Up</button>
42    <button class="down">Down</button>
43    This was initially the fifth element.
44 </div>
45
46 <script src="http://code.jquery.com/jquery-1.7.2.min.js"></script>
47
48 <script>
49 // please externalize this code to an external .js file
50 $(document).ready(function() {
51
52    $('.up').click(function() {
53    var parent = $(this).parent();
54    parent.insertBefore(parent.prev());
55    });
56    $('.down').click(function() {
57    var parent = $(this).parent();
58    parent.insertAfter(parent.next());
59    });
60
61 });
62 </script>
63 </body>
64 </html>
```

Hiding the first *up* button and the last *down* button is done by using the CSS style sheet on top of the HTML. Calling `insertBefore()` and `insertAfter()` automatically moves the element away from its current position.

Recipe: Removing Elements

When you detach() an element, it is gone from the screen and from the HTML document tree; however, it is still stored in memory. Listing 3.14 demonstrates the remove() and empty() functions to eliminate elements from both the document and from memory. The remove() function will return the removed elements, so you could store those in a variable and reinsert them into the page. Keep in mind that when doing this with the remove() function, all jQuery data and event information is lost.

Listing 3.14   **Demonstrating the Difference Between remove() and empty()**

```
00 <!DOCTYPE html>
01
02 <html lang="en">
03 <head>
04   <title>The remove() and empty() function</title>
05   <style>
06   /* please externalize this code to an external
07     .css file */
08   p {
09     border: 1px solid red;
10   }
11   </style>
12 </head>
13 <body>
14
15 <h1>Click on the paragraph to remove</h1>
16 <p id="remove">This text will have a different appearance after
17    clicking it</p>
18
19 <h1>Click on the paragraph to remove the spans</h1>
20 <p id="remove-spans">This text <span id="test">will</span>
21   have <span>a</span> different appearance after
22   <span>clicking</span> it</p>
23
24 <h1>Click on the paragraph to empty</h1>
25 <p id="empty">This text will have a different appearance
26    after clicking it</p>
27
28 <script src="http://code.jquery.com/jquery-1.7.2.min.js"></script>
29
30 <script>
31 // please externalize this code to an external .js file
32 $(document).ready(function() {
33
34   $('p#remove').click(function() {
```

Listing 3.14   **Demonstrating the Difference Between remove() and empty() (Continued)**

```
35      $(this).remove();
36    });
37
38    $('p#remove-spans').click(function() {
39      $(this).children('span').remove();
40
41      // Does not work:
42      //$(this).remove('span');
43
44      // Removes the element itself:
45      //$(this).remove(':has(span)');
46    });
47
48    $('p#empty').click(function() {
49      $(this).empty();
50    });
51
52  });
53  </script>
54  </body>
55  </html>
```

The remove() function on line 35 removes the complete paragraph element. On line 39, it removes the span elements directly under the paragraph. Similar to the other examples of the remove() function, this result can also be achieved by using $(this).children().remove('span'). When you call empty() on line 49, the paragraph element still exists; however, the text has been removed. If any child elements were contained within the paragraph element, they would also have been removed. Try this code example and take a look at the visual representation in the form of the red border.

Recipe: Wrapping and Unwrapping Elements

If you want to encapsulate an existing HTML element with a new HTML element, jQuery provides multiple functions to help you do it. Each of these functions has the word "wrap" in their title, but the exact details of their workings differ. Listing 3.15 demonstrates the most basic use of wrap().

Listing 3.15   **Wrapping and Unwrapping Paragraphs**

```
00  <!DOCTYPE html>
01
02  <html lang="en">
03  <head>
```

(Continues)

Listing 3.15   Wrapping and Unwrapping Paragraphs (Continued)

```
04    <title>The wrap() and unwrap() function</title>
05    <style>
06    /* please externalize this code to an external
07       .css file */
08    div.wrapper {
09      border: 1px solid red;
10    }
11    </style>
12  </head>
13  <body>
14
15  <h2>Paragraphs below are wrapped. Click the paragraphs to
16    test wrap()</h2>
17
18  <p>Paragraph to wrap</p>
19  <p>Paragraph to wrap</p>
20
21  <script src="http://code.jquery.com/jquery-1.7.2.min.js"></script>
22
23  <script>
24  // please externalize this code to an external .js file
25  $(document).ready(function() {
26
27    $('p').wrap('<div class="wrapper"/>');
28
29    $('p').click(function() {
30      $(this).unwrap('<div class="wrapper"/>');
31    });
32
33  });
34  </script>
35  </body>
36  </html>
```

In this example, each of the paragraphs is wrapped by its own wrapper div. Then, the unwrap() function removes these divs.

Listing 3.16 demonstrates the wrapInner() function.

Listing 3.16   Wrapping the Content of Paragraphs

```
00  <!DOCTYPE html>
01
02  <html lang="en">
03  <head>
04    <title>The wrapInner() function</title>
05    <style>
```

Listing 3.16   **Wrapping the Content of Paragraphs (Continued)**

```
06   /* please externalize this code to an external
07      .css file */
08   div.wrapper {
09     border: 1px solid red;
10   }
11   </style>
12 </head>
13 <body>
14
15 <h2>The paragraphs below are modified with wrapInner()</h2>
16
17 <p>Paragraph to wrap</p>
18 <p>Paragraph to wrap</p>
19
20 <script src="http://code.jquery.com/jquery-1.7.2.min.js"></script>
21
22 <script>
23 // please externalize this code to an external .js file
24 $(document).ready(function() {
25
26   $('p').wrapInner('<div class="wrapper"/>');
27
28   // This does not work with wrapInner() :
29   // $('p').click(function() {
30   //   $(this).unwrap('<div class="wrapper"/>');
31   // });
32
33 });
34 </script>
35 </body>
36 </html>
```

In this example, the paragraphs themselves are not wrapped. Instead, the contents of the paragraphs are wrapped. This means that the p now contains a div. The unwrap() function does not work in this example. Keep in mind that a div inside a paragraph is not only a bad practice but will cause your HTML to be invalid; this is just an example to demonstrate how wrapInner() works.

Listing 3.17 demonstrates the use of wrapAll().

Listing 3.17   **Wrapping a Set of Paragraphs**

```
00 <!DOCTYPE html>
01
02 <html lang="en">
03 <head>
```

(Continues)

Listing 3.17   **Wrapping a Set of Paragraphs (Continued)**

```
04   <title>The wrapAll() function</title>
05   <style>
06   /* please externalize this code to an external
07      .css file */
08   div.wrapper {
09     border: 1px solid red;
10   }
11   </style>
12 </head>
13 <body>
14
15 <h2>Paragraphs below are wrapped with wrapAll() Click
16     the paragraphs to unwrap()</h2>
17
18 <p>Paragraph to wrap</p>
19 <p>Paragraph to wrap</p>
20
21 <script src="http://code.jquery.com/jquery-1.7.2.min.js"></script>
22
23 <script>
24 // please externalize this code to an external .js file
25 $(document).ready(function() {
26
27   $('p').wrapAll('<div class="wrapper"/>');
28
29   $('p').click(function(){
30     $(this).unwrap('<div class="wrapper"/>');
31   });
32
33 });
34 </script>
35 </body>
36 </html>
```

In this example, a single wrapping div contains all the selected paragraphs. The unwrap() function removes this wrapper.

Summary

This chapter demonstrated the most important functions to manipulate the HTML document tree. This chapter started with classes, attributes, and properties. The majority of this chapter covered the various ways to modify elements inside the document: dynamic HTML, appending, prepending, inserting before and after, attaching, detaching, copying, and wrapping elements in various ways. By using the functions covered in this chapter, you can manipulate an HTML document any way you like.

Chapter 4

Listening and Responding to Events

Listening and responding to events using jQuery is relatively simple in terms of code. Regardless of the code's simplicity, however, handling events can still be complex. Large numbers of events are generated in seemingly unpredictable order. To be able to respond to events in a useful manner, you need a grasp of which events you can expect, under what circumstances. This chapter provides recipes with which you can log all events of a certain kind and experiment with your input to see what happens. It handles mouse events, keyboard events, form events, and some more general events such as scrolling. After investigating specific events, this chapter demonstrates the advantages of event delegation.

Recipe: Listening to Mouse Events

Mouse events probably outnumber any other event kind. You have to know what you are looking for in order to do something useful with so many events. To get a feel for what happens with different mouse events, Listing 4.1 simply displays events of certain kinds as they occur. There are too many mouse events to keep a log file and read it easily.

Listing 4.1 **Displaying Mouse Events**

```
00 <!DOCTYPE html>
01
02 <html lang="en">
03 <head>
04   <title>Mouse events</title>
05   <style>
06   /* please externalize this code to an external
07      .css file */
08   #target {
09 width: 150px;
10     height: 150px;
11     border: 1px solid red;
12   }
```

(Continues)

Listing 4.1   **Displaying Mouse Events (Continued)**

```
13   #block {
14 width: 50px;
15     height: 50px;
16     margin: 0px;
17     background-color: black;
18   }
19   </style>
20 </head>
21 <body>
22
23 <h2>Move the mouse over the block to see events</h2>
24
25 <div id="target">
26   <p id="block"></p>
27 </div>
28
29 <h3>Mouse Up / Down</h3>
30
31 <p class="mousedown mouseup"></p>
32
33 <h3>Mouse Move</h3>
34
35 <p class="mousemove"></p>
36
37 <h3>Mouse (Dbl)Click</h3>
38
39 <p class="click dblclick"></p>
40
41 <h3>Mouse Enter / Leave</h3>
42
43 <p class="mouseenter mouseleave"></p>
44
45 <h3>Mouse Over/Out</h3>
46
47 <p class="mouseover mouseout"></p>
48
49 <script src="http://code.jquery.com/jquery-1.7.2.min.js"></script>
50
51 <script>
52 // please externalize this code to an external .js file
53 $(document).ready(function() {
54
55   $.each(('click dblclick mousedown mouseup mousemove mouseover '
56         + 'mouseout mouseenter mouseleave').split(' '),
57     function( i, name ) {
58
59     $('#target').bind(name, function(event) {
```

Listing 4.1   **Displaying Mouse Events (Continued)**

```
60     $('.' + name).html('target = ' + event.target + ' ' +
61                'type = ' + event.type + ' ' +
62                'pageX = ' + event.pageX + ' ' +
63                'pageY = ' + event.pageY + ' ' +
64                'which = ' + event.which + ' ');
65     });
66   });
67
68 });
69 </script>
70 </body>
71 </html>
```

Most mouse events are fairly self-explanatory, and you can learn about them by playing around with the mouse and pointing to different parts of the test area. However, the difference between `mouseover` and `mouseout` versus `mouseenter` and `mouseleave` might not be apparent at first sight. Within most of the target `div`, the results are the same. Now, try moving the mouse over the block paragraph and notice the difference.

Note that this example uses the bind function for all event names. Of course, there are also shorthand functions you can use if you only listen to a smaller number of event types such as `mousedown()`, `mouseenter()`, `mouseleave()`, `mousemove()`, `mouseout()`, `mouseover()`, and `mouseup()`. If you find that you need to remove one of the events that you have attached, you can use the `unbind()` function to remove that particular event handler.

Example: Drawing on a Canvas

A different way to visualize mouse events is to use them to make drawings. If you have a modern browser that supports HTML5's `canvas` element, you can use Listing 4.2 to do some creative doodling.

Listing 4.2   **Listening to Mouse Events on a <canvas> Element and Drawing Pixels**

```
00 <!DOCTYPE html>
01
02 <html lang="en">
03 <head>
04   <title>Drawing in a canvas using mouse events</title>
05   <style>
06   /* please externalize this code to an external
07      .css file */
08   #target {
09     border: 1px solid red;
10   }
```

(Continues)

Listing 4.2   **Listening to Mouse Events on a <canvas> Element and Drawing Pixels (Continued)**

```
11    </style>
12  </head>
13  <body>
14
15  <h2>Draw pixels in the canvas:</h2>
16
17  <canvas id="target" width="150" height="150"></canvas>
18
19  <script src="http://code.jquery.com/jquery-1.7.2.min.js"></script>
20
21  <script>
22  // please externalize this code to an external .js file
23  $(document).ready(function() {
24
25    var context = $('#target')[0].getContext('2d');
26    var draw = false;
27
28    $('#target')
29      .mousedown(function() {
30      draw = true;
31    })
32      .mouseup(function() {
33      draw = false;
34    })
35      .mouseout (function() {
36      draw = false;
37    })
38    .mousemove(function(event) {
39      var pos = $(this).position();
40      if(draw){
41        context.fillRect(event.pageX - pos.left,
42                event.pageY - pos.top, 2, 2);
43      }
44    });
45
46  });
47  </script>
48  </body>
49  </html>
```

This example draws pixels when you press the mouse button. If you move the mouse fast, you see that there might be space between the pixels. If this was an actual drawing application, one way that could be solved is by watching the onmousemove event and then plotting all of the points in between the current position and previous position (to see some of the math involved see Bresenham's line algorithm at http://en.wikipedia.org/wiki/Bresenham%27s_line_algorithm). For demonstration purposes, it is good to know that there is space between mouse events in general.

Line 39 shows the use of the position() function, which returns the top and left coordinates relative to the offset of the parent inside of an object. Line 41 shows the object in action as the pos.left is used to ascertain the position from the left; in line 42, pos.top is used to establish the position from the top.

If you decide that your canvas element is going to be inside of parent defined by an absolute position, you should use the offset() function instead of the position() function. The offset() function returns the coordinate data relative to the document instead of the parent.

On lines 41 and 42, notice how the mouse position on the page needs to be translated to the mouse location within the canvas element.

Recipe: Listening to Keyboard Events

Similar to mouse events, you can learn a lot from watching keyboard events. In this case, it would have been feasible to log all events. This example still only shows the last event of each kind for the best overview though. Listing 4.3 separates keydown, keyup, and keypressed events. Play around with it, and take special care of characters like Ctrl, Alt, Shift, the arrow keys, F1–F12, and é, ü, î, ö.

Listing 4.3 **Displaying Keyboard Events from an <input> Element**

```
00 <!DOCTYPE html>
01
02 <html lang="en">
03 <head>
04   <title>Keyboard events</title>
05 </head>
06 <body>
07
08 <h2>Type in the text field below to see keyboard events</h2>
09
10 <input type="text">
11
12 <h1>Keydown</h1>
13
14 <p id="keydown"></p>
15
16 <h1>Keyup</h1>
17
18 <p id="keyup"></p>
19
```

(Continues)

```
20 <h1>Keypress</h1>
21
22 <p id="keypress"></p>
23
24 <script src="http://code.jquery.com/jquery-1.7.2.min.js"></script>
25
26 <script>
27 // please externalize this code to an external .js file
28 $(document).ready(function() {
29
30   $('input').keydown(function(event) {
31     $('#keydown').html('target = ' + event.target + '<br>' +
32              'type = ' + event.type + '<br>' +
33              'which = ' + event.which + '<br>');
34   });
35
36   $('input').keyup(function(event) {
37     $('#keyup').html('target = ' + event.target + '<br>' +
38              'type = ' + event.type + '<br>' +
39              'which = ' + event.which + '<br>');
40   });
41
42   $('input').keypress(function(event) {
43     $('#keypress').html('target = ' + event.target + '<br>' +
44              'type = ' + event.type + '<br>' +
45              'which = ' + event.which + '<br>');
46   });
47
48 });
49 </script>
50 </body>
51 </html>
```

If you watched closely, you might conclude that it is not possible to reproduce the `input` element's content from the keyboard events. Keyboard events are useful mostly for shortcuts such as those in Gmail or to create game controllers. The `event.which` that is used in this example is used to return the `keyCode` or `charCode`, as needed by the event type. You can learn more about the `keyCode`, `charCode`, and the `which` property at the Mozilla Developer Center (https://developer.mozilla.org/en-US/docs/DOM/event.keyCode).

Recipe: Listening to Form Events

If you want to know that a form has changed without tracking every keyboard or mouse event, you can listen for specific form-related events. Listing 4.4 demonstrates a form that will list the events that are triggered when the form is manipulated.

Listing 4.4   **Displaying All Events Generated in a Form**

```
00 <!DOCTYPE html>
01
02 <html lang="en">
03 <head>
04   <title>Form events</title>
05 </head>
06 <body>
07
08
09 <h2>Change the input in the boxes and see the event generated
10   while editing under the form</h2>
11
12 <form action="#" method="post">
13
14   <label for="first_field">First field</label>
15   <input type="text" name="first_field"
16       value="" id="first_field"><br>
17
18   <label for="second_field">Second field</label>
19   <input type="text" name="second_field"
20       value="" id="second_field"><br>
21
22   <label for="third_field">Third field</label>
23   <input type="text" name="third_field"
24       value="" id="third_field"><br>
25
26   <label for="fourth_field">Fourth field</label>
27   <input type="text" name="fourth_field"
28       value="" id="fourth_field"><br>
29
30   <input type="submit" name="submit" value="Submit" id="submit">
31
32 </form>
33
34 <p id="placeholder"></p>
35
36 <script src="http://code.jquery.com/jquery-1.7.2.min.js"></script>
37
38 <script>
39 // please externalize this code to an external .js file
40 $(document).ready(function() {
41
42   $('input').bind('blur change focus select submit',
43                   function(event) {
44
45     $('#placeholder').append('target = ' +
```

(Continues)

Listing 4.4   **Displaying All Events Generated in a Form (Continued)**

```
46          event.target.getAttribute('id') + ' ' +
47          'type = ' + event.type + ' <br/>');
48
49   });
50
51 });
52 </script>
53 </body>
54 </html>
```

The `blur`, `change`, and `focus` events can help you update validation and help messages as the visitor progresses through the form. In a more sophisticated form, you might enable or disable sets of form elements based on earlier input or submit (parts of) the form by using AJAX for quick feedback.

Recipe: Listening to Scroll Events

In some cases, you want to respond when the page is scrolled. Listing 4.5 demonstrates how to respond to `scroll` events.

Listing 4.5   **Displaying Scroll Events**

```
00 <!DOCTYPE html>
01
02 <html lang="en">
03 <head>
04   <title>Listening to scroll events</title>
05 </head>
06 <body>
07
08 <h2>Scroll the page to see scroll events</h2>
09
10 <div id="placeholder"></div>
11
12 <script src="http://code.jquery.com/jquery-1.7.2.min.js"></script>
13
14 <script>
15 // please externalize this code to an external .js file
16 $(document).ready(function() {
17
18   // make a long page so you can scroll without wasting
19   // too many pages in the book
20   var array = [];
21   for(var i = 0; i < 100; i++) {
```

Listing 4.5   **Displaying Scroll Events (Continued)**

```
22      array.push('<p>Element ' + i + '</p>');
23    }
24    $('#placeholder').html(array.join(''));
25
26    $(this).scroll(function(event) {
27      var scrollTop = $(window).scrollTop();
28      $('p').html('scrollTop: ' + scrollTop);
29    });
30
31  });
32  </script>
33  </body>
34  </html>
```

Be careful how you use this function. Repositioning your elements based on the scroll position by using this function is a bad idea for multiple reasons, the most important of which is that it feels slow to visitors.

Recipe: Adding Central Event Listeners by Using live() and die()

When you bind events to specific elements by using bind() or a shorthand function that uses bind(), under the hood, you sometimes create large numbers of hooks to event handlers. Especially if many elements share the same event handler, there might be a more efficient way: *event delegation.*

When using a version of jQuery previous to 1.7, the simplest way in which jQuery supports event delegation is by using the live() and die() methods. The live() function works similarly to bind() with one difference: Instead of binding to the element itself, it binds to the root of the document. When an event is generated on the element itself, it bubbles up the document tree until it reaches the root. When the root catches the event, it can still see that the event originated from a specific element down the tree. If the element matches the CSS query, the handler will be executed.

Functionally, there's little difference using live() instead of bind(), with one exception: If you add a new element that matches the search criteria, events on this element are ignored when using bind(). There is no event listener bound to the new element, and bind() only works on the moment it is called.

Listing 4.6 demonstrates that live() ensures that the events also work on elements that are created and added later on. When you want to remove an event that has been attached by using live(), you need to use the die() function. With this function, you can remove any events that have been attached by using live().

Listing 4.6   **Responding to Events on Newly Created Items**

```
00 <!DOCTYPE html>
01
02 <html lang="en">
03 <head>
04   <title>The live() and die() functions for
05     adding event listeners</title>
06 </head>
07 <body>
08
09 <h2>First click on Live, then click on li items
10   to generate events.</h2>
11
12 <ul id="main-list">
13   <li>One</li>
14   <li>Two</li>
15   <li>Three</li>
16 </ul>
17
18 <button id="live">Live</button>
19 <button id="die">Die</button>
20 <button id="add">Add a li item</button>
21
22 <p id="placeholder" />
23
24 <h2>And a seemingly unrelated list, you can also click on</h2>
25 <ul>
26   <li>Other element</li>
27   <li>And yet another</li>
28 </ul>
29
30
31 <script src="http://code.jquery.com/jquery-1.6.4.min.js"></script>
32
33 <script>
34 // please externalize this code to an external .js file
35 $(document).ready(function() {
36
37   $('#live').click(function() {
38     $('li').live('click', function() {
39       $('#placeholder').append(
40         'Clicked ' + $(this).html() + '<br/>');
41     });
42   });
43
44   $('#die').click(function() {
```

Listing 4.6   Responding to Events on Newly Created Items (Continued)

```
45     $('li').die('click');
46   });
47
48   $('#add').click(function() {
49     $('#main-list').append($('<li>Another</li>'));
50   });
51
52 });
53 </script>
54 </body>
55 </html>
```

The way the li selector on line 38 is written, the event listener responds to a click on any li element in the document as well as unrelated li elements. There are two ways to work around this: a more specific selection, or by using the delegate() function, as demonstrated in the next recipe.

Recipe: Delegating Events to Specific Ancestor Elements by Using delegate()

The concept of letting events bubble up the document tree until they meet an event listener is powerful. The way live() and die() implemented it, makes it transparent and easy to use for the programmer. However, listening for events on the root element makes the scope quite large.

In many cases, groups of related events are contained within a single parent element with a smaller scope. Listing 4.7 demonstrates how to use event delegation on a more specific container element by using delegate() and undelegate().

Listing 4.7   Listening for Events on <li> Items Within a Specific <ul>

```
00 <!DOCTYPE html>
01
02 <html lang="en">
03 <head>
04   <title>The delegate() and undelegate() functions for
05     adding event listeners</title>
06 </head>
07 <body>
08
09 <h2>First click on Delegate, then click on li items
10   to generate events.</h2>
11
```

(Continues)

Listing 4.7   Listening for Events on <li> Items Within a Specific <ul> (Continued)

```
12 <ul id="main-list">
13   <li>One</li>
14   <li>Two</li>
15   <li>Three</li>
16 </ul>
17
18 <button id="delegate">Delegate</button>
19 <button id="undelegate">Undelegate</button>
20 <button id="add">Add a li item</button>
21
22 <p id="placeholder" />
23
24 <h2>And a seemingly unrelated list, that does not
25   respond to clicks</h2>
26 <ul>
27   <li>Other element</li>
28   <li>And yet another</li>
29 </ul>
30
31 <script src="http://code.jquery.com/jquery-1.7.2.min.js"></script>
32
33 <script>
34 // please externalize this code to an external .js file
35 $(document).ready(function() {
36
37   $('#delegate').click(function() {
38     $('#main-list').delegate('li', 'click', function() {
39       $('#placeholder').append(
40         'Clicked ' + $(this).html() + '<br/>');
41     });
42   });
43
44   $('#undelegate').click(function() {
45     $('#main-list').undelegate('li', 'click');
46   });
47
48   $('#add').click(function() {
49     $('#main-list').append($('<li>Another</li>'));
50   });
51
52 });
53 </script>
54 </body>
55 </html>
```

The main difference between this listing and Listing 4.6 is that the li items below the set of buttons in Listing 4.7 no longer respond to click events. The event handler is bound to the first ul element. The notation of delegate() demands that the developer understands the principle of event delegation. The live() function might be used by developers without this knowledge. That can be dangerous if an element in the document blocks event bubbling.

jQuery 1.7 introduced a new way to handle and use event binding. As we have just learned with regard to using live(), die(), and delegate(), the new on() and off() functions replace these. Not only are these functions replaced, but even the bind() function uses the on() function behind the scenes. The on() function works in a similar fashion to the delegate() function. If you are already familiar with using the delegate() function, a simple way to remember how to use the on() function is to switch the places of the selector and events when calling the method. For comparison, Listing 4.8 shows the code for the delegate() example updated to use the on() function.

Listing 4.8   **Using the on() Function Instead of delegate()**

```
00 <!DOCTYPE html>
01
02 <html lang="en">
03 <head>
04   <title>The on() and off() functions for
05     adding event listeners</title>
06 </head>
07 <body>
08
09 <h2>First click on On, then click on li items
10   to generate events.</h2>
11
12 <ul id="main-list">
13   <li>One</li>
14   <li>Two</li>
15   <li>Three</li>
16 </ul>
17
18 <button id="on">On</button>
19 <button id="off">Off</button>
20 <button id="add">Add a li item</button>
21
22 <p id="placeholder" />
23
24 <h2>And a seemingly unrelated list, that does not
25   respond to clicks</h2>
```

(Continues)

Listing 4.8   **Using the on() Function Instead of delegate() (Continued)**

```
26 <ul>
27   <li>Other element</li>
28   <li>And yet another</li>
29 </ul>
30
31 <script src="http://code.jquery.com/jquery-1.7.2.min.js"></script>
32
33 <script>
34 // please externalize this code to an external .js file
35 $(document).ready(function() {
36
37   $('#on').click(function() {
38     $('#main-list').on('click', 'li', function() {
39       $('#placeholder').append(
40         'Clicked ' + $(this).html() + '<br/>');
41     });
42   });
43
44   $('#off').click(function() {
45     $('#main-list').off('click', 'li');
46   });
47
48   $('#add').click(function() {
49     $('#main-list').append($('<li>Another</li>'));
50   });
51
52 });
53 </script>
54 </body>
55 </html>
```

The on() function is a very efficient and powerful way to handle event binding in your code. When using the on() function, ensure that you use fast selectors such as an id ("#fast"), an element with class selector ("a.fast"), or element ("input"). As always, check the official documentation for updates and notices for tips on dealing with depreciated code by visiting http://api.jquery.com/on/.

Recipe: Changing the Execution Context of a Function by Using proxy()

If an event handler works on the event source element, you can use $(this) inside the handler to quickly access the element. However, if you want the handler to work on a different element, you need to select a different element within the function. If you have multiple similar handlers with multiple different origins and targets, this can lead to superfluous code.

Listing 4.9 demonstrates how a single handler can use $(this) with multiple different event sources and destinations.

Listing 4.9   Using an Event Handler with and Without proxy()

```
00 <!DOCTYPE html>
01
02 <html lang="en">
03 <head>
04   <title>Change the this object of a function</title>
05 </head>
06 <body>
07
08 <p>This text would change if a proxy is used pointing
09    to this paragraph</p>
10
11
12 <button id="regular">Regular button - changes
13   itself when pressed</button><br>
14
15 <button id="proxy">Proxy button - changes
16   the paragraph when pressed</button>
17
18 <script src="http://code.jquery.com/jquery-latest.min.js"></script>
19
20 <script>
21 // please externalize this code to an external .js file
22
23 $(document).ready(function() {
24
25   var handler = function() {
26     $(this).html('Changed');
27   }
28
29   $('#regular').click(handler);
30
31   $('#proxy').click($.proxy(handler, $('p')))
32
33 });
34 </script>
35 </body>
36 </html>
```

Line 26 does not know if the event was generated by a button or by a paragraph. As long as these elements can be manipulated with the `html()` function, the handler can be reused.

Summary

This chapter provided several examples by which you were able to investigate events sent to the browser. In addition to examples of simply logging and displaying events, one example provided a simple drawing tool. Finally, this chapter introduced the principle of event delegation and several methods to work with event delegation in jQuery.

Chapter 5

Communicating with the Server

This chapter discusses how to communicate with the server. To demonstrate this, a simple test server is written in Node.js, which is a server-side JavaScript execution environment. After that, various recipes show how to get JSON, HTML, XML, and JSONP from the server by using AJAX methods and functions. This chapter pays a lot of attention to error handling to assure the quality of the end result.

Recipe: Setting Up an Example Server in Node.js

To test the AJAX examples, you need a server. For the examples, it does not matter whether the server is written in PHP, Python, Ruby, Erlang, Dart, Go, .Net, or Java. Keep in mind, of course, that all servers take some setup time.

Because jQuery is JavaScript, this book assumes that you are already familiar with it. That is why the test server is provided in JavaScript code. To run the code, you need to download and install Node.js at http://nodejs.org.

There are no plugins or further modules needed for this example. For reference, the code in this chapter was developed and tested by using versions 0.4.11 and 0.6.19 of Node.js. After installing Node.js and putting the example in a file called 01-app.js, you can run the code from the following command line:

```
node 01-app.js
```

If this command does not start your node server, ensure that you have correctly added the node to your system path. When running the code, you can access subsequent examples at http://localhost:1337/02-ajax-get.html.

Listing 5.1 contains the implementation for the Node.js test server.

Listing 5.1   Listening for HTTP Requests Generated by Recipes in This Chapter and Responding Accordingly

```
00 var http = require('http'),
01   url = require('url'),
02   fs = require('fs');
03 http.createServer(function (req, res) {
04   var reqData = {
05     url: url.parse(req.url, true),
06     method: req.method,
07     headers: req.headers },
08   path = reqData.url.pathname;
09
10   if(path.match(/^\/[0-9a-z\-]+\.(html)|(json)|(xml)$/))
11     fs.readFile('.' + path, function (err, data) {
12       if (err) {
13         res.writeHead(404, {'Content-Type': 'text/plain'});
14         res.end('not found');
15       }
16       else {
17         if(path.split('.')[1] == 'html')
18           res.writeHead(200, {'Content-Type': 'text/html'});
19         else if(path.split('.')[1] == 'xml')
20           res.writeHead(200, {'Content-Type': 'application/xml'});
21         else
22           res.writeHead(200, {'Content-Type': 'application/json'});
23         res.end(data);
24       }
25     });
26   else if(path == '/return-http-headers') {
27     res.writeHead(200, {'Content-Type': 'application/json'});
28     res.end(JSON.stringify(reqData));
29   }
30   else if(path == '/sleep') {
31     var endTime = new Date().getTime() + 2000;
32     while (new Date().getTime() < endTime);
33     res.writeHead(500, {'Content-Type': 'text/plain'});
34     res.end('slow response');
35   }
36   else if(path == '/validate') {
37     var keys = [];
38     for(var key in reqData.url.query) {
39       if(reqData.url.query[key] == '')
40         keys.push(key);
41     }
42     res.writeHead(200, {'Content-Type': 'application/json'});
43     res.end(JSON.stringify(keys));
```

Listing 5.1 Listening for HTTP Requests Generated by Recipes in This Chapter and Responding Accordingly (Continued)

```
44    }
45    else if(path == '/redirect') {
46      res.writeHead(302, {
47        'Location': '/test-values.json' });
48      res.end();
49    }
50    else if(path == '/fail\-on\-purpose') {
51      res.writeHead(500, {'Content-Type': 'text/plain'});
52      res.end('unexpected" error');
53    }
54    else {
55      res.writeHead(404, {'Content-Type': 'text/plain'});
56      res.end('not found');
57    }
58 }).listen(1337, "localhost");
59 console.log('Server running at http://localhost:1337/');
```

HTML, JSON, and XML requests are passed to the file server. Some special cases you will encounter in the following recipes are handled each with their own specific response. Given the requested path, the responses should not be too surprising.

If the file cannot be found, or there is no handler and the request is not XML, JSON, or HTML, a 404 error is returned.

Recipe: Performing a GET Request

One of the simpler AJAX requests can be executed by using the shorthand method for GET. You can imagine performing a similar call for POST, PUT, and DELETE. Keep in mind that PUT and DELETE are not supported by all browsers, so it is wise to use GET and POST. Listing 5.2 shows the use of the get() method.

Listing 5.2 Fetching JSON Values by using the get() Shorthand Function

```
00 <!DOCTYPE html>
01
02 <html lang="en">
03 <head>
04   <title>The AJAX get() request function</title>
05 </head>
06 <body>
07
08 <h2>Press the button to perform the request.</h2>
```

(Continues)

Listing 5.2   **Fetching JSON Values by using the get() Shorthand Function (Continued)**

```
09
10 <button id="trigger">GET</button>
11 <br>
12 <div id="target"></div>
13
14 <script src="http://code.jquery.com/jquery-1.7.2.min.js"></script>
15
16 <script>
17 // please externalize this code to an external .js file
18 $(document).ready(function() {
19
20   $('#trigger').click(function() {
21
22     $.get('02a-test-values.json', function(data) {
23
24       $('#target').append('The returned value is: ' + data.name);
25
26     }, 'json');
27   });
28
29 });
30 </script>
31 </body>
32 </html>
```

Line 22 fetches the following JSON document:

```
{
  "name": "Adriaan de Jonge",
  "email" : "adriaandejonge@gmail.com"
}
```

When executed, this script returns the name of the author. In this example, the success handler function is a callback directly passed to the get() function. The last parameter passed in the get() is 'json'. This is an optional data-type parameter. In this instance, it informs jQuery that the data requested will be returned in JSON format. Later examples demonstrate an alternative approach for callback functions. If you use a web service or have some server-side logic set up to handle data coming in before handing back a response, you can pass an additional set of data to the server through the get() function. To learn more about sending data to the server by using get(), see the official documentation at http://api.jquery.com/jQuery.get/.

Recipe: Loading HTML Directly

Even simpler than the `get()` method is to use `load()` to gather a snippet of HTML and put it directly into the document. Listing 5.3 demonstrates how to do this.

Listing 5.3   **Filling a <div> with a Dynamic HTML Snippet**

```
00 <!DOCTYPE html>
01
02 <html lang="en">
03 <head>
04   <title>The AJAX load() request</title>
05 </head>
06 <body>
07
08 <h2>Press the button to perform the request.</h2>
09
10 <button id="trigger">GET</button>
11 <br>
12 <div id="target">
13
14 <script src="http://code.jquery.com/jquery-latest.min.js"></script>
15
16 <script>
17 // please externalize this code to an external .js file
18 $(document).ready(function() {
19
20   $('#trigger').click(function() {
21
22     $('#target').load('03a-test-snippet.html');
23
24   });
25
26 });
27 </script>
28 </body>
29 </html>
```

The HTML that will be loaded into the document is as follows:

```
<h1>Hello world from external HTML snippet</h1>
```

Line 22 demonstrates how the `load()` function works directly on a selection of elements without requiring a callback handler.

Recipe: Handling the Result by Using Promises

In Listing 5.2, you saw a callback handler being passed to the `get()` method to be called after a successful result from the AJAX request. The advantage of callbacks is asynchronous execution of code. The browser remains responsive while the AJAX request is working in the background. However, when you have many callbacks, the code starts looking like a Christmas tree. It is a callback inside a callback inside a callback. And what about failures?

Promises can solve this problem. Understanding promises involves some theory. First, let's explore how they work by looking in Listing 5.4.

Listing 5.4   **Demonstrating done(), fail(), and always()**

```
00 <!DOCTYPE html>
01
02 <html lang="en">
03 <head>
04   <title>The done() fail() always() function</title>
05 </head>
06 <body>
07
08 <h2>Press the button to perform the request.</h2>
09
10 <button id="trigger">GET</button>
11 <br>
12 <div id="target">
13
14 <script src="http://code.jquery.com/jquery-1.7.2.min.js"></script>
15
16 <script>
17 // please externalize this code to an external.js file
18 $(document).ready(function() {
19
20   $('#trigger').click(function() {
21
22     // avoid error() success() complete()
23     // those are deprecated in jQuery 1.8
24     // use done() fail() always() instead
25
26     $.ajax({url:' 02a-test-values.json', dataType: 'json'})
27     .done (function(data) {
28       $('#target').append('The returned value is: '
29                           + data.name + '<br>');
30     })
31     .fail(function() {
32       $('#target').append('The AJAX call failed.<br>');
33     })
```

Listing 5.4   **Demonstrating done(), fail(), and always() (Continued)**

```
34      .always(function() {
35          $('#target').append('finished anyway.');
36      });
37  });
38 });
39 </script>
40 </body>
41 </html>
```

Notice in this script that chained functions provide callbacks after calling the `ajax()` function. This is possible because `ajax()` returns a promise object. A promise is a safe version of a *deferred* object. Deferred objects are discussed in Chapter 11, "Creating Plugins." The difference is that a promise does not expose the internals of a deferred. Then, what does a promise do?

When you call the `done()` function with a callback handler and the `ajax()` request has not yet returned, the callback is stored in a queue. Once the `ajax()` request returns and the result is successful, all the queued callbacks under `done()` are called. When you call the `done()` function with a callback handler after the `ajax()` request has returned, if the result was successful, the callback is executed right away.

Callbacks passed to `fail()` and `always()` are handled similarly. Only `fail()` executes when the result was unsuccessful, of course.

There is a shorthand notation for `done()` and `fail()` called `then()`. The `then()` function takes two arguments: one callback in case of success and one in case of failure. The following snippet shows how you can use it to replace the `done()` and `fail()` methods used in Listing 5.4:

```
$.ajax({url:'02a-test-values.json', dataType: 'json'})
    .then(
      function(data) {
        $('#target').append('The returned value is: '
                          + data.name + '<br>');
      },
      function() {
        $('#target').append('The AJAX call failed.<br>');
      }
    );
```

Recipe: Handling Server Errors

To test the `fail()` handler, the test server from the first recipe provides a `fail-on-purpose` URL. Listing 5.5 calls this URL to see what happens.

Listing 5.5   **Catching Server Errors by Using fail()**

```
00 <!DOCTYPE html>
01
02 <html lang="en">
03 <head>
04   <title>Test case: failure</title>
05 </head>
06 <body>
07
08 <h2>Press the button to perform the request.</h2>
09
10 <button id="trigger">GET</button>
11 <br>
12 <div id="target">
13
14
15 <script src="http://code.jquery.com/jquery-1.7.2.min.js"></script>
16
17 <script>
18 // please externalize this code to an external .js file
19 $(document).ready(function() {
20
21   $('#trigger').click(function() {
22
23     $.ajax('fail-on-purpose')
24     .done(function(data, xhr) {
25       $('#target').append('Unexpected success. . . ' +
26                    '(actually not a good thing)');
27     })
28     .fail(function(xhr, text, error) {
29       $('#target').append('Failed as expected (good!). Code ' +
30                    xhr.status + ' and text ' + error);
31     });
32
33   });
34
35 });
36 </script>
37 </body>
38 </html>
```

As expected, the `fail()` callback is called. From the parameters passed to this callback handler, you can determine what went wrong and act accordingly.

Recipe: Catching Page-not-Found Results

Similarly, Listing 5.6 tests what happens when the page is not found.

Listing 5.6   **Recognizing a Page-not-Found Code**

```
00 <!DOCTYPE html>
01
02 <html lang="en">
03 <head>
04   <title>Test case: page not found</title>
05 </head>
06 <body>
07
08 <h2>Press the button to perform the request.</h2>
09
10 <button id="trigger">GET</button>
11 <br>
12 <div id="target">
13
14
15 <script src="http://code.jquery.com/jquery-1.7.2.min.js"></script>
16
17 <script>
18 // please externalize this code to an external .js file
19 $(document).ready(function() {
20
21   $('#trigger').click(function() {
22
23     $.ajax('not-found')
24     .done(function(data, xhr) {
25       $('#target').append('Unexpected success… ' +
26                '(actually not a good thing)');
27     })
28     .fail(function(xhr, text, error) {
29       $('#target').append('Failed as expected (good!). Code ' +
30       xhr.status + ' and text ' + error);
31     });
32
33   });
34
35 });
36 </script>
37 </body>
38 </html>
```

As expected, again, the `fail()` callback is called, only this time with different parameters. Although you could check the `xhr.status` for a specific error code, jQuery provides a setting in `ajax()` that looks specifically at HTTP codes. The following snippet of code could be used in the previous example, replacing line 23.

```
$.ajax('fail-on-purpose', {
    statusCode: {
        404: function() {//insert 404 handling function here},
        500: function() {//insert 500 handling function here}
    }
})
```

When you remove the comments and insert your own code, the code will be run when either a 404 or 500 HTTP status code is returned. If you leave the `fail()` method in place, it will also execute, giving you another error handling point.

Recipe: Handling Page Redirects

You might expect a similar result when you encounter a redirect code. Listing 5.7 investigates what happens in this case.

Listing 5.7   **Receiving Content After an Implicit Redirect**

```
00 <!DOCTYPE html>
01
02 <html lang="en">
03 <head>
04    <title>Test case: redirect</title>
05 </head>
06 <body>
07
08 <h2>Press the button to perform the request.</h2>
09
10 <button id="trigger">GET</button>
11 <br>
12 <div id="target">
13
14
15 <script src="http://code.jquery.com/jquery-1.7.2.min.js"></script>
16
17 <script>
18 // please externalize this code to an external .js file
19 $(document).ready(function() {
20
21    $('#trigger').click(function() {
22
```

Listing 5.7   **Receiving Content After an Implicit Redirect (Continued)**

```
23    $.ajax('redirect')
24    .done(function(data, xhr) {
25      $('#target').append('Successfully redirected. . . ' +
26                  'returned data is ' + data.name);
27    })
28    .fail(function(xhr, text, error) {
29      $('#target').append('Redirect failed. Code ' +
30                  xhr.status + ' and text ' + text);
31    });
32
33    });
34
35 });
36 </script>
37 </body>
38 </html>
```

In this case, the AJAX request is successfully redirected to the new URL. The resulting values are picked up by the done() handler. In this example, this is exactly what we want.

However, if you do not want to be redirected and know that something is wrong, you might be out of luck. It seems like jQuery has nothing to do with the automated redirect handling. The browser does this for you according to specification.

In some use cases, a redirect is used to ask for further details from the end user, such as login credentials. In these cases, you do not want the AJAX request to be redirected under the hood. Instead, you want to catch the redirect and pass it on to the full browser screen.

Under these circumstances, if you have no control over the server, you are out of luck. If you do have control over the server, you should find a different way to pass the direct back to the AJAX call. Consider making it part of the content payload. Some libraries have invented new non-standard HTTP status codes. That should be considered *bad practice* and can cause unexpected results with proxies and caches.

Recipe: Setting Request Timeouts

In a responsive interface, it is sometimes better to quickly say that you cannot answer in time than it is to wait for a long time. If the user is waiting for the results of an AJAX request, it is wise to add a timeout.

Listing 5.8 tries to fetch the result of the sleep function in one second. A quick glance at the first recipe in this chapter teaches us that the test server will never respond before two seconds have passed. You do not have to be psychic to predict the outcome here. . . .

Listing 5.8   **Failing If the Server Takes Longer Than One Second**

```
00 <!DOCTYPE html>
01
02 <html lang="en">
03 <head>
04   <title>The timeout property</title>
05 </head>
06 <body>
07
08 <h2>Press the button to perform the request.</h2>
09
10 <button id="trigger">GET</button>
11 <br>
12 <div id="target">
13
14
15 <script src="http://code.jquery.com/jquery-1.7.2.min.js"></script>
16
17 <script>
18 // please externalize this code to an external .js file
19 $(document).ready(function() {
20
21   $('#trigger').click(function() {
22
23     $.ajax({url: 'sleep',
24         timeout : 1000
25     })
26     .done(function(data, xhr) {
27       $('#target').append('Response in time after all: ' + data);
28     })
29     .fail(function(xhr, text, error) {
30       $('#target').append('Failed as expected: ' + error);
31     });
32
33   });
34
35 });
36 </script>
37 </body>
38 </html>
```

Once again, the `fail()` callback is called. And once again, it's called with different parameters, describing that this failure was caused by a timeout.

Recipe: Passing HTTP Headers

If you need control over HTTP headers—for example, those used for caching—you can pass anything with the AJAX request. To test how this works, the test server from the first example returns a JSON string containing exactly the headers it received during the request.

Listing 5.9 passes a simple ETag header and displays the result returned from the test server.

Listing 5.9 **Passing an ETag Header and Displaying the Returned Mirrored Headers from the Server**

```
00 <!DOCTYPE html>
01
02 <html lang="en">
03 <head>
04   <title>The headers property</title>
05 </head>
06 <body>
07
08 <h2>Press the button to perform the request.</h2>
09
10 <button id="trigger">GET</button>
11 <br>
12 <div id="target">
13
14
15 <script src="http://code.jquery.com/jquery-1.7.2.min.js"></script>
16
17 <script>
18 // please externalize this code to an external .js file
19 $(document).ready(function() {
20
21   $('#trigger').click(function() {
22
23     $.ajax({url: 'return-http-headers',
24         headers : {
25             ETag: '12345'
26       }
27     })
28     .done(function(data, xhr) {
29       $('#target').append(
30         $.map(data.headers, function(i, name) {
31             return name + ' = '+ data.headers[name] + '<br/>';
```

(Continues)

Listing 5.9   **Passing an ETag Header and Displaying the Returned Mirrored Headers from the Server (Continued)**

```
32              })
33              .join(' ')
34        );
35       })
36       .fail(function(xhr, text, error) {
37          $('#target').append('Failed unexpectedly');
38       });
39    });
40
41 });
42 </script>
43 </body>
44 </html>
```

The test server returns a little bit more than just the HTTP headers, which might be useful for different tests such as ETag configuration, compression support (gzip, deflate), and even agent identification.

Example: Validating Form Input on the Server Side

In Chapter 1, "Getting Started with jQuery," you saw the serialize() function. Chapter 4, "Listening and Responding to Events," demonstrated how to catch events on form elements. Combine these two with an AJAX request, and you can validate the input of a form before it is submitted.

The test server from the first recipe returns all the input element names that send an empty string. Listing 5.10 adds a red border to all element names returned by the validation function.

Listing 5.10   **Serializing and Sending the Form Input to the Server After Every Change**

```
00 <!DOCTYPE html>
01
02 <html lang="en">
03 <head>
04   <title>Use serialize() for side field validation</title>
05   <style>
06 /* please externalize this code to an external
07    .css file */
08    .error {
09      border-color: red;
10    }
```

Listing 5.10   **Serializing and Sending the Form Input to the Server After Every Change**
                (Continued)

```
11    </style>
12  </head>
13  <body>
14
15  <h2>Fill out the fields and see the result.</h2>
16
17  <form action="" method="post">
18    <label for="first_field">First field</label>
19    <input type="text" name="first_field"
20      value="" id="first_field"><br>
21
22    <label for="second_field">Second field</label>
23    <input type="text" name="second_field"
24      value="" id="second_field"><br>
25
26    <label for="third_field">Third field</label>
27    <input type="text" name="third_field"
28      value="" id="third_field"><br>
29
30    <label for="fourth_field">Fourth field</label>
31    <input type="text" name="fourth_field"
32      value="" id="fourth_field"><br>
33
34    <input type="submit" name="submit" value="Submit" id="submit">
35
36  </form>
37
38  <script src="http://code.jquery.com/jquery-1.7.2.min.js"></script>
39
40  <script>
41  // please externalize this code to an external .js file
42  $(document).ready(function() {
43
44    $('input').filter(':text').addClass('error');
45
46    $('input').change(function() {
47
48      $.get('validate', $('form').serialize())
49      .done(function(data) {
50
51        $('input').removeClass('error');
52
53        $.each(data, function(i, name) {
```

(Continues)

Listing 5.10   **Serializing and Sending the Form Input to the Server After Every Change (Continued)**

```
54          $('#' + name).addClass('error');
55       });
56
57    });
58
59  });
60
61 });
62 </script>
63 </body>
64 </html>
```

In a real-world example, you could imagine a more sophisticated validation function. Even if you can validate many things on the client by using JavaScript, good practice is to validate again on the server upon final submission. (Consider that a client can be easily replaced by rogue code in transit.) Having JavaScript code on both the client and the server, you can invent a scenario where you can reuse parts of the validation code.

Recipe: Loading XML

The original meaning of what was once the *acronym* AJAX was Asynchronous JavaScript And Xml. The XML part of this name slowly disappeared over time as HTML and JSON have become more popular alternatives (and thus, AJAX is technically no longer an acronym).

If you still want to communicate with the server by using XML, you certainly can. Listing 5.11 demonstrates that jQuery even makes it easy for you to read the XML. It works similarly to selecting HTML elements.

Listing 5.11   **Reading XML Values Returned by the Server by Using jQuery**

```
00 <!DOCTYPE html>
01
02 <html lang="en">
03 <head>
04   <title>Get XML from server</title>
05 </head>
06 <body>
07
08 <h2>Press the button to perform the request.</h2>
09
10 <button id="trigger">GET</button>
11 <br>
```

Listing 5.11   Reading XML Values Returned by the Server by Using jQuery (Continued)

```
12 <div id="target">
13
14
15 <script src="http://code.jquery.com/jquery-1.7.2.min.js"></script>
16
17 <script>
18 // please externalize this code to an external .js file
19 $(document).ready(function() {
20
21    $('#trigger').click(function() {
22
23      $.get('11a-test-values', function(data) {
24
25        $('#target').append('The returned value is: ' +
26            $(data).find('name').text());
27      });
28
29    });
30
31 });
32 </script>
33 </body>
34 </html>
```

Line 26 uses jQuery constructions to read from the XML. The following snippet contains the XML returned by the server:

```
<?xml version="1.0" encoding="UTF-8" ?>
<root>
   <name>Adriaan de Jonge</name>
   <email>adriaandejonge@gmail.com</email>
</root>
```

Imagine working with a larger XML example. Using jQuery functions such as those that have been shown, it remains manageable.

Recipe: Listening to AJAX Events

Similar to mouse, keyboard, and scroll events, in jQuery, AJAX requests generate AJAX events. You can use these to generate status indicators on screen so that the visitor knows that work is in progress. Listing 5.12 shows a basic event log for AJAX events.

Listing 5.12   **Displaying all AJAX Events**

```
00 <!DOCTYPE html>
01
02 <html lang="en">
03 <head>
04   <title>AJAX related event handlers</title>
05 </head>
06 <body>
07
08 <h2>Press the button to perform the request.</h2>
09
10 <button id="trigger">GET</button>
11 <br>
12 <div id="target"> </div>
13 <div id="log"> </div>
14
15 <script src="http://code.jquery.com/jquery-1.7.2.min.js"></script>
16
17 <script>
18 // please externalize this code to an external .js file
19 $(document).ready(function() {
20
21   $('#trigger').click(function() {
22     $('#target').load('test-snippet.html');
23   });
24
25   $.each(('ajaxError ajaxSend ajaxStart ajaxStop ' +
26         'ajaxSuccess ajaxComplete').split(' '),
27     function (i, name) {
28       $('#log').bind(name, function(event, xhr) {
29       $(this).append('Event: ' + event.type + '<br/>');
30     });
31   });
32 });
33 </script>
34 </body>
35 </html>
```

Watch the order in which the events arrive when you click the button. This means you can respond in several stages of the AJAX request. The events also allow you to modify or add request parameters if you need to from a central location.

Recipe: Reading JSONP from an External Server

Classic AJAX works with the XmlHttpRequest (XHR) object. Most browsers do not allow XHR to access other servers than the origin of the current page. To work around this limitation, JSONP was invented.

JSONP is JSON wrapped inside a function call. Instead of making an AJAX request, a `script` element pointing to the JSONP script is added inside the HTML document and a callback function is called to access the script.

Caution

The browser vendors who restricted the use of XHR had good reason to do so: security. Working around these restrictions with JSONP opens up new possibilities for hackers because JSONP does not allow validation before execution.

Listing 5.13 demonstrates how to retrieve data from Twitter by using JSONP. Keep in mind that error handling does not work with JSONP.

Listing 5.13   **Connecting to Twitter and Searching for jQuery-Related Posts**

```
00 <!DOCTYPE html>
01
02 <html lang="en">
03 <head>
04    <title>Get JSONP</title>
05 </head>
06 <body>
07
08 <h2>Press the button to perform the request.</h2>
09
10 <button id="trigger">GET</button>
11 <br>
12 <div id="target">
13
14
15 <script src="http://code.jquery.com/jquery-1.7.2.min.js"></script>
16
17 <script>
18 // please externalize this code to an external .js file
19 $(document).ready(function() {
20
21   $('#trigger').click(function() {
22
23     $.getJSON('http://search.twitter.com/search.json' +
24        '?q=jquery&callback=?', function(data) {
25
26       $.each(data.results, function(index, value) {
27
28         $('#target').append(value.text + '<br>');
29
30       });
31
32     });
33
```

(Continues)

Listing 5.13   **Connecting to Twitter and Searching for jQuery-Related Posts (Continued)**

```
34    });
35
36 });
37 </script>
38 </body>
39 </html>
```

By default, the JSONP handler in jQuery looks for a `callback=?` parameter in the query string. The `?` is replaced with a jQuery-generated callback function to be inserted into JSONP by the server.

You can modify settings if the parameter has another name than `callback` or when the callback method is not parameterized. If you insist, you can find these parameters in the jQuery online documentation.

The best advice is to avoid JSONP whenever possible.

Summary

This chapter covered the most common uses of AJAX. The recipes cover fetching JSON, HTML, and XML, as well as many error scenarios. You can pass HTTP headers, validate form input in the background, and listen for AJAX events in general. The last recipe showed a dirty hack to load data from other servers by using JSONP. Because of security risks and a lack of error handling, it is better to avoid JSONP.

PART II

UI

Chapter 6

Interacting with the User

jQuery UI is a set of standard jQuery plugins that help you add interactive behavior to your Web site. This chapter starts with the jQuery plugins that can be used on almost any HTML element to drag, drop, resize, select, or sort the elements. These plugins add behavior without drastically changing the HTML.

Downloading and Installing jQuery UI

To begin using jQuery UI components, you need to include a separate library. jQuery UI is set up in modules. Modules are programmed in the same way as are third-party plugins.

When you need just a single jQuery UI component, you can keep the size of your JavaScripts small by including only that specific plugin. On the jQuery UI Web site (http://jqueryui.com), you can make a selection of the jQuery components you need and download a custom JavaScript file.

When you want access to all available jQuery UI components or when code efficiency is not an issue, you can refer to a single JavaScript file containing all jQuery UI plugins in a similar way you refer to the jQuery Core library. When you use jQuery's Content Delivery Network (CDN), you include the following:

```
<script src="http://code.jquery.com/jquery-1.7.1.min.js"></script>
<script src="http://code.jquery.com/ui/1.8.16/jquery-ui.min.js">
</script>
```

To run jQuery UI, you still need to include jQuery Core.

If you like to write your own CSS, this is all you need to get started. However, if you are not a GUI designer and you prefer to reuse existing designs, you can include prefabricated CSS files, each with their own theme. This chapter uses the base theme, as shown here:

```
<link type="text/css" rel="stylesheet"
  href="http://code.jquery.com/ui/1.8.16/themes/base/jquery-ui.css">
```

Again, if you prefer a different style, you can replace the word *base* in the preceding code with one of the following theme names:

black-tie, blitzer, cupertino, dark-hive, dot-luv, eggplant,
excite-bike, flick, hot-sneaks, humanity, le-frog, mint-choc,
overcast, pepper-grinder, redmond, smoothness, south-street, start,
sunny, swanky-purse, trontastic, ui-darkness, ui-lightness, vader

This chapter avoids using the default CSS whenever it is relatively simple to work without it. In other cases, the base theme is used to avoid lengthy CSS listings. There are pointers on how to provide your own styling in these cases.

Recipe: Dragging Elements

jQuery UI can do many things without a CSS file. Listing 6.1, for example, provides a mechanism to make HTML elements draggable on the screen. In this example, you can try to move every part that is a separate element. To demonstrate, there is a paragraph that contains some bold text; you can move both the paragraph and the bold text to see how their movement is related.

Listing 6.1   **Making All Elements in a Page Draggable**

```
00 <!DOCTYPE html>
01
02 <html lang="en">
03 <head>
04   <title>jQuery UI Draggable</title>
05 </head>
06 <body>
07
08 <h2>Drag all elements around the screen</h2>
09 <p>More text <b>with bold</b> followed by text</p>
10 <h2>Another header</h2>
11 <ul>
12   <li>And a list</li>
13   <li>With items</li>
14 </ul>
15
16 <script src="http://code.jquery.com/jquery-1.7.1.min.js"></script>
17 <script src="http://code.jquery.com/ui/1.8.16/jquery-ui.min.js">
18 </script>
19
20 <script>
21 // please externalize this code to an external .js file
22 $(document).ready(function() {
23
24   $('body *').draggable();
25
26 });
```

Listing 6.1   **Making All Elements in a Page Draggable (Continued)**

```
27 </script>
28 </body>
29 </html>
```

The HTML in lines 8–14 is somewhat random. Any other HTML would have worked similarly well. Also for jQuery UI, scripts are loaded at the bottom of the page.

Styling the Draggable Element

Although moving elements around the screen like this opens up interesting new possibilities, it is not intuitive. The average visitor does not expect that these elements can be dragged.

Adding a few lines of CSS can change change this:

```
<style>
.ui-draggable {
  border: 1px dashed black;
}
.ui-draggable-dragging {
  border: 1px solid red;
}
</style>
```

Or perhaps you can think of even better styling yourself. Using this small snippet of CSS, all draggable elements receive their own dashed border, and when you start dragging the elements, the border becomes solid red until you stop dragging them.

Most styling in jQuery UI is done by using classes. As long as you can work with the HTML that is generated by the jQuery UI code, you have a lot of freedom to provide your own look and feel to the components.

When you are dragging an element, the draggable plugin adds a `style` attribute. The style attribute contains the following:

```
position: relative; left: 123px; top: 123px;
```

The `123px` is a random value here. In practice, the numbers will quickly change as you drag the element around the screen.

Setting Draggable Options

You can modify the behavior of the draggable elements by setting options when you are initializing the component. Table 6.1 lists the options that are set to change the default behavior. A code snippet is presented along with a description of the method.

Table 6.1   **Options for the Draggable Interaction**

Option	Description
`$('body *').draggable({disabled: true});`	By disabling a draggable component, you make it impossible to move the element. This does not seem particularly useful, but it might help setting all the classes to change the look and feel of the draggable and then quickly turn on and off the actual working of the element for applications that require this.
`$('body *').draggable({addClasses: false});`	When you set `addClasses` to false, none of the draggable elements are visualized using a `ui-draggable` class. However, when you do start dragging the element, it will get a `ui-draggable-dragging` class. If you have a large number of draggable elements, not adding these classes optimizes performance. You might already have your own styling provided by using HTML and CSS.
`$('body *').draggable({appendTo: 'body'});`	This option is used to set up the draggable helper's container that is used while dragging. By default the helper will be appended to the parent of the draggable.
`$('body *').draggable({axis: 'x'});`	By default, elements can be dragged over both the vertical and horizontal axis. By setting this option, you can restrict drag movements to only the *x* or *y* axis.
`$('body *').draggable({cancel: 'b'});`	By setting the `cancel` option, dragging cannot start when the mouse is on an element that matches the provided selector.
`$('body *').draggable({connectToSortable: 'ul#my-sortable'});`	When there is a *sortable* element set on the page—this is discussed later on in this chapter—you can allow draggable elements to become part of the sortable list. Think carefully before you use this option. Sortables can also be connected to each other. Only use this option if you need to drag elements from other sources into a sortable.

Table 6.1   **Options for the Draggable Interaction (Continued)**

Option	Description
`$('body b').` `draggable({containment: 'p'});`	Setting `containment` limits the freedom of movement of the draggable element. You can provide a CSS selector, a specific element, one of the words `parent`, `document`, or `window`, or you can provide an array of values `[x1, y1, x2, y2]`.
`$('body *').draggable({cursor:` `'move'});`	You can change the mouse cursor while dragging to any valid CSS cursor value: crosshair, e-resize, help, move, n-resize, ne-resize, nw-resize, pointer, progress, s-resize, se-resize, sw-resize, text, w-resize, or wait.
`$('body *').draggable({cursorAt:` `{left: 20, top: 50}});`	To change the position of the cursor while dragging, you can change the `cursorAt` option. Instead of `left` and `top`, you can also set the position with `right` and `bottom`, `left` and `bottom` or `right` and `top`.
`$('body *').draggable({delay:` `500});`	Set the time in milliseconds to wait before an element starts dragging.
`$('body *').draggable({distance:` `50});`	Set the distance over which an element should be dragged before the draggable component starts moving the element over the screen and fires the `dragstart` event.
`$('body *').draggable({grid:` `[20, 20]});`	Limit the positions of the dragged element to a grid of the specified proportion.
`$('body *').draggable({handle:` `'p'});`	Set the handle to control which part of the selector will be used to start the draggable.
`$('body *').draggable({helper:` `'clone'});`	By setting the `helper` option to `clone`, the dragged element is first cloned before it is dragged around the screen. This way, the original element remains in place.

(Continues)

Table 6.1   Options for the Draggable Interaction (Continued)

Option	Description
`$('body *').draggable({helper: function() {return $('b'). clone();}});`	Instead of making a clone of the dragged element, you can use any other element in the document as a helper. The selected element is the outcome of a function. Whether this is a clone or not is up to the function implementation.
`$('body *'). draggable({iframeFix: true});`	When you have an `iframe` on your page, dragged elements show strange behavior when you try to drag them over the `iframe`. By setting `iframeFix` to true, jQuery puts an overlay over all `iframes`.
`$('body *'). draggable({iframeFix: '#my-iframe'});`	It is also possible to select specific `iframes` instead of putting an overlay over all `iframes`. For this, you provide a CSS selector instead of setting `true`.
`$('body *').draggable({opacity: 0.5});`	Using `opacity`, you can create a see-through effect while dragging an element. The value ranges from 0 (invisible) to 1 (opaque).
`$('body *'). draggable({refreshPositions: true});`	On pages with a highly dynamic nature, you can set `refreshPositions` to `true` to increase the redraw interval to every mouse movement. This affects performance and responsiveness.
`$('body *').draggable({revert: 'invalid'});`	The `revert` option is particularly interesting when used in combination with the *droppable* component that is discussed later on in this chapter. In this example, the draggable will return to its original position when not dropped on a droppable area.
`$('body *'). draggable({revertDuration: 1000});`	Set the speed of the revert animation.
`$('body *').draggable({scope: 'my-scope'});`	Limit the scope of the draggable element. In setting this option, you require a droppable element with the same scope, otherwise you cannot drop the draggable anywhere.

Table 6.1   **Options for the Draggable Interaction (Continued)**

Option	Description
`$('body *').draggable({scroll: false});`	Prevent the container from scrolling when the visitor is dragging the element.
`$('body *').draggable({scrollSensitivity: 10});`	Set the number of pixels that the element needs to be dragged outside the current range before the container starts scrolling.
`$('body *').draggable({scrollSpeed: 50});`	Set the scroll speed.
`$('body *').draggable({snap: 'li'});`	Set a selector for elements that the draggable *snaps* to. When you drag the element close to another one that matches the selector, it will move to the border of that element.
`$('body *').draggable({snapMode: 'inner'});`	Set whether the element should snap to the inner border of the other element, the outer border, or both.
`$('body *').draggable({snapTolerance: 10});`	Set the snapping range. Increasing this value makes it easier to snap to an element but harder to drag the element to a position close to another element without snapping.
`$('body *').draggable({stack: '.my-stack'});`	Set a common CSS class to stack draggables of the same kind.
`$('body *').draggable({zIndex: -1});`	Manipulate the CSS `zIndex` of the draggable element.

Catching Draggable Events

When using draggable, event handling can be done in several places. The following code snippets demonstrate where it can occur.

These are two ways to add a handler for the same event. You can specify the event at the initialization of the draggable or you can set an event handler like any other event handler.

This event is thrown when draggable is initialized. Notice that you need to start listening for the `dragcreate` event *before* initializing it.

```
$('body *').draggable({create: function(event, ui) {
    // do event handling
}});
$('body *')
```

(Continues)

```
.on('dragcreate', function(event, ui) {
  // do event handling
})
.draggable();
```

You can add event handlers for the other events after initialization. The chance of missing an event between initialization and adding the handler is relatively small.

```
$('body *').draggable({drag: function(event, ui) {
  // do event handling
}});
$('body *')
  .draggable()
  .on('drag', function(event, ui) {
  // do event handling
  });
```

The event handler will receive two parameters: the event and a parameter object called ui. For the draggable events, ui contains the following values:

```
ui = {
  helper:{/* $(dragged obj) */},
  position:{top:12,left:12},
  originalPosition:{top:0,left:0},
  offset:{top:123,left:123}
}
```

The following shows two ways to specify an event to start dragging:

```
$('body *').draggable({start: function(event, ui) {
  // do event handling
}});
$('body *')
  .draggable()
  .on('dragstart', function(event, ui) {
  // do event handling
  });
```

The following shows two ways to specify an event to stop dragging:

```
$('body *').draggable({stop: function(event, ui) {
  // do event handling
  }});
$('body *')
  .draggable()
  .on('dragstop', function(event, ui) {
  // do event handling
  });
```

Invoking Methods on Draggable

Table 6.2 lists the code snippets that display the methods that can be used with draggable.

Table 6.2   **Methods for the Draggable Interaction**

Code	Methods Used with Draggable
`$('body *').draggable('destroy');`	Destroy the draggable component and revert the HTML to its original state.
`$('body *').draggable('disable');`	Disable the draggable. Prevent the draggable element from being dragged.
`$('body *').draggable('enable');`	Enable a disabled draggable element.
`$('body *').draggable('option', 'option-name', 'option-value');`	Set any of the options discussed in the section Setting Draggable Options.
`$('body *').draggable('option', {/*options*/});`	Set multiple options at the same time. This can also be used as a getter to retrieve values when the third argument is left off.
`$('body *').draggable('widget');`	Access the draggable element that serves as the `widget`.

Recipe: Dropping Elements

Dragging elements around the screen can be useful when you are trying to emulate a windows environment within the browser or in a limited number of use cases.

A draggable element becomes more useful when it is combined with a *droppable* area. Listing 6.2 demonstrates how to catch a draggable element when it is dropped on a designated droppable element.

Listing 6.2   **Catching Drop Events from a Target Area**

```
00 <!DOCTYPE html>
01
02 <html lang="en">
03 <head>
04   <title>jQuery UI Droppable</title>
05   <style>
06   .ui-draggable {
07     border: 1px dashed black;
08   }
09   .ui-draggable-dragging {
```

(Continues)

Listing 6.2   Catching Drop Events from a Target Area (Continued)

```
10      border: 1px solid red;
11    }
12    #target {
13      width: 400px;
14      height: 100px;
15      border: 2px solid black;
16    }
17    </style>
18  </head>
19  <body>
20
21  <h2>Drag the span to the rectangle below</h2>
22
23  <span>This is the SPAN</span>
24
25  <div id="target">Drop the span in this rectangle</div>
26
27  <script src="http://code.jquery.com/jquery-1.7.1.min.js"></script>
28  <script src="http://code.jquery.com/ui/1.8.16/jquery-ui.min.js">
29  </script>
30
31  <script>
32  // please externalize this code to an external .js file
33  $(document).ready(function() {
34
35    $('#target').droppable({drop: function() {
36      $(this).html('DROPPED!');
37    }, out: function() {
38      $(this).html('and gone again. . .');
39    }});
40
41    $('span').draggable();
42
43  });
44  </script>
45  </body>
46  </html>
```

Lines 35–39 change the #target div into a droppable area. It specifies two event handlers, one for dropping elements and one for when the draggable leaves the droppable area. In this implementation, the HTML of the droppable area is modified. You can easily replace this code with your own implementation.

Styling the Droppable Element

The droppable area is modified only slightly. jQuery UI adds a class `ui-droppable` that you could use to provide a different styling. In the options that follow, you can also add your own class when a draggable is dragged over the droppable, or when a draggable is being dragged. See `hoverClass` and `activeClass` for this.

Setting Droppable Options

The options `disable` and `addClasses` are explained in the Setting Draggable Options section. Table 6.3 presents other code snippets that demonstrate what options can be used with draggable.

Table 6.3   **Options for the Droppable Interaction**

Code	Options Used with Draggable
`$('#target').droppable({accept: 'span'});`	Accept only elements of the type `span`. You can also provide any other CSS selector in this filter, such as `#my-id` or `.my-class`.
`$('#target').droppable({activeClass: 'show-active'});`	Add your own class when a draggable that meets all requirements is being dragged. You can use CSS to change the looks of the droppable element when this is the case.
`$('#target').droppable({greedy: true});`	Prevent propagation on nested droppables. The default value is `false`. When set to `true`, the most specific droppable catches the draggable. In the default case, the droppable bubbles up the HTML tree to the most general droppable.
`$('#target').droppable({scope: 'my-scope'});`	Add your own class when a draggable that meets all requirements is dragged over the droppable. You can use CSS to change the looks of the droppable element when this is the case. This option can help you see the difference in behavior between the greedy and non-greedy options mentioned earlier.
`$('#target').droppable({hoverClass: 'show-hover'});`	Limit the accepted draggables to the specified scope. See also draggable.

(Continues)

Table 6.3   **Options for the Droppable Interaction (Continued)**

Code	Options Used with Draggable
`$('#target').droppable({scope: 'touch'});`	You can specify a scope of `fit`, `intersect`, `pointer`, or `touch`. These values signify which part of the draggable needs to be inside the droppable for a drop event to occur.
`$('#target').droppable({tolerance: 'fit'});`	The tolerance option is used to adjust the success or trigger of a draggable over the top of a droppable. The default is `intersect` which will trigger when 50 percent of the draggable is over the droppable. Other values are `fit`, `pointer`, and `touch`. The `fit` value requires that the draggable be 100 percent over the droppable. The `pointer` value looks for the mouse pointer to be over the droppable while dragging. The `touch` value will trigger when any portion of the draggable intersects the droppable.

Catching Droppable Events

Like draggable, there are two ways to specify droppable events. The first can be specified on initialization. The second can be set up as a normal event. These are the events for droppable.

A new droppable is created:

```
$('#target').droppable({create: function(event, ui) {
    // do event handling
}});
//or
$('#target')
  .on('dropcreate', function(event, ui) {
    // do event handling
  })
  .droppable();
```

A draggable that meets the requirements is being dragged:

```
$('#target').droppable({activate: function(event, ui) {
    // do event handling
}});
//or
$('#target').droppable()
  .on('dropactivate', function(event, ui) {
    // do event handling
  });
```

The draggable is no longer being dragged:

```
$('#target').droppable({deactive: function(event, ui) {
    // do event handling
}});
//or
$('#target').droppable()
    .on('dropdeactivate', function(event, ui) {
        // do event handling
  });
```

The draggable moves over the droppable:

```
$('#target').droppable({over: function(event, ui) {
    // do event handling
}});
//or
$('#target').droppable()
    .on('dropover', function(event, ui) {
        // do event handling
  });
```

The draggable moves out of the droppable:

```
$('#target').droppable({out: function(event, ui) {
    // do event handling
}});
//or
$('#target').droppable()
  .on('dropout', function(event, ui) {
    // do event handling
  });
```

The draggable is dropped on the droppable area:

```
$('#target').droppable({drop: function(event, ui) {
    // do event handling
}});
//or
$('#target').droppable()
  .on('drop', function(event, ui) {
    // do event handling
  });
```

Invoking Methods on Droppable

See the Invoking Methods on Draggable section for the methods that can be applied to droppable, because these methods are the same for droppable.

Recipe: Changing the Order of Elements by Using Sortable

Dragging and dropping elements by using draggable and droppable offers many possibilities. You can add interactive behavior on the entire screen. In some specific use cases, however, you do not need all this freedom. You would probably rather have a more specific component providing default behavior for you.

Sorting elements is an example of dragging and dropping elements for a specific use case. Listing 6.3 demonstrates how the sortable component helps you to transform a static, unordered list into a dynamic, sortable component.

Listing 6.3   **Transforming an Unordered List into a Sortable**

```
00 <!DOCTYPE html>
01
02 <html lang="en">
03 <head>
04   <title>jQuery UI Sortable</title>
05   <link type="text/css" rel="stylesheet" href=
06     "http://code.jquery.com/ui/1.8.16/themes/base/jquery-ui.css">
07   <style>
08   .ui-draggable {
09     border: 1px dashed black;
10   }
11   .ui-draggable-dragging {
12     border: 1px solid red;
13   }
14   ul {
15     border: 1px dashed gray;
16     padding: 10px 10px 10px 50px;
17     margin: 10px;
18   }
19   </style>
20 </head>
21 <body>
22
23 <h2>Move items in this list up and down</h2>
24 <ul id="target">
25   <li id="mykey-1">And a list</li>
26   <li id="mykey-2">With items</li>
27   <li id="mykey-3">And items containing subitems</li>
28   <li id="mykey-4">And more items containing subitems</li>
29 </ul>
30
31 <script src="http://code.jquery.com/jquery-1.7.1.min.js"></script>
32 <script src="http://code.jquery.com/ui/1.8.16/jquery-ui.min.js">
33 </script>
```

Listing 6.3   **Transforming an Unordered List into a Sortable (Continued)**

```
34
35 <script>
36 // please externalize this code to an external .js file
37 $(document).ready(function() {
38
39   $('ul').sortable();
40
41 });
42 </script>
43 </body>
44 </html>
```

On lines 24–29, you see that a standard unordered list is all the HTML you need to create a sortable. A simple call on line 39 is sufficient to instantiate a default sortable element.

Styling a Sortable

A `ui-sortable` class is added to the `ul` element. When dragging a `li` element, it gets the class `ui-sortable-helper`.

When dragging an `li` element, you can see that under the hood a style attribute is added with values for `width`, `height`, `position` (absolute), `z-index`, `left`, and `top`.

Setting Sortable Options

The following options are explained in the section Setting Draggable Options: `disabled`, `appendTo`, `cancel`, `containment`, `cursor`, `cursorAt`, `delay`, `distance`, `grid`, `handle`, `helper`, `opacity`, `scroll`, `scrollSensitivity`, `scrollSpeed`, and `zIndex`.

Other methods that can be used on sortable interactions are explained in Table 6.4.

Table 6.4   **Options for the Sortable Interaction**

Option	Description
`$('body *').draggable ({axis: 'x'});`	By default, elements can be dragged over both the vertical and horizontal axis. By setting this option, you can restrict drag movements to either the *x* or *y* axis (not both).
`$('ul#my-first-ul'). sortable({connectWith: 'ul#my-other-ul'});`	Allow two or more sortables to exchange elements by dragging the element from one sortable into the other.
`$('ul').sortable({dropOnEmpty: false});`	Prevent elements from being dragged into empty sortable containers when the containers are connected.

(Continues)

Table 6.4   **Options for the Sortable Interaction (Continued)**

Option	Description

`$('ul').`
`sortable({forceHelperSize:`
`true});`
	Ensure that the helper element has a size.

`$('ul').`
`sortable({forcePlaceholderSize:`
`true});`
	Ensure that the placeholder (where items can be dropped) has a size.

`$('ul').sortable({items: 'li'});`	This targets the element inside of the selector that should be sortable.
`$('ul').sortable({placeholder:` `'ui-state-highlight'});`	Change the class of the placeholder to make it stand out to the visitor.
`$('ul').sortable({revert: true});`	Let the element move to the placeholder with a smooth animation.
`$('#target').sortable({tolerance:` `'fit'});`	The tolerance option is used to adjust the behavior of the reordering while dragging. The rules are identical to that of the droppable; the default is `intersect` which will trigger when 50 percent of the draggable is over the droppable. Other values are `fit`, `pointer`, and `touch`. The `fit` value requires that the draggable be 100 percent over the droppable. The `pointer` value looks for the mouse pointer to be over the droppable while dragging. The `touch` value will trigger when any portion of the draggable intersects the droppable.

Catching Events on Sortable

The event handlers receive two parameters: `event` and `ui`. The event object is similar to all other event handers. The code snippets that follow are a demonstration of the events that can be used for event handling.

The `ui` object might contain the following fields, depending on which event is thrown:

```
ui = {
  helper: // element (a clone of the item)_
  item: // element (the item being dragged)
  offset: // [x, y] (absolute position)
  originalPosition: // [x, y]
  placeholder: // element (signifies where the item will be dropped)
```

```
    position: // [x, y]
    sender: // element (the parent sortable)
}
```

A new sortable is created:

```
$('ul').sortable({create: function(event, ui) {
    // do event handling
}});
//or
$('ul')
  .on('sortcreate', function(event, ui) {
    // do event handling
  })
  .sortable();
```

The visitor starts sorting the elements:

```
$('ul').sortable({start: function(event, ui) {
    // do event handling
}});
//or
$('ul').sortable()
  .on('sortstart', function(event, ui) {
    // do event handling
  });
```

The sortable element is being dragged. This event is called many times:

```
$('ul').sortable({sort: function(event, ui) {
    // do event handling
}});
//or
$('ul').sortable()
  .on('sort', function(event, ui) {
    // do event handling
  });
```

Dragging the sortable element causes the remaining elements in the list to change positions:

```
$('ul').sortable({change: function(event, ui) {
    // do event handling
}});
//or
$('ul').sortable()
  .on('sortchange', function(event, ui) {
```

(Continues)

```
    // do event handling
  });
```

The element is no longer being dragged; the placeholder still exists:

```
$('ul').sortable({beforeStop: function(event, ui) {
    // do event handling
}});
//or
$('ul').sortable()
  .on('sortbeforestop', function(event, ui) {
    // do event handling
  });
```

The element is no longer being dragged; the placeholder is removed:

```
$('ul').sortable({stop: function(event, ui) {
    // do event handling
}});
//or
$('ul').sortable()
  .on('sortstop', function(event, ui) {
    // do event handling
  });
The sortable element is in its new location.
$('ul').sortable({update: function(event, ui) {
    // do event handling
}});
//or
$('ul').sortable()
  .on('sortupdate', function(event, ui) {
    // do event handling
  });
```

An element is received from another, connected sortable:

```
$('ul').sortable({receive: function(event, ui) {
    // do event handling
}});
//or
$('ul').sortable()
  .on('sortreceive', function(event, ui) {
    // do event handling
  });
```

An element is removed and sent to another, connected sortable:

```
$('ul').sortable({remove: function(event, ui) {
    // do event handling
}});
//or
$('ul').sortable()
  .on('sortremove', function(event, ui) {
    // do event handling
  });
```

An element from another, connected sortable is dragged over this sortable:

```
$('ul').sortable({over: function(event, ui) {
    // do event handling
}});
//or
$('ul').sortable()
  .on('sortover', function(event, ui) {
    // do event handling
  });
```

An element from another, connected sortable was dragged over this sortable and is now dragged out again:

```
$('ul').sortable({out: function(event, ui) {
    // do event handling
}});
//or
$('ul').sortable()
  .on('sortout', function(event, ui) {
    // do event handling
  });
```

An element from another, connected sortable which could be placed inside this sortable is being dragged:

```
$('ul').sortable({activate: function(event, ui) {
    // do event handling
}});
//or
$('ul').sortable()
  .on('sortactivate', function(event, ui) {
    // do event handling
  });
```

An element from another, connected sortable which could be placed inside this sortable is no longer being dragged:

```
$('ul').sortable({deactivate: function(event, ui) {
    // do event handling
}});
//or
$('ul').sortable()
  .on('sortdeactivate', function(event, ui) {
    // do event handling
  });
```

Invoking Methods on Sortable

The following snippets show how to retrieve the values of the sortable as a serialized string.

```
$('ul').sortable('serialize');
```

The previous snippet will return a value such as mykey[]=1&mykey[]=0&mykey[]=2. If you want to use this value as a query string, you might consider changing the returned value as follows:

```
var numbered = $.map(
  $('ul').sortable('serialize').split(']'),
  function(value, index) {
      if(value.substr(-1) == '[')
        return value + index;
    else
      return value;
}).join(']');
```

With the previous code snippet, you get mykey[0]=2&mykey[1]=1&mykey[2]=3 as a return value.

Change the key value that is extracted from the element IDs into the provided key value:

```
$('ul').sortable('serialize', {key: 'myotherkey'});
```

Instead of serializing to a string, you can also serialize the sortable element into an array. This will return a value such as ['mykey-2', 'mykey-1', . . .]:

```
$('ul').sortable('toArray');
```

Recognize new items if they have not yet been recognized:

```
$('ul').sortable('refresh');
```

If a lot of action takes place on a page, you can call `refreshPositions` to ensure that the latest page state is reflected in the sortable element:

```
$('ul').sortable('refreshPositions');
```

Revert changes caused by sorting actions and revert the sortable to its original state. The `cancel` method can be called in `stop`, `receive`, and `change` events:

```
$('ul').sortable('cancel');
```

Example: Sorting Elements in a Tree Structure

You can create a simple tree structure and allow elements to be moved within the tree by nesting unordered lists and connecting them together. Listing 6.4 proves the principle by using three unordered lists.

Listing 6.4   **Connecting Unordered Lists in a Tree Structure**

```
00 <!DOCTYPE html>
01
02 <html lang="en">
03 <head>
04   <title>jQuery UI Sortable Tree</title>
05   <link type="text/css" rel="stylesheet" href=
06     "http://code.jquery.com/ui/1.8.16/themes/base/jquery-ui.css">
07   <style>
08   ul {
09     border: 1px dashed gray;
10     margin: 10px;
11     padding: 10px 10px 10px 30px;
12   }
13   </style>
14 </head>
15 <body>
16
17 <h2>Move elements in this tree</h2>
18 <ul id="target">
19   <li>And a list</li>
20   <li>With items</li>
21   <li>And items containing subitems
22     <ul class="child">
23       <li>Sub 1</li>
24       <li>Sub 2</li>
25     </ul>
26   </li>
27   <li>And more items containing subitems
```

(Continues)

Listing 6.4   **Connecting Unordered Lists in a Tree Structure (Continued)**

```
28        <ul class="child">
29          <li>Sub 4</li>
30          <li>Sub 5</li>
31        </ul>
32      </li>
33 </ul>
34
35 <script src="http://code.jquery.com/jquery-1.7.1.min.js"></script>
36 <script src="http://code.jquery.com/ui/1.8.16/jquery-ui.min.js">
37 </script>
38
39 <script>
40 // please externalize this code to an external .js file
41 $(document).ready(function() {
42
43   $('ul').sortable({connectWith: 'ul'});
44
45 });
46 </script>
47 </body>
48 </html>
```

With all unordered lists, you can also drag one unordered list into another unordered list. Or, you can flatten the tree structure. Increasing the number of unordered lists inside the tree could make the tree structure even more dynamic.

Recipe: Selecting Elements in an Unordered List

If you want to allow your visitor to select elements as input for your web application, you could consider offering a drop-down list or select element with which multiple values can be selected. The usability of such an interface might be questionable, however.

jQuery UI offers a more user-friendly way to select elements. Listing 6.5 demonstrates how to select elements from an unordered list by using jQuery.

Listing 6.5   **Making Elements Selectable**

```
00 <!DOCTYPE html>
01
02 <html lang="en">
03 <head>
04   <title>jQuery UI Selectable</title>
05   <style>
06   .ui-selectee {
07     background-color: rgba(20,20,20,0.2);
08   }
```

Listing 6.5   **Making Elements Selectable (Continued)**

```
09    .ui-selected {
10      background-color: yellow;
11    }
12    .ui-selecting {
13      background-color: rgba(20,20,20,0.5);
14    }
15
16    </style>
17  </head>
18  <body>
19
20  <h2>Select elements below</h2>
21  <ul id="target">
22    <li>And a list</li>
23    <li>With items</li>
24    <li>1</li>
25    <li>2</li>
26    <li>4</li>
27    <li>5</li>
28  </ul>
29
30  <script src="http://code.jquery.com/jquery-1.7.1.min.js"></script>
31  <script src="http://code.jquery.com/ui/1.8.16/jquery-ui.min.js">
32  </script>
33
34  <script>
35  // please externalize this code to an external .js file
36  $(document).ready(function() {
37
38    $('ul#target').selectable({
39      selected: function(event, ui) {
40        console.log(event);
41        console.log(ui);
42        $(ui.selected).html('SELECTED');
43      }
44    });
45
46  });
47  </script>
48  </body>
49  </html>
```

For elements to be selectable, they do not necessarily need to be in an unordered list that is presented in a top-down manner. You might just as well select elements from a two-dimensional grid that suits your requirements.

Styling Selectable Elements

If you want to style a selectable, there are five CSS classes you should take into account. First, there is the `ui-selectable` class on the root element of the selectable. Second, every element inside this root element has a `ui-selectee` class. Finally, depending on the current state of selection, the `ui-selecting`, `ui-unselecting`, or `ui-selected` classes will be added to the elements.

Setting Selectable Options

See Setting Draggable Options for an elaborate discussion of `disabled`, `cancel`, `delay`, and `distance`.

Table 6.5 shows several code-snippet options that can be used with selectable.

Table 6.5   **Options for the Selectable Interaction**

Option	Description
`$('ul#target').` `selectable({autoRefresh: false});`	Prevent selectable from setting classes on all selectable elements. This is mostly for performance optimization. You can provide styling by using cascading styling mechanisms inherent to CSS and additional classes are still added on selection.

`$('ul#target').`
`selectable({filter: 'li.my-fil-`
`ter'});`
	Within the selectable root container, you can filter which descending elements can be selected and which cannot by specifying a CSS selector as a filter parameter.

`$('ul#target').` `selectable({tolerance: 'fit'});`	The tolerance option is used to adjust the behavior of the reordering while dragging. The rules are similar to that of the droppable; the default is `touch` which will trigger when 50 percent of the draggable is over the droppable. The only other value is `fit`. This value requires that the draggable be 100 percent over the droppable. The `touch` value will trigger when any portion of the draggable intersects the droppable.

Catching Events on Selectable

The following code snippets demonstrate how event handling can be used with the selectable interaction:

```
$('ul#target').selectable({create: function(event, ui) {

    // do event handling
}});
```

```
//or
$('ul#target')
  .on('selectablecreate', function(event, ui) {
    // do event handling
  })
  .selectable();
```

Here, a tree of elements is set up as a selectable component.

After the selection operation is finished, the selected event is triggered for each element in the selection:

```
$('ul#target').selectable({selected: function(event, ui) {
    // do event handling
}});
//or
$('ul#target').selectable()
  .on('selectableselected', function(event, ui) {
    // do event handling
  });
```

The visitor is selecting one or more elements; this is called for each element that is added to the selection:

```
$('ul#target').selectable({selecting: function(event, ui) {
    // do event handling
}});
//or
$('ul#target').selectable()
  .on('selectableselecting', function(event, ui) {
    // do event handling
  });
```

The visitor starts selecting elements; this function is run when a visitor begins selecting elements:

```
$('ul#target').selectable({start: function(event, ui) {
    // do event handling
}});
//or
$('ul#target').selectable()
  .on('selectablestart', function(event, ui) {
    // do event handling
  });
```

The visitor stops selecting elements; this function runs at the end of a selection:

```
$('ul#target').selectable({stop: function(event, ui) {
    // do event handling
}});
//or
$('ul#target').selectable()
  .on('selectablestop', function(event, ui) {
    // do event handling
  });
```

The visitor has stopped selecting elements, and some elements are unselected in the new selection; This event is triggered for every element that is unselected:

```
$('ul#target').selectable({unselected: function(event, ui) {
    // do event handling
}});
//or
$('ul#target').selectable()
  .on('selectableunselected', function(event, ui) {
    // do event handling
  });
```

The visitor unselects elements in the selectable component:

```
$('ul#target').selectable({deactivate: function(event, ui) {
    // do event handling
}});
//or
$('ul#target').selectable()
  .on('unselecting', function(event, ui) {
    // do event handling
  });
```

Invoking Methods on Selectable

See the section Invoking Methods on Draggable for details about `destroy`, `disable`, `enable`, `option`, and `widget`.

Refresh the selectable component manually. In regular usage, you should not need this method. In highly dynamic Web pages, it can help you solve problems:

```
$('ul#target').selectable('refresh');
```

Example: Selecting Elements in a Tree Structure

Earlier in this chapter, you studied the example for sorting elements in a tree of nested unordered lists. Similarly, you can select elements that are in a tree of unordered lists. Listing 6.6 provides an example of such a selection.

Listing 6.6   **Making a Nested Unordererd List Selectable**

```
00 <!DOCTYPE html>
01
02 <html lang="en">
03 <head>
04   <title>jQuery UI Selectable Tree</title>
05   <link type="text/css" rel="stylesheet" href=
06     "http://code.jquery.com/ui/1.8.16/themes/base/jquery-ui.css">
07   <style>
08   .ui-selectee {
09     background-color: rgba(20,20,20,0.2);;
10   }
11   .ui-selected {
12     border: 1px dashed black;
13   }
14   .ui-selecting {
15     border: 1px solid red;
16   }
17
18   </style>
19 </head>
20 <body>
21
22 <h2>Select elements below</h2>
23 <ul id="target">
24   <li>And a list</li>
25   <li>With items</li>
26   <li>And items containing subitems
27     <ul class="child">
28       <li>Sub 1</li>
29       <li>Sub 2</li>
30     </ul>
31   </li>
32   <li>And more items containing subitems
33     <ul class="child">
34       <li>Sub 4</li>
35       <li>Sub 5</li>
36     </ul>
37   </li>
38 </ul>
39
40 <script src="http://code.jquery.com/jquery-1.7.1.min.js"></script>
41 <script src="http://code.jquery.com/ui/1.8.16/jquery-ui.min.js">
42 </script>
43
44 <script>
45 // please externalize this code to an external .js file
```

(Continues)

Listing 6.6   Making a Nested Unordererd List Selectable (Continued)

```
46 $(document).ready(function() {
47
48   $('ul#target').selectable();
49
50 });
51 </script>
52 </body>
53 </html>
```

When you try this example, pay special attention to the borders of the selections. Try to select only a child element and try to select only a parent element. Then, try to select both a parent and a single child. The combination of the tree model and the selectable interface offers a flexible interface.

Recipe: Resizing Elements

In rich Web applications, you can provide your visitors with the ability to resize elements inside the page. One of the ways to achieve this is by using jQuery UI resizable. Listing 6.7 demonstrates how to change a `div` element into a resizable component.

Listing 6.7   Making <div> Elements Resizable

```
00 <!DOCTYPE html>
01
02 <html lang="en">
03 <head>
04   <title>jQuery UI Resizable</title>
05   <link type="text/css" rel="stylesheet" href=
06     "http://code.jquery.com/ui/1.8.16/themes/base/jquery-ui.css">
07   <style>
08   #my-resizable {
09     width: 250px;
10     height: 100px;
11     border: 1px solid black;
12     overflow: hidden;
13   }
14   </style>
15 </head>
16 <body>
17
18 <div id="my-resizable">
19   <h2>Try to resize this div</h2>
20   <p>To help you a little bit, here is some text. Lorem ipsum dolor
21   sit amet, consectetur adipiscing elit. Aenean porttitor elit
22   iaculis orci lacinia sollicitudin. Maecenas neque justo,
23   vestibulum vitae viverra at, tincidunt vitae nisi. Vestibulum ante
```

Listing 6.7   **Making \<div\> Elements Resizable (Continued)**

```
24    ipsum primis in faucibus orci luctus et ultrices posuere cubilia
25    Curae; Suspendisse turpis erat, auctor eu posuere sit amet, tempor
26    at elit. Donec sodales, ante vitae luctus ultricies, sapien lectus
27    adipiscing lacus, non adipiscing felis mauris vel diam.</p>
28 </div>
29
30
31 <script src="http://code.jquery.com/jquery-1.7.1.min.js"></script>
32 <script src="http://code.jquery.com/ui/1.8.16/jquery-ui.min.js">
33 </script>
34
35 <script>
36 // please externalize this code to an external .js file
37 $(document).ready(function() {
38
39    $('#my-resizable').resizable();
40
41 });
42 </script>
43 </body>
44 </html>
```

The text on lines 20–28 helps you to test how realignment works when resizing the component. Line 39 instantiates the resizable component without restrictions.

Styling the Resizable Element

The resizable element itself gets a class `ui-resizable`. This way, you can provide your own styles for resizables in general. Inside the resizable component, jQuery UI adds several `div` elements that can be dragged over the screen to make the component resize.

```
<div class="ui-resizable-handle ui-resizable-e"></div>
<div class="ui-resizable-handle ui-resizable-s"></div>
<div class="ui-resizable-handle ui-resizable-se ui-icon ui-icon-
gripsmall -diagonal-se" style="z-index: 1001; "></div>
```

The first two elements signify the east and the south of the component, allowing horizontal and vertical resizing. The last element signifies the south-east of the element, displays an icon in the corner, and allows diagonal resizing.

Setting Resizable Options

See the Setting Draggable Options section for information about the `disabled`, `cancel`, `containment`, `delay`, `grid`, `helper`, and `distance` options.

Table 6.6 shows the code snippets that demonstrate the other options available for the resizable interaction.

Table 6.6   **Options for the Resizable Interaction**

Option	Description

`$('#my-resizable').`
`resizable({alsoResize:`
`'#other-resizable'});`
	Specify an additional element on the screen that should resize together with the current resizable component.

`$('#my-resizable').` `resizable({animate: true});`	Show an animation after resizing.

`$('#my-resizable').`
`resizable({animateDuration:`
`1000});`
	Set the animation speed. This can be the number of milliseconds or a string containing `slow`, `normal`, or `fast`.

Specify which animation should be used. You can choose from the following:

```
easeInOutBounce, easeOutBounce, easeInBounce, easeInOutBack,
easeOutBack, easeInBack, easeInOutElastic, easeOutElastic,
easeInElastic, easeInOutCirc, easeOutCirc, easeInCirc, easeInOutExpo,
easeOutExpo, easeInExpo, easeInOutSine, easeOutSine, easeInSine,
easeInOutQuint, easeOutQuint, easeInQuint, easeInOutQuart,
easeOutQuart, easeInQuart, easeInOutCubic, easeOutCubic, easeInCubic,
easeInOutQuad, easeOutQuad, easeInQuad, def, jswing, swing and linear.
$('#my-resizable').resizable({animateEasing: 'linear'});
```

There are two ways to set an aspect ratio. The first maintains the current aspect ratio on the screen. The second provides a new value. The aspect ratio is calculated as width/ height, so the example makes the component tall. If you need a wide component with similar proportions, you should set the aspect ratio to 4.

```
$('#my-resizable').resizable({aspectRatio: true});
//or
$('#my-resizable').resizable({aspectRatio: 0.25});
```

Show the resize handles only on `mouseover`:

```
$('#my-resizable').resizable({autoHide: true});
```

Introduce a semi-transparant helper when resizing:

```
$('#my-resizable').resizable({ghost: true});
```

Change the handles to a selection from the following values:

```
n, e, s, w, ne, se, sw, nw, all
$('#my-resizable').resizable({handles: 'n, w, nw'});
```

Restrict the dimensions of the resizable to minimum and maximum values:

```
$('#my-resizable').resizable({maxHeight: 200});
$('#my-resizable').resizable({maxWidth: 200});
$('#my-resizable').resizable({minHeight: 200});
$('#my-resizable').resizable({minWidth: 200});
```

Catching Events on Resizable

The following code snippets show what events are available for event handling.

An element is transformed into a resizable:

```
$('#my-resizable').resizable({create: function(event, ui) {
    // do event handling
}});
//or
$('#my-resizable')
  .on('resizecreate', function(event, ui) {
    // do event handling
  })
  .resizable();
```

The visitor starts resizing the component:

```
$('#my-resizable').resizable({start: function(event, ui) {
    // do event handling
}});
//or
$('#my-resizable').resizable()
  .on('resizestart', function(event, ui) {
    // do event handling
  });
```

The visitor further resizes the component:

```
$('#my-resizable').resizable({resize: function(event, ui) {
    // do event handling
}});
//or
$('#my-resizable').resizable()
  .on('resize', function(event, ui) {
    // do event handling
  });
```

The visitor is done resizing the component:

```
$('#my-resizable').resizable({stop: function(event, ui) {
    // do event handling
}});
//or
$('#my-resizable').resizable()
  .on('resizestop', function(event, ui) {
    // do event handling
  });
```

Invoking Methods on Resizable

All methods available on resizable are discussed in the section Invoking Methods on Draggable: `destroy`, `disable`, `enable`, `option`, and `widget`.

Summary

This chapter discussed the user interactions that are available with jQuery UI to make interactive web pages. It showed the simple mechanisms to add interaction to almost any HTML element. This includes dragging, dropping, sorting, selecting, and resizing.

This chapter contains many small code snippets with options, events, and methods to modify each component. It also provides the HTML structures and CSS classes required to add your own styling to the components.

Chapter 7

Interacting with Widgets

Now that you've been introduced to the basics of user interaction with the help of jQuery UI, in this chapter you'll learn about a set of components with a more specific HTML structure. Accordions, tabs, auto-complete suggestions, date pickers, buttons, sliders, dialogs, and progress bars are part of the widgets that are included in jQuery UI.

Widgets are jQuery UI components that require more specific HTML as input and can generate more complex HTML structures as an output.

Recipe: Grouping Content by Using the Accordion

Listing 7.1 introduces the accordion widget, with which you can group content under headers and show only a single selected group at a time. Clicking another header closes the current group and opens the group under the selected header.

Listing 7.1 **Transforming <h3> and <div> Elements into an Accordion**

```
00 <!DOCTYPE html>
01
02 <html lang="en">
03 <head>
04   <title>jQuery UI Accordion</title>
05   <link type="text/css" rel="stylesheet" href=
06     "http://code.jquery.com/ui/1.8.16/themes/base/jquery-ui.css">
07   <style>
08     div#my-accordion {
09         font-size: 14px;
10     }
11   </style>
12 </head>
13 <body>
14
15 <div id="my-accordion">
```

(Continues)

Listing 7.1   Transforming <h3> and <div> Elements into an Accordion (Continued)

```
16    <h3>
17      <a href="#first">Try to switch to the next part</a>
18    </h3>
19    <div>
20      The content
21    </div>
22    <h3>
23      <a href="#second">Next</a>
24    </h3>
25    <div>
26      More content
27    </div>
28    <h3>
29      <a href="#third">Last</a>
30    </h3>
31    <div>
32      and the last content
33    </div>
34 </div>
35
36 <script src="http://code.jquery.com/jquery-1.7.1.min.js"></script>
37 <script src="http://code.jquery.com/ui/1.8.16/jquery-ui.min.js">
38 </script>
39
40 <script>
41 // please externalize this code to an external .js file
42 $(document).ready(function() {
43
44    $('#my-accordion').accordion();
45
46 });
47 </script>
48 </body>
49 </html>
```

On lines 15–34, you see a `div` with a specific HTML structure. You should recognize a pattern of an `h3` with an anchor followed by a `div` and then an `h3` again. The `h3` elements serve as group headers and the `div`s can be hidden in order to collapse a group.

Styling the Accordion

The introduction of this chapter already mentioned that the accordion generates a more elaborate HTML structure. To be more accurate, it extends the existing HTML structure. After applying the `accordion` to the `div`, the HTML looks like that in the snippet which follows. (Note: The next HTML is *generated*. You do not need to type it in anywhere.)

```html
<div id="my-accordion"
  class="ui-accordion ui-widget ui-helper-reset ui-accordion-icons"
  role="tablist">
  <h3
    class="ui-accordion-header ui-helper-reset ui-state-active
        ui-corner-top"
    role="tab"
    aria-expanded="true"
    aria-selected="true"
    tabindex="0">
    <span class="ui-icon ui-icon-triangle-1-s"></span>
    <a href="#first">First</a>
  </h3>
  <div
    class="ui-accordion-content ui-helper-reset ui-widget-content
        ui-corner-bottom ui-accordion-content-active"
    style="display: block; height: 18px; padding-top: 14px;
        padding-bottom: 14px; overflow-x: auto; overflow-y: auto; "
    role="tabpanel">Content for first section</div>
  <h3
    class="ui-accordion-header ui-helper-reset ui-state-default
        ui-corner-all"
    role="tab"
    aria-expanded="false"
    aria-selected="false"
    tabindex="-1">
  <span class="ui-icon ui-icon-triangle-1-e"></span>
    <a href="#second">Second</a>
  </h3>
  <div
    class="ui-accordion-content ui-helper-reset ui-widget-content
        ui-corner-bottom"
    style="overflow-x: auto; overflow-y: auto; display: none;
        height: 18px; padding-top: 14px; padding-bottom: 14px; "
    role="tabpanel">Content for second section</div>
```

The code in bold signifies the changes from the original HTML. The highlighted parts of the code are options that will change when the visitor clicks a different accordion header.

Setting Accordion Options

There are many different options that can be set and used with the accordion widget. Table 7.1 presents examples of setting the option, along with descriptions of what the each option does.

Table 7.1   **Options for the Accordion Widget**

Option	Description
`$('#my-accordion').` `accordion({disabled: true});`	The default option for `disabled` is `false`. Setting the option to `true` disables the accordion and stops it from working. You can set this option at any time including during initialization.
`$('#my-accordion').` `accordion({active: false});`	Setting `active` to `false` closes all groups upon initialization. This only works if collapsible is `true`. Instead of a Boolean, you can also provide a selector, a jQuery element, or an HTML element to open.
`$('#my-accordion').` `accordion({animated: 'blind'});`	The animated option displays an animation when opening and closing groups. The default value is `slide`, but the you can use the following values, instead: `blind`, `bounce`, `clip`, `drop`, `explode`, `fade`, `fold`, `highlight`, `puff`, `pulsate`, `scale`, `shake`, `size`, and `transfer`.
`$('#my-accordion').` `accordion({autoHeight: false});`	Disables group height adjusting. This way each group has the height of its content instead of keeping the height of the total accordion component constant. The default value for `autoHeight` is `true`.
`$('#my-accordion').` `accordion({clearStyle: true,` `autoHeight: false});`	The `clearStyle` option cleans any height style elements after animation, which is useful for loading dynamic content. Note that it does not work with the `autoHeight` option.
`$('#my-accordion').` `accordion({collapsible: true});`	You can use the `collapsible` option cause all of the accordion sections to be collapsed at the same time. This option can work together with `active: false` to provide an accordion that is completely closed upon initialization. The default value is `false`.
`$('#my-accordion').` `accordion({event: 'dblclick'});`	Changes the event that opens accordion groups. You can also consider events such as `mouseover` or the default `click`.

Table 7.1   **Options for the Accordion Widget (Continued)**

Option	Description
`$('#my-accordion').` `accordion({fillSpace: true});`	Overrides `autoHeight` and fills the complete parent element. This is useful for creating a Visual Studio–like sidebar with option groups. The default value is `false`.
`$('#my-accordion').` `accordion({header: 'h3'});`	By default, the accordion uses every other item in the component as a group header. In the example snippet, this option is set to explicitly configure `h3` elements as the group headers.

`$('#my-accordion').accordion({`
`icons: {`
`    'header': 'ui-icon-circle-`
`plus',`
`    'headerSelected': 'ui-icon-`
`circle-minus'`
`}});`
	With the icons option, you can provide additional icons on group headers. You can find a list of all available icons in Chapter 8, Changing the Look and Feel.

`$('#my-accordion').` `accordion({navigation: true});`	Opens the section with the anchor selected in the URL. This requires the `a` `href` elements to provide a unique local hash tag. The default value is `false`.

`$('#my-accordion').accordion({`
`navigation: true,`
`  navigationFilter:`
`function(index) {`
`    return index == 2;`
`}});`
	Instead of opening the group from the hash tag from the URL, you can also implement your own function that specifies which group should be opened. The function is called for every group, with the group index as a function parameter. It should return true for the group that should be open. The implementation can be more sophisticated than this example.

Catching Events on Accordion

The following is an example of the values you might receive in the `ui` parameter:

```
ui = {
newContent: // element
newHeader: // element
```

(Continues)

```
oldContent: // element
oldHeader: // element
options: Object
  active: 3
  animated: "slide"
  autoHeight: true
  change: function (event, ui) {
  clearStyle: false
  collapsible: false
  disabled: false
  duration: undefined
  event: "click"
  fillSpace: false
  header: "> li > :first-child,> :not(li):even"
  icons: Object
  navigation: true
  navigationFilter: function (index) {
  proxied: "slide"
  proxiedDuration: undefined
}
```

The following shows where event handling takes place when a new accordion component is instantiated:

```
$('#my-accordion').accordion({create: function(event, ui) {
    // do event handling
}});
//or
$('#my-accordion')
  .on('accordioncreate', function(event, ui) {
    // do event handling
  })
  .accordion();
```

The following shows a new accordion group being selected and a place to handle the event after the component is done animating:

```
$('#my-accordion').accordion({change: function(event, ui) {
    // do event handling
}});
//or
$('#my-accordion').accordion()
  .on('accordionchange', function(event, ui) {
    // do event handling
  });
```

The following shows a new accordion group being selected and handling the event when the animation is just starting:

```
$('#my-accordion').accordion({changestart: function(event, ui) {
    // do event handling
}});
//or
$('#my-accordion').accordion()
  .on('accordionchangestart', function(event, ui) {
    // do event handling
  });
```

Methods

The `accordion` widget also contains several methods that can be used to change values and behavior. Table 7.2 lists available methods.

Table 7.2   **Methods for the Accordion Widget**

Method	Description
`$('#my-accordion').` `accordion('destroy');`	Removes all accordion functionality and returns the selected element back to its original state.
`$('#my-accordion').` `accordion('disable');`	Disables the accordion functionality, but does not remove the element from the page.
`$('#my-accordion').` `accordion('enable');`	Enables a disabled accordion.

`$('#my-accordion').`
`accordion('option', optionName,`
`[value]);`
	Use this to get or set values used in the accordion. If you leave it blank it will act as a getter; when populated it becomes a setter.

`$('#my-accordion').` `accordion('option', options);`	By passing an `options` object, you can set multiple options at the same time.
`$('#my-accordion').` `accordion('widget');`	This returns the `.ui-accordion` element.
`$('#my-accordion').` `accordion('activate', 1);`	Select the second group.
`$('#my-accordion').` `accordion('resize');`	Recalculate the accordion height based on the current HTML elements.

Recipe: Suggesting Input Values by Using Autocomplete

On some Web sites, you can find selection drop-down menus that contain extremely long lists of choices. In many cases you can help your visitor by replacing the drop-down menu with an input element featuring an autocomplete. Instead of scrolling, the visitor types the first characters of his desired choice, and autocomplete does the rest.

Listing 7.2 provides an autocomplete example that completes the first words from a text called *Lorem Ipsum*. This is a text from two millennia ago that is still used by graphic designers and the typesetting industry (often called "dummy" or "filler" text, with all due apologies to Latin scholars everywhere) to see the effect of their design choices.

Listing 7.2   **Suggesting Lorem Ipsum Values**

```
00 <!DOCTYPE html>
01
02 <html lang="en">
03 <head>
04   <title>jQuery UI Draggable</title>
05   <link type="text/css" rel="stylesheet" href=
06     "http://code.jquery.com/ui/1.8.16/themes/base/jquery-ui.css">
07   <style>
08     .ui-widget {
09         font-size: 12px;
10     }
11   </style>
12 </head>
13 <body>
14
15 <div id="my-container">
16   <label for="my-autocomplete">Type to see how this works</label>
17   <input type="text" id="my-autocomplete">
18 </div>
19
20 <script src="http://code.jquery.com/jquery-1.7.1.min.js"></script>
21 <script src="http://code.jquery.com/ui/1.8.16/jquery-ui.min.js">
22 </script>
23
24 <script>
25 // please externalize this code to an external .js file
26 $(document).ready(function() {
27
28   var loremIpsum = [
29 'Lorem', 'ipsum', 'dolor', 'sit', 'amet', 'consectetur',
30   'adipiscing', 'elit', 'Donec', 'fermentum', 'tortor', 'et',
31   'ante', 'ullamcorper', 'eget', 'posuere', 'ligula'
```

Listing 7.2   **Suggesting Lorem Ipsum Values (Continued)**

```
32    ];
33
34    $('#my-autocomplete').autocomplete({source: loremIpsum});
35
36 });
37 </script>
38 </body>
39 </html>
```

When you run this example, notice that the suggestions in the autocomplete box are ordered exactly as they appear on lines 29–31. The `autocomplete()` is called on line 34 and is given an option of `source` with a value `loremIpsum` which is the array created on line 28. If you need a different sorting order—alphabetical or by popularity—you need to implement it yourself before feeding the values to the autocomplete box.

Styling the Autocomplete Component

After calling the `autocomplete` command, the HTML of the input box changes to this:

```
<input type="text" id="my-autocomplete" class="ui-autocomplete-input"
  autocomplete="off" role="textbox" aria-autocomplete="list"
  aria-haspopup="true">
```

When you start typing in the autocomplete box, a set of temporary HTML elements is appended to the bottom of the document to facilitate the selection list.

```
<ul
  class="ui-autocomplete ui-menu ui-widget ui-widget-content
    ui-corner-all"
  role="listbox" aria-activedescendant="ui-active-menuitem"
  style="z-index: 1; width: 149px; top: 32px; left: 181px;
  display: none;">
  <li class="ui-menu-item" role="menuitem">
   <a class="ui-corner-all" tabindex="-1">Lorem</a>
  </li>
  <li class="ui-menu-item" role="menuitem">
   <a class="ui-corner-all" tabindex="-1">dolor</a>
  </li>
  . . . etc . . .
</ul>
```

You can use the class names from these HTML snippets to manually style the autocomplete component.

Setting Autocomplete Options

Table 7.3 lists the options that can be set with the `autocomplete` widget.

Table 7.3   **Options for the Autocomplete Widget**

Option	Description
```$('#my-autocomplete').autocomplete({ source: '/retrieve-suggestions'});```	Makes a call to the specified URL to retrieve autocomplete values. The `autocomplete` element adds a `?term={yourvalue}` query to the URL.
```[{id: 'my-id', label: 'my-label', value: 'my-value'}, {id: '2nd-id', label: '2nd-label', value: '2nd-value'}, //etc]```	The returned data can be a JSON data structure, similar to the previous code.
```$('#my-autocomplete').autocomplete(source: function(req, res) { res([' {id: 'my-id', label: 'my-label', value: 'my-value'}, {id: '2nd-id', label: '2nd-label', value: '2nd-value'} //etc]); }});```	In addition to server-side queries and static arrays, you can also provide a function.
```$('#my-autocomplete'). autocomplete({disabled: true});```	Setting the disabled option to `true` causes autocompete stop working. The default value is `false`.
```$('#my-autocomplete'). autocomplete({appendTo: '#another-autocomplete'});```	Using the `appendTo` option, you can initialize an autocomplete on the value that's passed to the `appendTo` option. The default value is `body`.
```$('#my-autocomplete'). autocomplete({delay: 500});```	With the delay option, you can set up a timer that will trigger the activation of the autocomplete. The default value is `300`.

Table 7.3   **Options for the Autocomplete Widget (Continued)**

Option	Description
``$('#my-autocomplete').
autocomplete({autoFocus: true, source:
loremIpsum});```	Preselects the first item from the autocomplete list. By combining it with the source option, you can choose what data to display first. The default value for `autoFocus` is `false`.
``$('#my-autocomplete').
autocomplete({minLength: 3, source:
loremIpsum});```	Specifies a required minimum number of typed characters (in this example, 3) before displaying an autocomplete. This prevents extremely long lists or heavy database queries.
``$('#my-autocomplete').autocomplete({
position: {
my: 'left top',
at: 'right top' },
source: loremIpsum});```	Sets the position of the selection list to the specified location. The position option can be viewed in detail at http://docs.jquery.com/UI/Position.

Catching Events on Autocomplete

There are many places where event handling can take place while using autocomplete. The following code snippets give an example of where it can be done.

A new autocomplete component is initialized:

```
$('#my-autocomplete').autocomplete({create: function(event, ui) {
    // do event handling
}});
//or
$('#my-autocomplete')
  .on('autocompletecreate', function(event, ui) {
    // do event handling
  })
  .autocomplete();
```

The visitor typed a search value that is at least `minLength` long. Return `false` to cancel the search:

```
$('#my-autocomplete').autocomplete({search: function(event, ui) {
    // do event handling
}});
//or
```

(Continues)

```
$('#my-autocomplete').autocomplete()
  .on('autocompletesearch', function(event, ui) {
    // do event handling
  });
```

The selection menu is opened:

```
$('#my-autocomplete').autocomplete({open: function(event, ui) {
    // do event handling
}});
//or
$('#my-autocomplete').autocomplete()
  .on('autocompleteopen', function(event, ui) {
    // do event handling
  });
```

An element in the drop-down menu receives focus. Return `false` to prevent the input field from updating already:

```
$('#my-autocomplete').autocomplete({focus: function(event, ui) {
    // do event handling
}});
//or
$('#my-autocomplete').autocomplete()
  .on('autocompletefocus', function(event, ui) {
    // do event handling
  });
An item is selected.$('#my-autocomplete').autocomplete({select: function(event,
ui) {
 // do event handling
}});
//or
$('#my-autocomplete').autocomplete()
  .on('autocompleteselect', function(event, ui) {
    // do event handling
  });
```

The autocomplete is closed:

```
$('#my-autocomplete').autocomplete({close: function(event, ui) {
    // do event handling
}});
//or
```

```
$('#my-autocomplete').autocomplete()
  .on('autocompleteclose', function(event, ui) {
    // do event handling
  });
```

When the visitor moves to the next element on screen, if the input value has changed, this event is triggered:

```
$('#my-autocomplete').autocomplete({change: function(event, ui) {
    // do event handling
}});
//or
$('#my-autocomplete').autocomplete()
  .on('autocompletechange', function(event, ui) {
    // do event handling
  });
```

Invoking Methods on Autocomplete

The following snippets present examples of using methods with autocomplete.

Bind to `click` event, leaving the value parameter out to use current value, and use `minLength: 0` to display all values:

```
$('#my-autocomplete')
  .autocomplete({minLength: 0, source: loremIpsum})
  .click(function() {
    $(this).autocomplete('search');
  });
```

Close the current suggestion:

```
$('#my-autocomplete').autocomplete('close');
```

Recipe: Transforming Elements into Buttons

In general, HTML provides several ways to create elements that look like buttons, even without CSS styling or JavaScript. Consider, for example, the `button` element and input types `button` and `submit`.

With a combination of CSS and JavaScript, any other element can be made to look and feel like a button. Listing 7.3 demonstrates how jQuery UI helps you to create buttons.

Listing 7.3   **Selecting a List of Elements and Styling Them as Buttons**

```
00 <!DOCTYPE html>
01
02 <html lang="en">
03 <head>
04   <title>jQuery UI Button</title>
05   <link type="text/css" rel="stylesheet" href=
06     "http://code.jquery.com/ui/1.8.16/themes/base/jquery-ui.css">
07 </head>
08 <body>
09
10 <div id="target">
11   <button>My button</button>
12   <input type="submit" id="my-submit" value="My submit">
13   <a href="http://www.google.com">My link</a>
14   <p>
15     My paragraph
16   </p>
17   <ul>
18     <li>My unordered list</li>
19     <li>This might not be the best idea ... </li>
20   </ul>
21 </div>
22
23 <script src="http://code.jquery.com/jquery-1.7.1.min.js"></script>
24 <script src="http://code.jquery.com/ui/1.8.16/jquery-ui.min.js">
25 </script>
26
27 <script>
28 // please externalize this code to an external .js file
29 $(document).ready(function() {
30
31   $('#target')
32     .children()
33     .button()
34     .click(function() {
35       alert($(this).html());
36     });
37
38 });
39 </script>
40 </body>
41 </html>
```

In this listing, lines 11–20 contain a set of HTML elements of different types. After applying lines 31–36, all are styled as buttons and look roughly similar.

Styling Buttons

If you want to apply your own CSS styling, here is the HTML structure you can use after you generate the buttons:

```
<div id="target">
  <button class="ui-button ui-widget ui-state-default ui-corner-all
      ui-button-text-only" role="button" aria-disabled="false">|
    <span class="ui-button-text">My button</span>
  </button>
  <input type="submit" id="my-submit" value="My submit"
    class="ui-button ui-widget ui-state-default ui-corner-all"
    role="button" aria-disabled="false">
  <a href=http://www.google.com
    class="ui-button ui-widget ui-state-default ui-corner-all
      ui-button-text-only" role="button">
    <span class="ui-button-text">My link</span>
  </a>
  <p class="ui-button ui-widget ui-state-default ui-corner-all
    ui-button-text-only" role="button">
    <span class="ui-button-text">
      My paragraph
    </span>
  </p>
  <ul class="ui-button ui-widget ui-state-default ui-corner-all
      ui-button-text-only" role="button">
    <span class="ui-button-text">
      <li>My unordered list</li>
      <li>This might not be the best idea. . .</li>
    </span>
  </ul>
</div>
```

The button component adds many classes that can be used for styling or reused from existing themes. In addition, an extra span is nested to wrap the content inside the button component.

When a visitor interacts with it, the button acquires temporary extra classes:

`ui-state-hover, ui-state-active, ui-state-disabled, ui-button-disabled`

Setting Button Options

The `disabled` option was discussed in the previous chapter. However, especially within the context of buttons, it is worth repeating, because disabling buttons is done more frequently than disabling draggable items. The following scenarios show how to disable a button, display an icon on a button, and change a button's label.

Disable a button:

```
$('button').button({ disabled: true});
```

Show two icons on the button instead of text:

```
$('button').button({
    text: false,
    icons: {
      primary:'ui-icon-signal',
      secondary:'ui-icon-signal-diag'}
});
```

Change the label of the button to the specified value:

```
$('button').button({ label: 'Say something different'});
```

Catching Events on Buttons

Just like the other widgets, event handling can be done with button widgets during creation, and initialization. The following snippets are examples of how you can handle events with buttons.

Handling an event when a new button is initialized:

```
$('button').button({create: function(event, ui) {
    // do event handling
}});
//or
$('button')
  .on('buttoncreate', function(event, ui) {
    // do event handling
  })
  .button();
```

You might be surprised not to find any other events here. The most important event on a button is the click event. The click event already exists on any HTML element, so it does not need reinventing by the jQuery UI framework.

Methods

The methods available for the button widget are similar to those available for the accordion widget covered at the beginning of this chapter as well as draggable covered in Chapter 6, Interacting with the User. I recommend that you refer back the sections detailing destroy, disable, enable, option, and widget.

To manually refresh the button based on the current state of the page:

```
$('button').button('refresh');
```

Example: Styling Radio Buttons by Using a Buttonset

In addition to `buttons`, jQuery UI offers `buttonsets`. Listing 7.4 demonstrates how to use a button set to style a set of radio buttons as a set of normal buttons from which only one can be selected at a time.

Listing 7.4   **Styling a Set of Radio Buttons**

```
00 <!DOCTYPE html>
01
02 <html lang="en">
03 <head>
04   <title>jQuery UI Radio</title>
05   <link type="text/css" rel="stylesheet" href=
06     "http://code.jquery.com/ui/1.8.16/themes/base/jquery-ui.css">
07 </head>
08 <body>
09
10 <div id="target">
11   <label for="first">First</label>
12   <input type="radio" name="my-radio" id="first"><br>
13   <label for="second">Second</label>
14   <input type="radio" name="my-radio" id="second"><br>
15   <label for="third">Third</label>
16   <input type="radio" name="my-radio" id="third"><br>
17 </div>
18
19 <script src="http://code.jquery.com/jquery-1.7.1.min.js"></script>
20 <script src="http://code.jquery.com/ui/1.8.16/jquery-ui.min.js">
21 </script>
22
23 <script>
24 // please externalize this code to an external .js file
25 $(document).ready(function() {
26
27   $('#target').buttonset();
28
29 });
30 </script>
31 </body>
32 </html>
```

You can set up similar code for check boxes or sets of conventional buttons.

Recipe: Choosing Dates by Using the Datepicker

Before HTML5, selecting dates in a Web page was painful. And even with HTML5, there still are browser that do not offer a usable implementation of a date picker.

Listing 7.5 demonstrates the `datepicker` provided by jQuery UI, which works with conventional input fields.

Listing 7.5   **Helping the Web Site Visitors Type a Date**

```
00 <!DOCTYPE html>
01
02 <html lang="en">
03 <head>
04   <title>jQuery UI Datepicker</title>
05   <link type="text/css" rel="stylesheet" href=
06     "http://code.jquery.com/ui/1.8.16/themes/base/jquery-ui.css">
07 </head>
08 <body>
09
10 <input type="text" id="my-date">
11
12 <script src="http://code.jquery.com/jquery-1.7.1.min.js"></script>
13 <script src="http://code.jquery.com/ui/1.8.16/jquery-ui.min.js">
14 </script>
15
16 <script>
17 // please externalize this code to an external .js file
18 $(document).ready(function() {
19
20   $('#my-date').datepicker();
21
22 });
23 </script>
24 </body>
25 </html>
```

Lines 10 and 20 are all that is required to initialize a simple date picker. And this is just the tip of the iceberg. Beneath the surface, there are many options to adjust preferences and accommodate different countries.

Styling the Datepicker

The HTML, CSS, and JavaScript generated by the `datepicker` is not its most admirable part. These are the classes and HTML elements you need to know if you want to provide custom styling.

```
<div class="ui-datepicker ui-widget ui-widget-content
    ui-helper-clearfix ui-corner-all" id="ui-datepicker-div"
  style="position: absolute; top: 0px; left: 8px; z-index: 1;
    display: block;">
  <div class="ui-datepicker-header ui-widget-header ui-helper-clearfix
    ui-corner-all">
  <a title="Prev"
    onclick="DP_jQuery_1322422893896.datepicker
      .adjustDate('#my-date', -1, 'M');"
    class="ui-datepicker-prev ui-corner-all">
    <span class="ui-icon ui-icon-circle-triangle-w">Prev</span>
  </a>
  <a title="Next"
    onclick="DP_jQuery_1322422893896.datepicker
      .adjustDate('#my-date', +1, 'M');"
    class="ui-datepicker-next ui-corner-all">
    <span class="ui-icon ui-icon-circle-triangle-e">Next</span>
  </a>
  <div class="ui-datepicker-title">
    <span class="ui-datepicker-month">November</span> 
    <span class="ui-datepicker-year">2011</span>
  </div>
</div>
<table class="ui-datepicker-calendar">
  <thead>
    <tr>
      <th class="ui-datepicker-week-end">
        <span title="Sunday">Su</span>
      </th>
      <th>
        <span title="Monday">Mo</span>
      </th>
      <th>
        <span title="Tuesday">Tu</span>
      </th>
      <th>
        <span title="Wednesday">We</span>
      </th>
      <th>
        <span title="Thursday">Th</span>
      </th>
      <th>
        <span title="Friday">Fr</span>
      </th>
      <th class="ui-datepicker-week-end">
        <span title="Saturday">Sa</span>
```

```
      </th>
    </tr>
  </thead>
  <tbody>
    <tr>
      <td class="ui-datepicker-week-end ui-datepicker-other-month
          ui-datepicker-unselectable ui-state-disabled">
         
      </td>
      <td class="ui-datepicker-other-month ui-datepicker-unselectable
          ui-state-disabled">
         
      </td>
      <td onclick="DP_jQuery_1322422893896.datepicker
          .selectDay('#my-date',10,2011, this);return false;"
        class="">
        <a href="#" class="ui-state-default">1</a>
      </td>
      <td onclick="DP_jQuery_1322422893896.datepicker
          .selectDay('#my-date',10,2011, this);return false;"
        class="">
        <a href="#" class="ui-state-default">2</a>
      </td>
      <td onclick="DP_jQuery_1322422893896.datepicker
          .selectDay('#my-date',10,2011, this);return false;"
        class="">
        <a href="#" class="ui-state-default">
          . . . etc until last day of the month .
        </a>
      </td>
    <tr>
    . . . etc until last week of the month . . .
    </tr>
  </tbody>
</table>
```

The current date can be recognized with the class `ui-state-highlight`.

Setting Datepicker Options

In the following snippet, you can see that the `disabled` option works just like it does for the other objects and widgets. It can be used on initialization and enabled later. By default, the value of this option is `false`.

```
$('#my-date').datepicker({disabled: true});
```

The `altField` option searches for another field to update when a date is selected. The `altFormat` option changes the way the date is returned. Contrary to what you would expect, the yy returns a four-digit year. If you type yyyy, the function returns 23-06-20122012 instead of 23-06-2012.

```
$('#my-date').datepicker({
  altField: '#dutch-notation',
  altFormat: 'dd-mm-yy'
});
```

This text is appended after the input field to indicate the date format that the visitor should type into the text field, as shown in the following:

```
$('#my-date').datepicker({appendText: '(mm/dd/yyyy)'});
```

Resize the input field to make the current date fit. The default value is `false`:

```
$('#my-date').datepicker({autoSize: true});
```

With the knowledge of other jQuery UI components, you would have expected to provide a class name as a value, for example `ui-icon-calendar`. Instead, you need to provide a hard coded path to an image, as demonstrated here:

```
$('#my-date').datepicker({buttonImage: '/images/my-image.png'});
```

Remove the text from the button. The default value is `false`:

```
$('#my-date').datepicker({buttonImageOnly: true});
```

The `buttonText` option changes the text on the button. You use the `showOn` option to change when the `datepicker` is shown. The default is `focus`, which is triggered when the field has focus. Using the value of `button` causes the `datepicker` to wait until a button is clicked, and using both values requires that both events are triggered before `datepicker` is displayed.

Set the `datepicker` button text to `choose` when clicked:

```
$('#my-date').datepicker({buttonText: 'choose', showOn: 'button'});
```

Change the implementation for week number calculation. The default is ISO 8601 compliant. This means that the first week of the year depends on the first Thursday of the year:

```
$('#my-date').datepicker({calculateWeek: function(date) {
  // calculate week number from date
  return calculatedWeekNr;
}});
```

Provide drop down lists for month and year instead of just the month selection arrows. The default value for each of these options is `false`:

```
$('#my-date').datepicker({changeMonth: true, changeYear: true});
```

These options change the text values on buttons in the `datepicker`. The `closeText` option changes the text on the close button; the default value is `Done`. The `currentText` option changes the text used on the current day; the default value is `Today`. The `prevText` option changes the value of the previous month link; the default value is `Prev`. The `nextText` option changes the value of the next month link; the default value is `Next`. The `showButtonPanel` option simply toggles whether the button panel is shown; the default value is `false`.

Change the text on the close button of the `datepicker` to `Close`, the current day text to `Current`, the previous month link text to `Earlier`, the next month link text to `Later`, and enable the button panel:

```
$('#my-date').datepicker({closeText: 'Close',
  currentText: 'Current', prevText: 'Earlier',
  nextText: 'Later', showButtonPanel: true});
```

Setting `constrainInput` to `false` allows input that does not match the current date format. The default value is `true`:

```
$('#my-date').datepicker({constrainInput: false});
```

You might live in a small country in Northwest Europe and you're not sure whether English will be the lingua franca of the twenty-first century. Of course, there is a good chance that Chinese will become more important than English, eventually. But Chinese is a difficult language and it still has to conquer the world.

To be on the safe side of the English versus Chinese debate, you'd better stay neutral and write all your texts and dates in an obscure and obsolete language called Dutch. The Dutch do everything a bit different. For instance, they write their dates as dd-mm-yy instead of mm/dd/yy. There is good news for you: using the jQuery UI `datepicker`, you can write dates in any format you like. The following example implements a Dutch version of the `datepicker`:

```
$('#my-date').datepicker({
  dateFormat: 'dd-mm-yy', dayNames: ['Maandag', 'Dinsdag', 'Woensdag',
  'Donderdag', 'Vrijdag', 'Zaterdag', 'Zondag'],
  dayNamesMin: ['Ma', 'Di', 'Wo', 'Do', 'Vr', 'Za', 'Zo'],
  dayNamesShort: ['Maa', 'Din', 'Woe', 'Don', 'Vri', 'Zat', 'Zon'],
  monthNames: ['Januari', 'Februari', 'Maart', 'April', 'Mei',
  'Juni', 'Juli', 'Augustus', 'September', 'Oktober', 'November',
  'December'],
  monthNamesShort: ['Jan', 'Feb', 'Mrt', 'Apr', 'Mei', 'Jun', 'Jul',
  'Aug', 'Sep', 'Okt', 'Nov', 'Dec']});
```

The `duration` option sets the speed with which the date picker appears. This can also be set as a number in milliseconds:

```
$('#my-date').datepicker({duration: 'slow'});
```

Configure so that the week starts on Wednesday instead of Sunday. The default value for `firstDay` is 0, which is Sunday. The rest of the days of the week continues forward; 1 is Monday, 2 is Tuesday, and so on:

```
$('#my-date').datepicker({firstDay: 3});
```

If there is a `minDate` and/or `maxDate`, hide the previous and next buttons instead of disabling them. The default value is `false`:

```
$('#my-date').datepicker({hideIfNoPrevNext: true});
```

If you are rendering a `datepicker` for a language such as Arabic, you want to set the rendering of the dates to pick so that they read from right to left. (Note: RTL stands for *right to left*.) The default value is `false`:

```
$('#my-date').datepicker({isRTL: true});
```

The following snippet restricts the dates to the provided minimum and maximum date range. In this example, the character w stands for weeks. You can also use d, m, and y for days, months and years, respectively, or you can provide a date string in the current date format:

```
$('#my-date').datepicker({ maxDate: '+5w', minDate: '-4w'});
```

The `numberOfMonths` option in the following example is set to display three months at a time. The default value is 1. The `showCurrentAtPos` option in this example is set to show the current month at the second position. The default value is 0 and counts up from the top/left month.

```
$('#my-date').datepicker({numberOfMonths: 3,
    showCurrentAtPos: 1});
```

Select and show the first days of the next month and the last days of the previous month. These options are shown together because the `selectOtherMonths` option will only work if the `showOtherMonths` option is set to `true`. The default value for both options is `false`:

```
$('#my-date').datepicker({selectOtherMonths: true,
    showOtherMonths: true});
```

Determine the point at which a two-digit year is considered to be in the current century and when it is assumed to be in the previous century. The default value is +10:

```
$('#my-date').datepicker({shortYearCutoff: '+20'});
```

Use the `showAnim` option to employ animations with the `datepicker`. The options are blind, bounce, clip, drop, explode, fade, fold, highlight, puff, pulsate, scale, shake, size, slide, and transfer. The default value is show:

```
$('#my-date').datepicker({showAnim: 'blind'});
```

Change the header of the `datepicker` and turn the month and year around. This option is also a localization option. The default value is `false`:

```
$('#my-date').datepicker({showMonthAfterYear: true});
```

Provide additional parameters for the `showAnim` option. The default value is set to the default value of the animation used as the value of the `showAnim` option:

```
$('#my-date').datepicker({showAnim: 'slide', showOptions: {direction: 'down' }});
```

Show week numbers. The default value is `false`:

```
$('#my-date').datepicker({showWeek: true});
```

Use `stepMonths` to quickly scroll through the months when multiple months are showing. The default value is `1`:

```
$('#my-date').datepicker({stepMonths: 2});
```

Change the week header (this is useful for internationalization):

```
$('#my-date').datepicker({weekHeader: 'w'});
```

Restrict the range of years from which to to choose. The following example is useful for selecting birth dates for adults. The restriction requires the year selector drop-down menu to work:

```
$('#my-date').datepicker({yearRange: 'c-120:c-18', changeYear: true});
```

Add extra text after the year:

```
$('#my-date').datepicker({yearSuffix: ' A.D.'});
```

Catching Events on Datepicker

There are many places where event handling can take place while using a `datepicker`. The following code snippets show examples.

Event handling when a new `datepicker` is initialized:

```
$('#my-date').datepicker({create: function(event, ui) {
    // do event handling
}});
//or
$('#my-date')
    .on('datepickercreate', function(event, ui) {
    // do event handling
  })
  .datepicker();
```

Provide an options field just before the `datepicker` is shown. The input field and the `datepicker` instance serve as function parameters. This makes it possible to make options depend on the current user input:

```
$('#my-date').datepicker({beforeShow: function(input, inst) {
  return {yearSuffix: ' A.D.'};
}});
```

Use `beforeShowDay` to provide custom details for your date chooser. This function is useful if you offer a service where the customer price depends on the specific date. As an example, consider hotel bookings or similar applications:

```
$('#my-date').datepicker({beforeShowDay: function() {
  return [
    true, // date is selectable
    'my-class', // add my-class for styling
    'Probably NOT X-Mas' // date description for mouseover
  ];
}});
```

Perform custom actions when the month or year is changed. You could update your entire browser screen to reflect the current selected month. You could change your screen themes with the seasons or anything you like:

```
$('#my-date').datepicker({
  onChangeMonthYear: function(year, month, inst) {
    alert(year + '-' + month);
}});
```

Define your own function when the `datepicker` is closed, regardless of whether a date was selected or not. The `dateText` is empty if no date has been selected. To access the input field, you can use this:

```
$('#my-date').datepicker({
  onClose: function(dateText, inst) {
    alert(dateText);
}});
```

Similar to the `onClose` event, only `onSelect` always returns a date:

```
$('#my-date').datepicker({
  onSelect: function(dateText, inst) {
    alert(dateText);
}});
```

Invoking Methods on the Datepicker

The `datepicker` widget has methods similar to the `accordion` widget covered at the beginning of this chapter and the draggable interactions covered in Chapter 6, which are `destroy`, `disable`, `enable`, `option`, and `widget`.

Open a `datepicker` as a dialog box in the middle of the screen. You can add an `onSelect` function, an object with additional settings, and an array with `[x, y]` coordinates for the dialog location on the screen:

```
$('#my-date').datepicker('dialog', '02/05/2013');
```

Return whether or not the `datepicker` is currently disabled:

```
('#my-date').datepicker('isDisabled');
```

Hide the `datepicker`:

```
$('#my-date').datepicker('hide');
```

Show the `datepicker` if it is hidden:

```
$('#my-date').datepicker('show');
```

Refresh the `datepicker` after the screen has changed:

```
$('#my-date').datepicker('refresh');
```

Return the date that is currently selected (or null if none is selected yet):

```
$('#my-date').datepicker('getDate');
```

Change the selected date. You can also add values such as `'+1m +2y'` to go two years and one month forward in time.

```
$('#my-date').datepicker('setDate', '02/02/2013');
```

Recipe: Attracting Attention with the Dialog

If you want a small piece of your Web page to stand out to the visitor, there are several ways to achieve it. One way is to open the content in the form of a dialog. jQuery UI provides such a dialog component. Listing 7.6 demonstrates how you can create a dialog from a conventional paragraph element.

Listing 7.6   **Transforming a Paragraph into a Dialog**

```
00 <!DOCTYPE html>
01
02 <html lang="en">
03 <head>
04   <title>jQuery UI Dialog</title>
05   <link type="text/css" rel="stylesheet" href=
06     "http://code.jquery.com/ui/1.8.16/themes/base/jquery-ui.css">
07 </head>
```

Listing 7.6   **Transforming a Paragraph into a Dialog (Continued)**

```
08 <body>
09
10 <p id="my-dialog">This is the text of my dialog</p>
11
12 <button>Open dialog</button>
13
14 <script src="http://code.jquery.com/jquery-1.7.1.min.js"></script>
15 <script src="http://code.jquery.com/ui/1.8.16/jquery-ui.min.js">
16 </script>
17
18 <script>
19 // please externalize this code to an external .js file
20 $(document).ready(function() {
21
22   $('button').click(function() {
23     $('#my-dialog').dialog();
24   });
25
26 });
27 </script>
28 </body>
29 </html>
```

Lines 22–24 connect the dialog initialization routine to a click handler on the button in the document instead of creating the dialog on page load. This illustrates that after loading the document, the dialog content is a conventional paragraph. The paragraph seems to disappear from the document after dialog initialization.

Styling the Dialog

The dialog generates a large list of HTML elements around the original. Therefore, in the following example, the original item is highlighted instead of the changed parts. Note that this is generated HTML. You do not need to type this code anywhere. It will result from Listing 7.6.

```
<div style="display: block; z-index: 1001; outline: 0px none;
 position: absolute; height: auto; width: 300px; top: 46px;
 left: 391px;"
  class="ui-dialog ui-widget ui-widget-content ui-corner-all
    ui-draggable ui-resizable"
  tabindex="-1" role="dialog"
  aria-labelledby="ui-dialog-title-my-dialog">
  <div class="ui-dialog-titlebar ui-widget-header ui-corner-all
```

```
      ui-helper-clearfix">
      <span class="ui-dialog-title"
        id="ui-dialog-title-my-dialog"> </span>
        <a href="#" class="ui-dialog-titlebar-close ui-corner-all"
         role="button">
          <span class="ui-icon ui-icon-closethick">close</span>
        </a>
    </div>
    <p id="my-dialog" class="ui-dialog-content ui-widget-content"
     style="width: auto; min-height: 56.0333px; height: auto;"
       scrolltop="0" scrollleft="0">
        This is the text of my dialog
    </p>
    <div class="ui-resizable-handle ui-resizable-n"></div>
    <div class="ui-resizable-handle ui-resizable-e"></div>
    <div class="ui-resizable-handle ui-resizable-s"></div>
    <div class="ui-resizable-handle ui-resizable-w"></div>
    <div class="ui-resizable-handle ui-resizable-se ui-icon
     ui-icon-gripsmall-diagonal-se ui-icon-grip-diagonal-se"
       style="z-index: 1001;"></div>
    <div class="ui-resizable-handle ui-resizable-sw"
       style="z-index: 1002;"></div>
    <div class="ui-resizable-handle ui-resizable-ne"
       style="z-index: 1003;"></div>
    <div class="ui-resizable-handle ui-resizable-nw"
       style="z-index: 1004;"></div>
</div>
```

You might recognize the resizable handles from the `resizable` component.

Setting Dialog Options

The dialog has many options that can be set and used to alter data and even the text that is displayed in the dialog. Table 7.4 presents code examples as well as descriptions for the options that are available in the `dialog` widget.

Table 7.4   **Available Options and Descriptions for the Dialog Widget**

Option	Description
`$('#my-dialog').dialog({disabled: true});`	Disables the dialog. The default value is `false`.
`$('#my-dialog').dialog({autoOpen: false});`	Keeps the dialog closed until it is explicitly asked to be opened. Creating the dialog hides the original HTML element from the screen. The default value is `true`.

Table 7.4 Available Options and Descriptions for the Dialog Widget (Continued)

Option	Description

`$('#my-dialog').dialog({buttons: {`
`  'My Button': function()`
`{alert('My button was pressed');}`
`}});`
	Provides a custom button set and implement event handlers for these buttons.

`$('#my-dialog').` `dialog({closeOnEscape: false});`	Prevents the Esc key from closing the dialog. The default value is `true`.
`$('#my-dialog').` `dialog({closeText: 'X'});`	Changes the text for the close link. This is useful for internationalization. The default value is `close`.

`$('#my-dialog').`
`dialog({dialogClass:`
`'my-dialog'});`
	Adds classes to style the dialog.

`$('#my-dialog').` `dialog({draggable: false});`	Prevents the visitor from dragging the dialog over the screen. The default value is `true`.
`$('#my-dialog').dialog({height:` `200, width: 200});`	Changes the dialog dimensions. The default value is `auto`.
`$('#my-dialog').dialog({hide:` `'bounce'});`	Changes the animation when hiding the dialog. The bounce effect in this example might be a bit over the top.

`$('#my-dialog').`
`dialog({maxHeight: 300, maxWidth:`
`300});`
	Binds the dimensions to a maximum. The default value for both options is `false`, meaning that users can resize the dimension to any size they want.

`$('#my-dialog').`
`dialog({minHeight: 100, minWidth:`
`300});`
	Binds the dimensions to a minimum. The default for both options is `150`.

`$('#my-dialog').dialog({modal:` `true});`	Makes the dialog modal. This prevents the visitor from accessing other screen elements while the dialog box is open. The default option is `false`.
`$('#my-dialog').dialog({position:` `[100, 100]});`	You can also provide string values such as `center`, or arrays or string values such as `['left', 'top']`. The default value is `center`.

(Continues)

Table 7.4   **Available Options and Descriptions for the Dialog Widget (Continued)**

Option	Description
`$('#my-dialog').` `dialog({resizable: false});`	Prevents the visitor from resizing the dialog. The default value is `true`.
`$('#my-dialog').dialog({show:` `'bounce'});`	Shows the dialog using an animation, similar to `hide`.
`$('#my-dialog').dialog({stack:` `false});`	Prevents the dialog from overlapping other dialogs. The default value is `true`.
`$('#my-dialog').dialog({title:` `'My title'});`	Provides a custom title for the dialog header.
`$('#my-dialog').dialog({zIndex:` `1001});`	Changes the `zIndex`. The default value is 1000.

Catching Events on the Dialog

The following code snippets provide examples of how to handle events by using the `dialog` widget.

Event handling when a new dialog is initialized:

```
$('#my-dialog').dialog({create: function(event, ui) {
    // do event handling
}});
//or
$('#my-dialog')
  .on('dialogcreate', function(event, ui) {
    // do event handling
  })
  .dialog();
```

Handle an event when the visitor tries to close the dialog. Returning `false` prevents it from closing.

```
$('#my-dialog').dialog({beforeClose: function(event, ui) {
    // do event handling
}});
//or
$('#my-dialog').dialog()
  .on('dialogbeforeclose', function(event, ui) {
    // do event handling
  });
```

Event handling when the dialog is opened:

```
$('#my-dialog').dialog({open: function(event, ui) {
    // do event handling
}});
//or
$('#my-dialog').dialog()
  .on('dialogopen', function(event, ui) {
    // do event handling
  });
```

Handling an event when the dialog receives focus:

```
$('#my-dialog').dialog({focus: function(event, ui) {
    // do event handling
}});
//or
$('#my-dialog').dialog()
  .on('dialogfocus', function(event, ui) {
    // do event handling
  });
```

Handling and event when the visitor starts dragging the dialog:

```
$('#my-dialog').dialog({dragStart: function(event, ui) {
    // do event handling
}});
//or
$('#my-dialog').dialog()
  .on('dialogdragstart', function(event, ui) {
    // do event handling
  });
```

Event handling when the visitor drags the dialog farther:

```
$('#my-dialog').dialog({drag: function(event, ui) {
    // do event handling
}});
//or
$('#my-dialog').dialog()
  .on('dialogdrag', function(event, ui) {
    // do event handling
  });
```

Event handling when the visitor is done dragging the dialog:

```
$('#my-dialog').dialog({dragStop: function(event, ui) {
    // do event handling
}});
//or
$('#my-dialog').dialog()
  .on('dialogdragstop', function(event, ui) {
    // do event handling
  });
```

Event handling when the visitor starts resizing the dialog:

```
$('#my-dialog').dialog({resizeStart: function(event, ui) {
    // do event handling
}});
//or
$('#my-dialog').dialog()
  .on('dialogresizestart', function(event, ui) {
    // do event handling
  });
```

Event handling when the visitor further resizes the dialog:

```
$('#my-dialog').dialog({resize: function(event, ui) {
    // do event handling
}});
//or
$('#my-dialog').dialog()
  .on('dialogresize', function(event, ui) {
    // do event handling
  });
```

Event handling when the visitor is done resizing the dialog:

```
$('#my-dialog').dialog({resizeStop: function(event, ui) {
    // do event handling
}});
//or
$('#my-dialog').dialog()
  .on('dialogresizestop', function(event, ui) {
    // do event handling
  });
```

Event handling when the visitor closes the dialog:

```
$('#my-dialog').dialog({close: function(event, ui) {
    // do event handling
}});
//or
$('#my-dialog').dialog()
  .on('dialogclose', function(event, ui) {
    // do event handling
  });
```

Invoking Methods on the Dialog

The `dialog` widget has methods similar to the `accordion` widget covered at the beginning of this chapter and the draggable interactions covered in Chapter 6, which are `destroy`, `disable`, `enable`, `option`, and `widget`.

Removes the dialog completely from the page:

```
$('#my-dialog').dialog('destroy');
```

Disables the dialog:

```
$('#my-dialog').dialog('disable');
```

Enables the dialog:

```
$('#my-dialog').dialog('enable');
```

Get or set the value of the dialog:

```
$('#my-dialog').dialog('option', options);
```

Returns the dialog element:

```
$('#my-dialog').dialog('widget');
```

Close a currently open dialog. You can consider this to be a hide function. The dialog can be reused after closing:

```
$('#my-dialog').dialog('close');
```

Returns whether the dialog is currently open:

```
$('#my-dialog').dialog('isOpen');
```

Moves the dialog to the front if it is hidden under other dialogs:

```
$('#my-dialog').dialog('moveToTop');
```

Open a previously closed dialog or a dialog that was created by using the option `autoOpen: false`:

```
$('#my-dialog').dialog('open');
```

Recipe: Displaying Status of a Process by Using the Progressbar

When your Web application performs an action with a duration longer than roughly two seconds, it is a good practice to show the status of the action to your visitor. When you do not know the status of the action, usually you change the mouse cursor or show a spinner.

In some cases you do know the progress of the process. In such cases, it is better to be as accurate as possible to manage the visitor's expectations. Listing 7.7 introduces the jQuery UI's `progressbar`, which you can use for precisely this purpose.

Listing 7.7　**Transforming a <div> Element into a Progressbar**

```
00 <!DOCTYPE html>
01
02 <html lang="en">
03 <head>
04   <title>jQuery UI Progressbar</title>
05   <link type="text/css" rel="stylesheet" href=
06     "http://code.jquery.com/ui/1.8.16/themes/base/jquery-ui.css">
07 </head>
08 <body>
09
10 <div id="my-progress"></div>
11
12 <script src="http://code.jquery.com/jquery-1.7.1.min.js"></script>
13 <script src="http://code.jquery.com/ui/1.8.16/jquery-ui.min.js">
14 </script>
15
16 <script>
17 // please externalize this code to an external .js file
18 $(document).ready(function() {
19
20   var el = $('#my-progress');
21
22   el.on('progressbarcreate', function(event, ui) {
23     el.after('<p>Start value: ' + el.progressbar('value') + '</p>');
24   });
25
26   el.progressbar();
27
28   // animate progress
29   var count = 0;
30   setInterval(function() {
31     if(count++ > 100) count = 0;
32     el.progressbar('value', count);
```

Listing 7.7   Transforming a <div> Element into a Progressbar (Continued)

```
33    },100);
34
35 });
36 </script>
37 </body>
38 </html>
```

This example uses JavaScript's built-in function `setInterval` to simulate actual progress. Determining the progress on actual processes might require some clever thinking and calculations.

Styling the Progressbar

jQuery UI expands the target `div` with several classes and attributes and adds a child `div` that represents the progress. Avoid writing text in the progress bar `div`, because it will push the progress indicator down.

```
<div id="my-progress"
  class="ui-progressbar ui-widget ui-widget-content ui-corner-all"
  role="progressbar" aria-valuemin="0" aria-valuemax="100"
  aria-valuenow="90">
  <div class="ui-progressbar-value ui-widget-header ui-corner-left"
    style="display: block; width: 90%; "></div>
</div>
```

Setting Progressbar Options

The following snippets show you how to set options when using `progressbar`.

Disable the progress bar on creation:

```
$('#my-progress').progressbar({disabled: true});
```

Create a progress bar that is filled for 25 percent.

```
$('#my-progress').progressbar({value: 25});
```

Catching Progressbar Events

The following snippets demonstrate handling events when using `progressbar`.

A new progress bar is initialized:

```
$('#my-progress').progressbar({create: function(event, ui) {
    // do event handling
}});
```

```
//or
$('#my-progress')
  .on('progressbarcreate', function(event, ui) {
    // do event handling
  })
  .progressbar();
```

Event handling when the status on the `progressbar` changes:

```
$('#my-progress').progressbar({change: function(event, ui) {
    // do event handling
}});
//or
$('#my-progress').progressbar()
  .on('progressbarchange', function(event, ui) {
    // do event handling
  });
```

Event handling when the `progressbar` reaches 100 percent. You can catch this event to change the appearance of the `progressbar`, to perhaps highlight its status:

```
$('#my-progress').progressbar({complete: function(event, ui) {
 // do event handling
}});
//or
$('#my-progress').progressbar()
 .on('progressbarcomplete', function(event, ui) {
 // do event handling
 });
```

Invoking Methods on the Progressbar

The `progressbar` uses the same methods as the draggable interaction found in Chapter 6, as well as the `dialog` widget and `accordion` widgets found in this chapter. See their entries for details on `destroy`, `disable`, `enable`, `option`, and `widget`.

Update the value of the progress bar to the specified parameter:

```
$('#my-progress').progressbar('value', 50});
```

Recipe: Retrieving Numbers by Using a Slider

On client-side applications, you sometimes find sliders as input elements for numbered values. The advantage of a slider is that it is more visual and intuitive than an input element with a number.

Listing 7.8 shows how to change a div element into a slider component.

Listing 7.8   Transforming a \<div\> Element into a Slider and Displaying Its Value

```
00 <!DOCTYPE html>
01
02 <html lang="en">
03 <head>
04   <title>jQuery UI Slider</title>
05   <link type="text/css" rel="stylesheet" href=
06     "http://code.jquery.com/ui/1.8.16/themes/base/jquery-ui.css">
07   <style>
08   #my-slider {
09     width: 250px;
10   }
11   </style>
12 </head>
13 <body>
14
15 <h2>The slider</h2>
16 <div id="my-slider"></div>
17
18 <h2>The slider value</h2>
19 <input type="text" id="slider-value">
20
21 <script src="http://code.jquery.com/jquery-1.7.1.min.js"></script>
22 <script src="http://code.jquery.com/ui/1.8.16/jquery-ui.min.js">
23 </script>
24
25 <script>
26 // please externalize this code to an external .js file
27 $(document).ready(function() {
28
29   $('#my-slider').slider({
30     change: function() {
31       $('#slider-value').attr('value', $(this).slider("value"));
32     }
33   });
34
35 });
36 </script>
37 </body>
38 </html>
```

In addition to initializing the slider, this code implements an event handler that listens for change events. All changes are reflected in a conventional input element.

Styling the Slider Element

Compared to other jQuery UI components, the `slider` component generates a relatively small HTML structure. In the snippet that follows, some classes are added to the div to make it look like a slider and an anchor is added representing the slider handle.

```
<div id="my-slider"
   class="ui-slider ui-slider-horizontal ui-widget ui-widget-content
     ui-corner-all">
   <a class="ui-slider-handle ui-state-default ui-corner-all"
     href="#" style="left: 0%; "></a>
</div>
```

Setting Slider Options

There are several options that can be adjusted when using a `slider` widget. Table 7.5 presents code examples as well as descriptions for the options that are available in the `slider` widget.

Table 7.5   **Options for the slider Widget**

Option	Description
`$('#my-slider').slider({disabled: true});`	Creates a slider that is disabled upon startup. The default value is `false`.
`$('#my-slider').slider({animate: 'slow'});`	Animates the slider when the visitor clicks a location instead of dragging the handler. The values can be `slow`, `normal`, `fast`, or the number of milliseconds for the animation. The default value is `false`.
`$('#my-slider').slider({min: 25, max: 250});`	Provides the range of values from which to select. Default: `0-100`. The default value for `min` is `0` and the default value for `max` is `100`.
`$('#my-slider').slider({orientation: 'vertical'});`	Changes the horizontal slider to vertical.
`$('#my-slider').slider({ range: true, values: [25, 50]});`	Uses two sliders to select a range. Other values for the range can be `min` or `max`. Then a single slider is sufficient. The default value for range is `false`.

Table 7.5   **Options for the slider Widget (Continued)**

Option	Description
`$('#my-slider').slider({step: 10});`	Restricts the slider values to 0, 10, 20, and so on.
`$('#my-slider').slider({value: 10});`	Sets the initial slider value, unless you need a range, then you should set values with an array of two integers. The default value is 0.

Catching Slider Events

Sliders have several places where event handling can be tied in. The following code snippets are examples of where this can be done.

Event handling when a new `slider` component is initialized:

```
$('#my-slider').slider({create: function(event, ui) {
    // do event handling
}});
//or
$('#my-slider')
  .on('slidecreate', function(event, ui) {
    // do event handling
  })
  .slider();
```

Event handling when the visitor starts sliding the handle:

```
$('#my-slider').slider({start: function(event, ui) {
    // do event handling
}});
//or
$('#my-slider').slider()
  .on('slidestart', function(event, ui) {
    // do event handling
  });
```

Event handling when the visitor continues to slide the handle:

```
$('#my-slider').slider({slide: function(event, ui) {
    // do event handling
}});
//or
```

(Continues)

```
$('#my-slider').slider()
  .on('slide', function(event, ui) {
    // do event handling
  });
```

Event handling when the value of the slider has changed:

```
$('#my-slider').slider({change: function(event, ui) {
    // do event handling
}});
//or
$('#my-slider').slider()
  .on('slidechange', function(event, ui) {
    // do event handling
  });
```

Event handling when the visitor stops sliding the handle:

```
$('#my-slider').slider({stop: function(event, ui) {
    // do event handling
}});
//or
$('#my-slider').slider()
  .on('slidestop', function(event, ui) {
    // do event handling
  });
```

Invoking Methods on the Slider

The `slider` widget uses the same methods as the draggable interaction found in
Chapter 6 as well as those for the `dialog` and `accordion` widgets. See their entries for
more details about `destroy`, `disable`, `enable`, `option`, and `widget`.

Update the slider to the value 10:

```
$('#my-slider').slider('value', 10);
```

Update the slider range to the range 10–20:

```
$('#my-slider').slider('values', [10, 20]);
```

Recipe: Navigating a Page by Using Tabs

Earlier in this chapter, the `accordion` component was introduced to group larger sets of
content and show only one group at a time. The `tab` element has a similar function with
a few subtle differences. Although not necessarily always true, an `accordion` is well
suited to serve as an extra element on the side of a main screen, whereas a `tab` element
serves best as the main screen itself.

Listing 7.9 transforms a relatively simple HTML structure into a set of tabs. One of the differences between the `accordion` and the `tab` element is that the list of tab headers and the content groups are separated from one another; with the `accordion`, the group header and the group itself belong together.

Listing 7.9   **Transforming an Unordered List into a Tab Pane**

```
00 <!DOCTYPE html>
01
02 <html lang="en">
03 <head>
04   <title>jQuery UI Tabs</title>
05   <link type="text/css" rel="stylesheet" href=
06     "http://code.jquery.com/ui/1.8.16/themes/base/jquery-ui.css">
07   <style>
08     body {
09       font-size: 12px;
10     }
11   </style>
12 </head>
13 <body>
14
15 <div id="my-tabs">
16   <ul>
17     <li>
18       <a href="#first">First</a>
19     </li>
20     <li>
21       <a href="#second">Second</a>
22     </li>
23     <li>
24       <a href="#third">Third</a>
25     </li>
26   </ul>
27   <div id="first">
28     This is the text of the first tab
29   </div>
30   <div id="second">
31     You have switched to the second tab
32   </div>
33   <div id="third">
34     And finally, you have switched to the third tab
35   </div>
36 </div>
37
38 <script src="http://code.jquery.com/jquery-1.7.1.min.js"></script>
39 <script src="http://code.jquery.com/ui/1.8.16/jquery-ui.min.js">
40 </script>
```

(Continues)

Listing 7.9   **Transforming an Unordered List into a Tab Pane (Continued)**

```
41
42 <script>
43 // please externalize this code to an external .js file
44 $(document).ready(function() {
45
46    $('#my-tabs').tabs();
47
48 });
49 </script>
50 </body>
51 </html>
```

In Listing 7.9, the content of the tabs is in the `div` elements on lines 27–35. You can easily modify this example to fetch content from the server by using an AJAX call. In this case, you need to replace the `a href` attributes with references to the server-side location of the content that you want in the tab. The content needs to be on the same server as the current HTML. When you provide these references, under the hood, the `tab` component automatically calls jQuery's `load()` function to load the HTML. This function is demonstrated in Chapter 5, Communicating with the Server.

Styling the Tab Element

The `tab` element does not make many changes in the HTML. It does add many classes with which you can style `tab` with either a *theme roller* theme or with your own CSS styling.

```
<div id="my-tabs"
  class="ui-tabs ui-widget ui-widget-content ui-corner-all">
  <ul class="ui-tabs-nav ui-helper-reset ui-helper-clearfix
      ui-widget-header ui-corner-all">
    <li class="ui-state-default ui-corner-top ui-tabs-selected
        ui-state-active">
      <a href="#first">First</a>
    </li>
    <li class="ui-state-default ui-corner-top">
      <a href="#second">Second</a>
    </li>
    <li class="ui-state-default ui-corner-top">
      <a href="#third">Third</a>
    </li>
  </ul>
  <div id="first" class="ui-tabs-panel ui-widget-content
      ui-corner-bottom">
    This is the text of the first tab
```

```
</div>
<div id="second" class="ui-tabs-panel ui-widget-content
    ui-corner-bottom ui-tabs-hide">
  You have switched to the second tab
</div>
<div id="third" class="ui-tabs-panel ui-widget-content
    ui-corner-bottom ui-tabs-hide">
  And finally, you have switched to the third tab
</div>
</div>
```

The bold values are added by the `tab` component. The underlined values depend on which tab is currently open. In this example, the first tab is open.

Setting Options on the Tabs Widget

Just as with the other widgets in jQuery UI, the `tabs` widget has several options that can be edited to change the default behavior. Table 7.6 presents code examples as well as descriptions for the options that are available in the `tabs` widget.

Table 7.6   **Options for the tab Widget**

Option	Description

`$('#my-tabs').`
`tabs({ajaxOptions:{timeout:`
`2000}});`
	Uses any option from `$.ajax`. These options are presented in Chapter 5.

`$('#my-tabs').tabs({cache: true});`	Enables caching of requests. The default value is `false`.
`$('#my-tabs').tabs({collapsible:` `true});`	Allows closing the current tab by clicking the current tab again. The default value is `false`.

`$('#my-tabs').tabs({cookie: {`
`  expires: 7, path: '/',`
`  secure: true, name: 'my-cookie'`
`}});`
	Stores the tab that is currently open in a cookie.

`$('#my-tabs').tabs({disabled: [0,` `1]});`	Disables specific tabs in an array of tab indices.
`$('#my-tabs').tabs({event:` `'mouseover'});`	Changes the event that triggers tab selection from `click` to `mouseover`. The default value is `click`.

(Continues)

Table 7.6   **Options for the tab Widget (Continued)**

Option	Description
``$('#my-tabs').tabs({fx:
[{opacity:'toggle',
duration:'normal'},
{opacity:'toggle',
duration:'fast'}]});```	Specifies the effect and the speed of the effect for hiding the old tab and showing the new tab.
``$('#my-tabs').tabs({idPrefix:
'id-fix-'});```	Changes the prefix of generated id attributes for remote tabs. Default value is `ui-tabs-`
``$('#my-tabs').tabs({panelTemplate:
'<p></p>'});```	Changes the panel from the default `<div></div>` into a paragraph.
```$('#my-tabs').tabs({selected: 2});```	Changes the currently selected tab upon initialization. This is zero-based, so in this example, the third tab would be selected. The default value is `0`. To set all tabs to unselected use a value of `-1`.
``$('#my-tabs').tabs({spinner: '<p
class='my-spinner'>Please wait</
p>'});```	Changes the element that is shown while loading the remote content for the tabs. You can use CSS to create your own spinning icon. The default value is `<em>Loading#8230;</em>`.
``$('#my-tabs').tabs({tabTemplate:
'<li><a
href="#{href}"><span>#{label}
</span></a></li>'});```	Changes this template to generate HTML that is different from the current default. This template is used together with the add method. The default value is `<li><a href="#{href}"><span>#{label}</span></a></li>`.

Catching Events on the Tabs Component

The tabs widget has many places where events can be handled or triggered. The following is a list of code snippets that can be used as examples for handling events.

Event handling when a new tabs widget is initialized:

```
$('#my-tabs').tabs({create: function(event, ui) {
   // do event handling
}});
//or
$('#my-tabs')
  .on('tabscreate', function(event, ui) {
```

```
    // do event handling
  })
  .tabs();
```

Event handling when a different tab is clicked:

```
$('#my-tabs').tabs({select: function(event, ui) {
    // do event handling
}});
//or
$('#my-tabs').tabs()
  .on('tabsselect', function(event, ui) {
    // do event handling
  });
```

Event handling when remote content has been loaded:

```
$('#my-tabs').tabs({load: function(event, ui) {
    // do event handling
}});
//or
$('#my-tabs').tabs()
  .on('tabsload', function(event, ui) {
    // do event handling
  });
```

Event handling when a different tab is shown:

```
$('#my-tabs').tabs({show: function(event, ui) {
    // do event handling
}});
//or
$('#my-tabs').tabs()
  .on('tabsshow', function(event, ui) {
    // do event handling
  });
```

Event handling when a tab is added:

```
$('#my-tabs').tabs({add: function(event, ui) {
    // do event handling
}});
//or
$('#my-tabs').tabs()
  .on('tabsadd', function(event, ui) {
    // do event handling
  });
```

Event handling when a tab is removed:

```
$('#my-tabs').tabs({remove: function(event, ui) {
    // do event handling
}});
//or
$('#my-tabs').tabs()
  .on('tabsremove', function(event, ui) {
    // do event handling
  });
```

Event handling when a formerly disabled tab is enabled:

```
$('#my-tabs').tabs({enable: function(event, ui) {
    // do event handling
}});
//or
$('#my-tabs').tabs()
  .on('tabsenable', function(event, ui) {
    // do event handling
  });
```

Event handling when a formerly enabled tab is disabled:

```
$('#my-tabs').tabs({disable: function(event, ui) {
    // do event handling
}});
//or
$('#my-tabs').tabs()
  .on('tabsdisable', function(event, ui) {
    // do event handling
  });
```

Invoking Methods on the Tabs Component

The `tabs` widget uses the same methods as the draggable interaction found in Chapter 6 as well as those for the `dialog` and `accordion` widgets presented in this chapter. See their entries for details about `destroy`, `disable`, `enable`, `option`, and `widget`.

Add a new tab at the specified position with the specified URL and tab label:

```
$('#my-tabs').tabs('add', '/my-url', 'My Tab Label', 1);
```

Remove the tab at the specified index:

```
$('#my-tabs').tabs('remove', 1);
```

Enable the specified tab index:

```
$('#my-tabs').tabs('enable', 1);
```

Disable the specified tab index:

```
$('#my-tabs').tabs('disable', 1);
```

Select the specified tab index:

```
$('#my-tabs').tabs('select', 1);
```

Reload the content of the specified tab:

```
$('#my-tabs').tabs('load', 1);
```

Load the specified URL on the specified tab index:

```
$('#my-tabs').tabs('url', 1, '/my-url');
```

Get the number of tabs in the tab component:

```
$('#my-tabs').tabs('length');
```

Abort all AJAX requests:

```
$('#my-tabs').tabs('abort');
```

Automatically cycle through the tabs every 2000 milliseconds. When a user selects a tab, it stops rotating because `continuing` is `false`:

```
$('#my-tabs').tabs('rotate', 2000, false);
```

Summary

This chapter introduced the widget components in jQuery UI that support Web developers with common tasks, such as grouping content into tabs, accordions, sliders, and progress bars, auto-complete, date pickers, dialogs, and buttons.

This chapter contains many examples of how to implement widgets and the options that are available to you to extend their use.

PART III

Mobile

Chapter 8

Changing the Look and Feel

This chapter starts with a quick introduction of jQuery's ability to work with your own CSS styling. The remainder of this chapter demonstrates the animation functions of both jQuery Core and jQuery UI. Some of the recipes focus on demonstrating all possible function arguments rather than the functions themselves. These recipes can be used as reference material when developing with jQuery UI.

Changing the Styling of jQuery UI Components

There are various ways to change the look and feel of jQuery UI components. One way is to select a different standard theme. Chapter 6, Interacting with the User, already mentioned the standard themes. Themes are defined in the CSS file reference, as illustrated here:

```
<link type="text/css" rel="stylesheet"
  href="http://code.jquery.com/ui/1.8.16/themes/base/jquery-ui.css">
```

To change the theme, replace the word **base** in the preceding snippet with one of the following theme names:

```
black-tie, blitzer, cupertino, dark-hive, dot-luv, eggplant,
excite-bike, flick, hot-sneaks, humanity, le-frog, mint-choc,
overcast, pepper-grinder, redmond, smoothness, south-street, start,
sunny, swanky-purse, trontastic, ui-darkness, ui-lightness, vader
```

Another way to change the look and feel of jQuery UI components is to search the Internet for third-party themes. You might find some that are created by skilled designers.

For creating your own theme, you can use jQuery's *ThemeRoller* to create a custom theme. Using this tool, you can to change a limited number of default properties such as colors, distances, and the size of rounded corners. You can find ThemeRoller at http://jqueryui.com/themeroller/.

If you feel that ThemeRoller does not give you sufficient freedom and you want to have more influence on the look and feel of the UI components, you can create your own CSS file. You can do this based on existing CSS files or, if you're feeling industrious, start one from scratch.

The generated HTML and CSS classes can be found in Chapter 6 under each component. Some components create a lot of HTML; others only add a few class names.

Many of the class names added to the components are specific to that particular component. Think of `ui-resizable` for example. If you see class names like that in other plugins, you can safely assume that the resizable component is used under the hood.

Several generic classes are used in more than one component. These classes start with `ui-widget`, `ui-helper`, `ui-state`, `ui-corner`, and `ui-priority`.

The generic classes are truly generic and widely used, so it is wise to avoid changing them any more than ThemeRoller allows.

For the component-specific HTML and CSS, you can safely write your own styling and test the component independently on all browsers.

Creating Animations by Using jQuery Core

You do not necessarily need jQuery UI to start adding animations and effects. jQuery Core already offers some basic animation functions even without jQuery UI. This part of jQuery Core is discussed under jQuery UI because it fits better with the rest of this chapter.

Listing 8.1 demonstrates how the height, width and position of a `div` can be modified and change gradually through the use of an animation.

Listing 8.1 **Animating the Size and Position of a Rectangle**

```
00 <!DOCTYPE html>
01
02 <html lang="en">
03 <head>
04   <title>The jQuery animate() function</title>
05   <style>
06   #my-animate {
07     border: 1px solid black;
08     width: 100px;
09     height: 100px;
10     position: absolute;
11     left: 50px;
12     top: 100px;
13   }
14   </style>
15 </head>
16 <body>
```

Listing 8.1   **Animating the Size and Position of a Rectangle (Continued)**

```
17
18 <h2>Click the div below to animate it</h2>
19
20 <div id="my-animate">
21 Click
22 </div>
23
24 <script src="http://code.jquery.com/jquery-1.7.1.min.js"></script>
25
26 <script>
27 // please externalize this code to an external .js file
28 $(document).ready(function() {
29
30   $('#my-animate').click(function() {
31     $(this).animate({height: '+=50'}, 500)
32     .animate({ backgroundColor: 'black'}, 1000)
33     .animate({left: '+=50', width: '+=100'}, 500)
34     .animate({top: '+=25'}, 500);
35   });
36
37 });
38 </script>
39 </body>
40 </html>
```

On line 31, the value +=50 means that the current height should increase by 50 pixels. If you specify a fixed value without the relative qualifier +=, the height will change to that exact value.

The values 500 and 1000 signify the numbers of milliseconds that the animations will take. You can also specify strings slow and fast, implying 600 and 200 milliseconds, respectively.

On line 32, there is also an attempt to change the background color by using an animation. In this example, this will not work. You need jQuery UI for color animations.

Recipe: Animating Colors by Using jQuery UI

When you add the jQuery UI libraries to your page, the animate function becomes more intelligent. It is extended under the hood, so you can do more with it without changes in the interface. Listing 8.2 demonstrates how you can use the animate function to gradually change colors on screen.

Listing 8.2   **Changing Colors in an Animation**

```
00 <!DOCTYPE html>
01
02 <html lang="en">
03 <head>
04 <title>The jQuery UI animate() function</title>
05   <style>
06     #my-animate {
07       border: 1px solid black;
08       width: 100px;
09       height: 100px;
10       position: absolute;
11       left: 50px;
12       top: 100px;
13     }
14   </style>
15 </head>
16 <body>
17
18 <h2>Click the div below to animate it</h2>
19
20 <div id="my-animate">
21 Click
22 </div>
23
24 <script src="http://code.jquery.com/jquery-1.7.1.min.js"></script>
25 <script src="http://code.jquery.com/ui/1.8.16/jquery-ui.min.js">
26 </script>
27
28 <script>
29 // please externalize this code to an external .js file
30 $(document).ready(function() {
31
32   $('#my-animate').click(function() {
33     $(this).animate({height: '+=50'}, 500)
34     .animate({ backgroundColor: 'black'}, 1000)
35     .animate({left: '+=50', width: '+=100',
36         backgroundColor: 'red'}, 500)
37     .animate({top: '+=25'}, 500);
38   });
39
40 });
41 </script>
42 </body>
43 </html>
```

On lines 35 and 36, you can see how the color and positions can be animated at the same time. Every other animation will start when the previously specified animation has ended. The `animate` function adds the animations to a queue called `fx`. (More about this queue later in this chapter.)

Recipe: Hiding Elements by Using Fade and Slide in jQuery Core

In addition to the animation function, you can also show and hide elements by using jQuery Core, without jQuery UI. Again, these functions are more relevant in the context of jQuery UI because this library extends the possibilities for easing functions. Listing 8.3 demonstrates how to fade in and out, slide up and down, and delay further animations.

Listing 8.3   **Fading and Sliding Elements**

```
00 <!DOCTYPE html>
01
02 <html lang="en">
03 <head>
04   <title>The jQuery fade and slide functions</title>
05   <style>
06   #my-animate {
07     border: 1px solid black;
08     width: 100px;
09     height: 100px;
10     position: absolute;
11     left: 50px;
12     top: 100px;
13   }
14   </style>
15 </head>
16 <body>
17
18 <h2>Click the div below to animate it</h2>
19
20 <div id="my-animate">
21 Click
22 </div>
23
24 <script src="http://code.jquery.com/jquery-1.7.1.min.js"></script>
25
26 <script>
27 // please externalize this code to an external .js file
28 $(document).ready(function() {
```

(Continues)

Listing 8.3   **Fading and Sliding Elements (Continued)**

```
29
30   $('#my-animate').click(function() {
31      $(this).fadeOut(1000)
32      .delay(500)
33      .fadeIn(1000, 'swing')
34      .slideUp(500)
35      .slideDown(1000, 'swing');
36   });
37
38 });
39 </script>
40 </body>
41 </html>
```

Lines 33 and 35 specify the *easing* function swing. jQuery UI includes 32 different easing options, which are presented in the following list:

linear	easeInOutSine
swing	easeInExpo
easeInQuad	easeOutExpo
easeOutQuad	easeInOutExpo
easeInOutQuad	easeInCirc
easeInCubic	easeOutCirc
easeOutCubic	easeInOutCirc
easeInOutCubic	easeInElastic
easeInQuart	easeOutElastic
easeOutQuart	easeInOutElastic
easeInOutQuart	easeInBack
easeInQuint	easeOutBack
easeOutQuint	easeInOutBack
easeInOutQuint	easeOutBound
easeInSine	easeInOutBounce
easeOutSine	

The jQuery UI team maintains a very good interactive demonstration page that shows diagrams of each easing style. Visit http://jqueryui.com/demos/effect/easing.html to give them a try.

Without jQuery UI, you can only choose between linear and swing. Later in this chapter, you will find a recipe that draws all easing functions available in jQuery UI.

When you add the jQuery UI library to this example, you can extend it with all the other easing functions.

Recipe: Adding Graphical Effects by Using jQuery UI

So far, the basic animation functions were already available in jQuery Core and extended by jQuery UI. However, the `effect` function is only available in jQuery UI. You can use this function to attract attention to newly added or removed elements on screen. Listing 8.4 quickly demonstrates all available effects so that you can choose which one is best for your use case.

Listing 8.4   **Recursively Executing All Available Effects**

```
00 <!DOCTYPE html>
01
02 <html lang="en">
03 <head>
04 <title>The jQuery UI effect() function</title>
05   <style>
06     #my-animate {
07       border: 1px solid black;
08       width: 100px;
09       height: 100px;
10       position: relative;
11       left: 80px;
12       top: 80px;
13     }
14    </style>
15 </head>
16 <body>
17
18 <h2>Click the div below to animate it</h2>
19
20 <div id="my-animate">
21 Click
22 </div>
23
24 <script src="http://code.jquery.com/jquery-1.7.1.min.js"></script>
25 <script src="http://code.jquery.com/ui/1.8.16/jquery-ui.min.js">
26 </script>
27
28 <script>
29 // please externalize this code to an external .js file
30 $(document).ready(function() {
```

(Continues)

Listing 8.4   **Recursively Executing All Available Effects (Continued)**

```
31
32    var effects = 'blind bounce clip drop explode fold highlight ' +
33      'puff pulsate scale shake size slide';
34
35    var recursiveEffects = function(effs) {
36      var eff = effs.pop();
37      if(eff) $('#my-animate')
38        .html(eff)
39        .effect(eff, {}, 'slow', function() {
40          recursiveEffects(effs);
41        });
42    };
43
44    $('#my-animate').click(function() {
45      recursiveEffects(effects.split(' ').reverse());
46    });
47
48 });
49 </script>
50 </body>
51 </html>
```

The construction in this code is slightly different than usual. In earlier examples, you already did find parameterized examples in which the parameters come from splitting a larger string into an array. Usually, $.each is used to iterate over the array.

Instead, this example uses a recursive function to iterate over the array. At the start of the function, the last item in the array is popped. This item is set both as text for the HTML and used as the name for the effect function. Within the effect function, the last argument is a callback. This callback makes a recursive call to the current function. This will keep running until the array is empty. Then, the code will fall through the if(eff) test and break.

Recipe: Animating Addition and Removal of CSS Classes by Using jQuery UI

Until this point, all animation code directly specified changes in CSS properties as input for animations. Although technically this does works, it has a big downside; styling becomes mixed with your JavaScript code.

A better and more maintainable solution leaves all styling inside CSS files and provides just enough JavaScript to switch a class on an HTML element. In jQuery Core, this already works as you have seen in Chapter 3, Modifying the Page. However, then you do not have an animation.

jQuery UI makes it possible to animate changes from one CSS class to another as long as the changing properties are either numeric values or colors. Listing 8.5 demonstrates the possibilities offered by jQuery UI's for adding and removing CSS classes.

Listing 8.5   Toggling, Adding, Removing, and Switching CSS Classes

```
00 <!DOCTYPE html>
01
02 <html lang="en">
03 <head>
04 <title>The jQuery UI Change Classes</title>
05   <style>
06     .my-animate {
07       border: 1px solid black;
08       width: 100px;
09       height: 100px;
10     }
11     .my-toggle {
12       border: 50px dashed red;
13       width: 200px;
14       height: 400px;
15       font-size: 50px;
16       padding: 50px;
17     }
18     .my-add {
19       border-radius: 100px;
20       -moz-border-radius: 100px;
21     }
22     .my-switch {
23       background-color: yellow;
24     }
25     </style>
26 </head>
27 <body>
28
29 <h2>Click the div below to animate it</h2>
30
31 <button>Toggle fx</button>
32
33 <div class="my-animate">
34 Click
35 </div>
36
37 <script src="http://code.jquery.com/jquery-1.7.1.min.js"></script>
38 <script src="http://code.jquery.com/ui/1.8.16/jquery-ui.min.js">
39 </script>
```

(Continues)

Listing 8.5   **Toggling, Adding, Removing, and Switching CSS Classes (Continued)**

```
40
41 <script>
42 // please externalize this code to an external .js file
43 $(document).ready(function() {
44
45   $('.my-animate').click(function() {
46     $(this).toggleClass('my-toggle', 2000)
47       .addClass('my-add', 2000)
48       .removeClass('my-toggle', 2000)
49       .switchClass('my-add', 'my-switch', 2000);
50   });
51
52   $('button').click(function() {
53     $.fx.off = !$.fx.off;
54     $.fx.interval = 500;
55   });
56
57 });
58 </script>
59 </body>
60 </html>
```

Pressing the button once turns off the animations. Pressing it twice turns the animation back on but keeps the long interval. The default interval is 13 milliseconds.

To demonstrate the limitations of animated CSS class switching, the my-toggle class defines a dashed border instead of a solid one. As you try this example, you will find out that the animation goes first and the actual class change takes place at the end of the animation.

Lines 53 and 54 demonstrate how you can turn off animations or change the animation interval.

Recipe: Displaying all Easing Functions in jQuery UI as Charts

In this chapter, you can see how to use the toggle and fade functions allow to specify an easing function as a parameter. In Chapter 6, you can use the easing functions as a parameter in the resizable component.

The idea of an easing function is to gradually go from y=0 to y=1 as x=0 goes to x=1. By default, this can be done in a linear fashion by using y=x. Most easing functions provide non-linear alternatives that give a different *feel* to animations. You might be familiar with elastic, bouncing, starting fast and ending slowly, or the other ways around easing styles.

Listing 8.6 does not demonstrate the animations themselves. Instead, it draws the easing functions on the screen in a simplified point chart. It does this by plotting a large number of div elements in a row, where the vertical position depends on the easing function. It must be said that this is not a proper use of divs and borders; this is just for demonstration purposes.

Listing 8.6   **Drawing Easing Functions on Screen**

```
00 <!DOCTYPE html>
01
02 <html lang="en">
03 <head>
04 <title>The jQuery UI easing functions</title>
05   <style>
06     .placeholder {
07       width: 100px;
08     }
09     .col {
10       margin: 50px 0px 50px 0px;
11       padding: 0px;
12       width: 1px;
13       height: 100px;
14       position: relative;
15       float: left;
16     }
17     .point {
18       margin: 0px;
19       padding: 0px;
20       border: 1px solid black;
21       width: 1px;
22       height: 1px;
23       position: relative;
24       float: left;
25     }
26   </style>
27 </head>
28 <body>
29
30 <h2>Display All Easing Functions</h2>
31
32 <div class="placeholder">
33 </div>
34
35 <script src="http://code.jquery.com/jquery-1.7.1.min.js"></script>
36 <script src="http://code.jquery.com/ui/1.8.16/jquery-ui.min.js">
37 </script>
```

(Continues)

Listing 8.6   **Drawing Easing Functions on Screen (Continued)**

```
38
39 <script>
40 // please externalize this code to an external .js file
41 $(document).ready(function() {
42
43   $.each($.easing, function(index, value) {
44     if(! /def|linear|jswing/.test(index)) {
45     var current = $('.placeholder').append('<div>'+index+'</div>');
46
47     for(var i = 0; i < 100; i++) {
48       current.append('<div class="col">' +
49       '<div class="point" style="top: '+
50       (100 - value(0, i, 0, 100, 100)) +
51       'px; left: '+ i + 'px ;"></div></div>');
52     }}
53   });
54
55 });
56 </script>
57 </body>
58 </html>
```

Line 43 fetches the easing functions directly from the library. Line 44 excludes the default, linear, and swing function from the drawings. Next, 100 columns are created and in each column, there will be a single small `div` with a vertical position specified by the easing function.

Recipe: Displaying All Icons in jQuery UI

In Chapter 7, Interacting with Widgets, There are some examples of icons from jQuery UI. You can set them in the corners of `resizables` or `dialogs`. You can add them to `buttons`, `accordions`, `tabs`, or `datechoosers`. Or, you can use them anywhere you like, regardless of jQuery UI components.

Listing 8.7 creates a flat list of icons and their respective names as a catalog from which to choose your icons. If you change the theme, you can quickly see the changes in the icon list.

Listing 8.7   **Naming and Displaying a Large List of Icons**

```
00 <!DOCTYPE html>
01
02 <html lang="en">
03 <head>
04 <title>The jQuery UI Icons</title>
```

Listing 8.7   **Naming and Displaying a Large List of Icons (Continued)**

```
05 <link type="text/css" rel="stylesheet" href=
06   "http://code.jquery.com/ui/1.8.16/themes/base/jquery-ui.css">
07 <style>
08   span {
09     float: left;
10   }
11 </style>
12 </head>
13 <body>
14
15 <h2>Display All Icons</h2>
16
17 <div class="placeholder">
18 </div>
19
20 <script src="http://code.jquery.com/jquery-1.7.1.min.js"></script>
21 <script src="http://code.jquery.com/ui/1.8.16/jquery-ui.min.js">
22 </script>
23
24 <script>
25 // please externalize this code to an external .js file
26 $(document).ready(function() {
27
28   var icons = 'carat-1-n carat-1-ne carat-1-e carat-1-se ' +
29     'carat-1-s carat-1-sw carat-1-w carat-1-nw carat-2-n-s ' +
30     'carat-2-e-w triangle-1-n triangle-1-neckgr triangle-1-e ' +
31     'triangle-1-seckgr triangle-1-s triangle-1-swckgr ' +
32     'triangle-1-w triangle-1-nwckgr triangle-2-n-sckg ' +
33     'triangle-2-e-wckg arrow-1-n arrow-1-ne arrow-1-e arrow-1-se ' +
34     'arrow-1-s arrow-1-sw arrow-1-w arrow-1-nw arrow-2-n-s ' +
35     'arrow-2-ne-swckgr arrow-2-e-w arrow-2-se-nwckgr ' +
36     'arrowstop-1-nckgr arrowstop-1-eckgr arrowstop-1-sckgr ' +
37     'arrowstop-1-wckgr arrowthick-1-nckg arrowthick-1-neck ' +
38     'arrowthick-1-eckg arrowthick-1-seck arrowthick-1-sckg ' +
39     'arrowthick-1-swck arrowthick-1-wckg arrowthick-1-nwck ' +
40     'arrowthick-2-n-sc arrowthick-2-ne-sw arrowthick-2-e-wc ' +
41     'arrowthick-2-se-nw b arrowthickstop-1-n arrowthickstop-1-e ' +
42     'arrowthickstop-1-s arrowthickstop-1-w arrowreturnthick-1-w ' +
43     'arrowreturnthick-1-n arrowreturnthick-1-e ' +
44     'arrowreturnthick-1-s arrowreturn-1-wck arrowreturn-1-nck ' +
45     'arrowreturn-1-eck arrowreturn-1-sck arrowrefresh-1-wc ' +
46     'arrowrefresh-1-nc arrowrefresh-1-ec arrowrefresh-1-sc ' +
47     'arrow-4p arrow-4-diag extlinkp newwin refreshp shufflep ' +
48     'transfer-e-w transferthick-e-w folder-collapsedc ' +
```

(Continues)

Listing 8.7   **Naming and Displaying a Large List of Icons (Continued)**

```
49      'folder-open document document-b notesi mail-closed ' +
50      'mail-open suitcase commentp person prints trashs locked ' +
51      'unlocked bookmark tagsit homesi flagsi calendar cartsi ' +
52      'pencil clocks disksi calculator zoomin zoomoutp search ' +
53      'wrench gearsi hearts starsi linksi cancel plussi plusthick ' +
54      'minuss minusthick closes closethick keysit lightbulb ' +
55      'scissors clipboard copysi contactp images videos script ' +
56      'alerts infosi notice helpsi checks bullet radio-on ' +
57      'radio-off pin-ws pin-ss playsi pauses seek-next ' +
58      'seek-prev seek-end seek-start seek-first stopsi ' +
59      'ejects volume-off volume-on powers signal-diag signal ' +
60      'battery-0 battery-1 battery-2 battery-3 circle-plus ' +
61      'circle-minus circle-close circle-triangle-e ' +
62      'circle-triangle-s circle-triangle-w circle-triangle-n ' +
63      'circle-arrow-eckg circle-arrow-sckg circle-arrow-wckg ' +
64      'circle-arrow-nckg circle-zoominckgr circle-zoomoutckg ' +
65      'circle-check circlesmall-plusc circlesmall-minus ' +
66      'circlesmall-close squaresmall-plusc squaresmall-minus ' +
67      'squaresmall-close grip-dotted-vertical ' +
68      'grip-dotted-horizontal grip-solid-vertical ' +
69      'grip-solid-horizontal  gripsmall-diagonal-se ' +
70      'grip-diagonal-sec';
71
72   $.each(icons.split(' '), function(index, value) {
73       $('.placeholder').append('<br>' +
74         '<span class="ui-icon ui-icon-'+ value +'"></span>' +
75         '<span>ui-icon-' + value +'</span><br>');
76   });
77
78 });
79 </script>
80 </body>
81 </html>
```

This long list of icons is not the most elegant code snippet in this book. Unfortunately, there is no way to retrieve all icons like you can retrieve all easing functions.

Recipe: Executing Code at the End of an Animation with a Promise

In Chapter 5, Communicating with the Server, the concept of Observables was first introduced. You can use an observable to schedule a function for execution after another operation is finished. This works well for implementing handlers for server-side responses from AJAX requests.

It can also be used to execute code when all animations are finished. If you were to use the callback handler inside effects or animations for this purpose, there is a risk that another animation is added to the queue and the code is run too early. The Deferred construction helps you to avoid this.

A Deferred exposes the `promise` function which only allows access to those functions that are relevant from an outsider's perspective. This way, it prevents other code from manipulating the internals of the Deferred process.

Listing 8.8 adds a callback to the `done` function of the `promise` / `deferred` interface. It also demonstrates the `stop` function from jQuery Core and its cooperation with the Deferred interface.

Listing 8.8   Implementing a Promise

```
00 <!DOCTYPE html>
01
02 <html lang="en">
03 <head>
04 <title>The jQuery promise() and stop() functions</title>
05   <style>
06     #my-animate {
07       border: 1px solid black;
08       width: 100px;
09       height: 100px;
10     }
11   </style>
12 </head>
13 <body>
14
15 <h2>Click the div below to animate it</h2>
16
17 <div id="my-animate">
18 Click
19 </div>
20
21 <button>Stop</button>
22
23 <script src="http://code.jquery.com/jquery-1.7.1.min.js"></script>
24 <script src="http://code.jquery.com/ui/1.8.16/jquery-ui.min.js">
25 </script>
26
27 <script>
28 // please externalize this code to an external .js file
29 $(document).ready(function() {
30
31   $('#my-animate').click(function() {
32     $(this).effect('slide', {}, 5000);
```

(Continues)

Listing 8.8   **Implementing a Promise (Continued)**

```
33     $(this).promise().done(function() {
34       alert('animation is done');
35     });
36   });
37
38   $('button').click(function() {
39     $('#my-animate').stop();
40   });
41
42 });
43 </script>
44 </body>
45 </html>
```

After you press the stop button, you immediately see the `alert` box. If you do not press the stop button, this will take five seconds.

Recipe: Executing Code Within Animations by Using Queue and Dequeue

In most cases, queuing several animations in a row will be more than enough to decorate your Web page. Too much animation and too many moving elements can drive the visitors crazy.

In a few exceptional use cases, you want to go beyond graphical animations and also execute different code when one animation ends but before the next one starts.

Promises execute when all animations are finished. Working with a promise for this purpose would seem like hacking. Callbacks could work. The problem with larger callback chains is that your code begins to look like a Christmas tree.

An alternative is to work with the queuing mechanism that is used by animations under the hood. Listing 8.9 demonstrates how to add your own function on the animation queue.

Listing 8.9   **Changing HTML in Between Animations with Queues**

```
00 <!DOCTYPE html>
01
02 <html lang="en">
03 <head>
04 <title>The jQuery UI queue() and dequeue() functions</title>
05 <style>
06   .my-animate {
07     border: 1px solid black;
08     width: 150px;
09     height: 150px;
```

Listing 8.9   **Changing HTML in Between Animations with Queues (Continued)**

```
10    }
11    .my-toggle {
12      background-color: yellow;
13    }
14    </style></head>
15 <body>
16
17 <h2>Click the div below to animate it</h2>
18
19 <div class="my-animate">
20 Click
21 </div>
22
23 <script src="http://code.jquery.com/jquery-1.7.1.min.js"></script>
24 <script src="http://code.jquery.com/ui/1.8.16/jquery-ui.min.js">
25 </script>
26
27 <script>
28 // please externalize this code to an external .js file
29 $(document).ready(function() {
30
31    $('.my-animate').click(function() {
32      $(this)
33        .toggleClass('my-toggle', 'fast')
34        .queue(function() {
35          $(this).html('Queue . . . And then dequeue, otherwise ' +
36            'the animation will not continue');
37          $(this).dequeue();
38        })
39        .toggleClass('my-toggle', 'fast')
40        .queue(function() {
41          $(this).html('This is what you get when you forget '
42            + 'to dequeue . . .');
43          // forget $(this).dequeue(); on purpose
44        })
45        .toggleClass('my-toggle', 'fast')
46        .promise().done(function() {
47        $(this).html('This function will never be called because ' +
48          'the second queued function does NOT dequeue . . .');
49      });
50    });
51
52 });
53 </script>
54 </body>
55 </html>
```

The `queue` function can take an additional parameter, a string signifying the queue name. By default, the queue name is `fx`. When you run code inside the queue, the animations will not continue until `dequeue` is called. Lines 37 and 43 demonstrate the effects of adding `dequeue` and forgetting to add it.

Summary

This chapter started with a discussion about the possibilities you can realize by adding your own CSS styling to jQuery UI. The easiest method is to reuse standard CSS themes. Or with a little bit of extra work, you can create your own variant with the theme roller. If you want more freedom, jQuery UI does not stop you from creating your own CSS file or downloading third-party themes from the Internet.

The animation functions of both jQuery Core and jQuery UI are thoroughly demonstrated in this chapter. Some of the recipes can serve as reference material to look up animations, easing functions, and icons before using them.

Chapter 9

Navigating Pages by Using jQuery Mobile

This chapter introduces the basics of jQuery Mobile. It describes the framework for setting up pages, navigating to other pages, loading content via AJAX requests, and providing smooth transition animations. Within the page, there are certain basic elements, such as headers and footers, that behave differently based on the options you specify. This page setup, combined with basics such as columns, events, and a minimum of custom JavaScript code serve as the fundamentals for using jQuery Mobile.

Recipe: Setting Up jQuery Mobile Basics

jQuery Mobile is different from jQuery Core and jQuery UI. You can use most features of jQuery mobile without writing a single line of JavaScript. Instead, you need to add attributes to the HTML. All attributes start with the syntax `data-`, similar to what you saw in Chapter 1, Getting Started with jQuery, when the `data()` function was explained. jQuery Mobile uses the `jqmData()` function, instead. This is discussed later in this chapter.

jQuery Mobile requires you to set up your HTML in a specific way. Listing 9.1 provides the basic setup for a page with a header and a minimum of content.

Listing 9.1 Displaying a Simple Page with a Header

```
00 <!DOCTYPE html>
01 <html>
02 <head>
03   <title>jQuery Mobile: Basics</title>
04   <meta name="viewport"
05     content="width=device-width, initial-scale=1">
06   <link rel="stylesheet" href=
07   "http://code.jquery.com/mobile/1.1.0/jquery.mobile-1.1.0.min.css">
08   <script type="text/javascript"
09     src="http://code.jquery.com/jquery-1.7.1.min.js">
```

(Continues)

Listing 9.1   Displaying a Simple Page with a Header (Continued)

```
10   </script>
11   <script type="text/javascript" src=
12     "http://code.jquery.com/mobile/1.1.0/jquery.mobile-1.1.0.min.js">
13   </script>
14 </head>
15 <body>
16
17 <div data-role="page">
18
19   <div data-role="header">
20     <h1>My Title</h1>
21   </div>
22
23   <div data-role="content">
24     <p>Hello world</p>
25   </div>
26
27 </div>
28
29 </body>
30 </html>
```

In this HTML, you notice a couple of things. First, lines 4 and 5 specify a `viewport`. This code asks your mobile device to adjust the zoom level and page size to fit the current content on the screen. This is extremely important when dealing with mobile devices. The default width for the `viewport` is browser dependent, but is generally around 980 pixels. When your device has a small or wider resolution than the default setting, the page layout can become distorted. It will appear as either too small for the screen, or the zoom level will be adjusted so that the text is hard to read and you need to zoom in to make use of the page. By setting the width and initial-scale, you are able to size the content of your site to match the screen size of the device.

Lines 6 and 7 provide a CSS file. You can use this to change colors. If you are brave, you can also change the complete look and feel. In that case, you must consider the number of devices for which you want to test. jQuery Mobile is tested on a large number of devices, by default.

On lines 8–13, you find the JavaScript sources for both jQuery Core and jQuery Mobile. In the rest of this book, JavaScripts are loaded at the bottom of the HTML for performance reasons. In jQuery Mobile, it is recommended to load HTML from the header. When you link to another page, jQuery Mobile loads it by using an AJAX request, as you will see later in this chapter. When this page is loaded, scripts inside the header are to be ignored. Any scripts that you do want to load because they are specific to that page should be placed inside the body.

Lines 17–27 contain the actual code. Most of it is simple HTML. In every `div` element, you find a `data-role` attribute of either `page`, `header`, or `content`.

These roles are used by the jQuery Mobile framework to assign styles, themes, and behavior. When you view this from a browser—preferably a mobile browser—you can see the result.

Recipe: Serving Multiple Pages from a Single HTML File

You can add multiple pages to a single HTML file. This way, there is no need to create a new request to the server, so the interface is more responsive. In addition, the navigation keeps working when you are offline. Listing 9.2 demonstrates how to link to a second page.

This works well for a limited number of pages. At some point, though, depending on the specifications of the devices you are targeting, memory consumption becomes a problem. Linking to external pages is discussed later.

Listing 9.2   **Navigating to a Second Page**

```
00 <!DOCTYPE html>
01 <html>
02   <head>
03     <title>Pages</title>
04     <meta name="viewport"
05       content="width=device-width, initial-scale=1">
06     <link rel="stylesheet" href=
07       "http://code.jquery.com/mobile/1.1.0/jquery.mobile-1.1.0.min.css">
08     <script type="text/javascript"
09       src="http://code.jquery.com/jquery-1.7.1.min.js">
10     </script>
11     <script type="text/javascript" src=
12       "http://code.jquery.com/mobile/1.1.0/jquery.mobile-1.1.0.min.js">
13     </script>
14   </head>
15 <body>
16
17 <div data-role="page">
18
19   <div data-role="header">
20     <h1>First</h1>
21   </div>
22
23   <div data-role="content">
24     <p>Hello world <a href="#second">and go to the second</a></p>
25   </div>
26
27   <!--
28   Either/or ... the result is in the LINK, not the DIV
29
```

(Continues)

Listing 9.2   **Navigating to a Second Page (Continued)**

```
30   <div data-role="content">
31     <p>Or ... <a href="#second" data-rel="dialog"
32      data-transition="pop">show the exact same page as a
33      dialog!</a></p>
34   </div>
35     -->
36 </div>
37
38 <div data-role="page" id="second">
39
40   <div data-role="header">
41     <h1>Second</h1>
42   </div>
43   <div data-role="content">
44     Hello, again!
45   </div>
46
47 </div>
48
49 </body>
50 </html>
```

Let's start at the bottom of the HTML. Lines 38–45 contain the div with the second page. It has its own header and its own content. More importantly, the div element contains an id attribute.

Lines 23–25 contain the main content of the first page. There is a link to the second page. The id attribute serves as an anchor that can be referenced by putting a # in front to make it a hash-tag. Watch the URL bar of your mobile browser when you click the link. You can use the new URL to bookmark the page and open the second page directly when you click the bookmark.

Finally, lines 27–35 contain an alternative to lines 23–25. It is currently disabled with `<!-- -->` comment tags. If you replace lines 23–25 with this content, the second page opens as a dialog instead of a new page. As you can see, it is the link that specifies whether the page should be opened as normal page or as a dialog.

It is recommended that you do not mix the way a single page is opened. Either open it as a page or as a dialog. Switching this within a single HTML file can lead to unexpected behavior.

Recipe: Changing the Title Element

A single HTML file contains a single title element. When you provide multiple pages inside a single HTML file, this can lead to undesired behavior. Pages within a single HTML file might require their own HTML titles.

Listing 9.3 shows how to provide different titles for different pages within a single HTML file.

Listing 9.3   **Providing Separate Titles for Every Page**

```
00 <!DOCTYPE html>
01 <html>
02 <head>
03   <title>Page Title</title>
04   <meta name="viewport"
05     content="width=device-width, initial-scale=1">
06   <link rel="stylesheet" href=
07     "http://code.jquery.com/mobile/1.1.0/jquery.mobile-1.1.0.min.css">
08   <script type="text/javascript"
09     src="http://code.jquery.com/jquery-1.7.1.min.js">
10   </script>
11   <script type="text/javascript" src=
12     "http://code.jquery.com/mobile/1.1.0/jquery.mobile-1.1.0.min.js">
13   </script>
14 </head>
15 <body>
16
17 <div data-role="page" id="first" data-title="My First Title">
18   <!-- Title not set at first loading! If left out: original
19     title, otherwise the specified-->
20
21   <div data-role="header">
22     <h1>First</h1>
23   </div>
24
25   <div data-role="content">
26     <p><a href="#second">and go to the second</a></p>
27   </div>
28
29 </div>
30
31 <div data-role="page" id="second" data-title="My Second Title">
32
33   <div data-role="header">
34     <h1>Second</h1>
35   </div>
36
37   <div data-role="content">
38     <p><a href="#first">and go to the first</a></p>
39   </div>
40
41 </div>
```

(Continues)

Listing 9.3   **Providing Separate Titles for Every Page (Continued)**

```
42
43 </body>
44 </html>
```

On line 3, you see the default `title` element. This title is loaded by default. On lines 17 and 31, you find titles specific to each page. As soon as you navigate to the first page, the title of the browser changes to the `data-title` attribute from line 31.

When you press the back button, the title goes back to the default title from line 3. If you want to get the title from the `data-title` attribute on line 17, you need to create a link referencing the first page. This is done on line 38. You can test the example and see what happens.

Recipe: Loading External Pages Using AJAX

Until this point, the examples have been loading pages that were already available inside the HTML. All of them worked with hash tags to reference `id`s that were already inside the DOM tree.

As your Web site grows, it becomes impossible to load all pages in a single HTML. Using jQuery Mobile, it is just as easy to create links to other HTML pages as it is in normal Web applications. As Listing 9.4 shows, the links are exactly the same.

The difference is in the way that links are handled by jQuery Mobile. When links point to the same domain as the current page, by default they are loaded with an AJAX request. This can be turned off with specific settings as demonstrated later in this chapter. Also, if a link points to a different domain, it will be treated as a link in a normal Web site.

The advantages of loading with AJAX is the possibility to provide smooth transition animations. Also, the pages are stored inside a DOM tree. This allows quick navigation back to the previous page without accessing the server. The downside of this is memory consumption. On devices with limited resources, this can become an issue.

> **Note**
>
> When developing locally, you should be using a Web server. If you are trying to use jQuery Mobile without a server, the AJAX requests will fail and you will be shown an error, either on the screen or in your console. Although some browsers might let you load local files even through AJAX calls, it is always best to replicate production circumstances whenever possible.

Listing 9.4   **Linking to External Pages**

```
00 <!DOCTYPE html>
01 <html>
02   <head>
03     <title>Linking AJAX</title>
04     <meta name="viewport"
```

Listing 9.4   **Linking to External Pages (Continued)**

```
05        content="width=device-width, initial-scale=1">
06      <link rel="stylesheet" href=
07        "http://code.jquery.com/mobile/1.1.0/jquery.mobile-1.1.0.min.css">
08      <script type="text/javascript"
09        src="http://code.jquery.com/jquery-1.7.1.min.js">
10      </script>
11      <script type="text/javascript" src=
12        "http://code.jquery.com/mobile/1.1.0/jquery.mobile-1.1.0.min.js">
13      </script>
14    </head>
15  <body>
16
17  <div data-role="page">
18
19    <div data-role="header">
20        <h1>Linking AJAX</h1>
21    </div>
22
23    <div data-role="content">
24      <p><a href="04b-link.html">Link to an external file</a></p>
25      <p><a href="04b-link.html" data-prefetch>Prefetch the
26        external file</a></p>
27    </div>
28
29  </div>
30
31  </body>
32  </html>
```

Lines 24 and 25 provide two different ways to link to an external file. In reality, you might not want to use `data-prefetch` on all of your links, because this creates an extra HTTP request per link and will slow down the rendering and delivery of your site. Save them for links that you are sure will be visited. The first link will load the page when it is clicked. The second link will preload the data behind the link as soon as it can to speed up navigation.

Listing 9.5 provides an example of an external page to load.

Listing 9.5   **Providing an External Page to Load**

```
00  <!DOCTYPE html>
01  <html>
02    <head>
03    <title>Linked Page</title>
04    </head>
```

(Continues)

Listing 9.5   **Providing an External Page to Load (Continued)**

```
05 <body>
06
07 <div data-role="page">
08
09   <div data-role="header">
10     <h1>Linked File</h1>
11   </div>
12
13   <div data-role="content">
14     <p>
15       <a href="04-linking-ajax.html">
16         Link to an original file
17       </a>
18     </p>
19   </div>
20
21 </div>
22
23 </body>
24 </html>
```

Note that this example does not contain any CSS or JavaScript inside the header. In this example, this is mostly done to prove that the page is loaded by using AJAX and that the scripts and CSS files from the first page will still be there.

In production, it is better to provide the script and CSS after all, because someone might directly access the link to this file. You can try, but the page will miss the look and feel from jQuery Mobile.

Pay special attention to what happens in the URL bar. Although pages are loaded with AJAX, the URL still changes to the new location. This helps with "bookmarkability" and navigation.

Recipe: Displaying Page Loading Messages

When the server you contact is slow, or more likely on a mobile device, when the connection is slow, you typically see page loading messages when clicking a link containing a jQuery Mobile page.

These indicators can also be used for different purposes than clicking links (for example, when you provide your own JavaScript code that either contacts a server via AJAX or performs a heavy computation itself). Listing 9.6 demonstrates how to display page loading messages.

Listing 9.6   **Turning the Load Message On and Off**

```
00 <!DOCTYPE html>
01 <html>
02   <head>
```

Listing 9.6 **Turning the Load Message On and Off (Continued)**

```
03    <title>Loading Messages</title>
04    <meta name="viewport"
05      content="width=device-width, initial-scale=1">
06    <link rel="stylesheet" href=
07      "http://code.jquery.com/mobile/1.1.0/jquery.mobile-1.1.0.min.css">
08    <script type="text/javascript"
09      src="http://code.jquery.com/jquery-1.7.1.min.js">
10    </script>
11    <script type="text/javascript" src=
12      "http://code.jquery.com/mobile/1.1.0/jquery.mobile-1.1.0.min.js">
13    </script>
14    <script>
15    $(document).ready(function() {
16      $('#show').on('click', function() {
17        $.mobile.showPageLoadingMsg();
18      });
19      $('#hide').on('click', function() {
20        $.mobile.hidePageLoadingMsg();
21      });
22    });
23    </script>
24    </head>
25  <body>
26
27  <div data-role="page">
28
29    <div data-role="header">
30        <h1>Show/Hide Loading Message</h1>
31    </div>
32
33    <div data-role="content">
34      <a href="#" id="show" data-role="button">Show Loading
35        Message</a>
36      <a href="#" id="hide" data-role="button">Hide Loading
37        Message</a>
38    </div>
39
40  </div>
41
42  </body>
43  </html>
```

Line 34–37 provide two buttons to turn on and off loading messages. These buttons
are attached to custom JavaScript code. Although most jQuery Mobile code does not
require writing custom JavaScript, a number of exceptions remain. Lines 17 and 20
display and hide the loading message. By pressing these buttons, you notice that there
actually is no connection between a loading message and actual work being done.

Although it is possible to turn the loading message on and off at any time, you should reserve using it for times when you are actually doing work in the background or loading page assets.

Note that using `$(document).ready(function() {})` only works once: at the initial loading of the HTML. Once you load new pages with AJAX, this event will not be fired again. If you want code to be executed for every page, you need to call `$(document).on('pageinit', function() {})`.

Recipe: Linking to External Pages without AJAX

By default, jQuery mobile transforms all links to AJAX requests, as long as they refer to files on the same domain. However, there might be situations in which you want to avoid this behavior. For example, you might have parts of your site using a different mobile JavaScript framework that conflicts when you try to load it with AJAX. Listing 9.7 demonstrates multiple ways to disable AJAX loading behavior on a link.

Listing 9.7   **Providing Links to External Pages Indicating No AJAX**

```
00 <!DOCTYPE html>
01 <html>
02   <head>
03     <title>Linking Without AJAX</title>
04     <meta name="viewport"
05       content="width=device-width, initial-scale=1">
06     <link rel="stylesheet" href=
07       "http://code.jquery.com/mobile/1.1.0/jquery.mobile-1.1.0.min.css">
08     <script type="text/javascript"
09       src="http://code.jquery.com/jquery-1.7.1.min.js">
10     </script>
11     <script type="text/javascript" src=
12       "http://code.jquery.com/mobile/1.1.0/jquery.mobile-1.1.0.min.js">
13     </script>
14   </head>
15 <body>
16
17 <div data-role="page">
18
19   <div data-role="header">
20     <h1>Linking Without AJAX</h1>
21   </div>
22
23   <div data-role="content">
24     <p><a href="04b-link.html" data-ajax="false">Link to an
25       external file</a></p>
26     <!-- OR:
27     <p><a href="04b-link.html" rel="external">Link to an
```

Listing 9.7   Providing Links to External Pages Indicating No AJAX (Continued)

```
28       external file</a></p>
29    -->
30  </div>
31
32 </div>
33
34 </body>
35 </html>
```

On line 24, the `data-ajax` attribute is introduced to specify whether AJAX should be used. The default value is `true`. If you set it to `false`, AJAX will be disabled.

Line 27 provides the `rel="external"` attribute. The behavior inside jQuery Mobile is the same: AJAX will be disabled. This notation is according to the HTML recommendation. Using this can have side effects, though. Someone might specify CSS rules that give a different look and feel to links that point to external locations. For example, an icon might be added to these links.

Recipe: Specifying the Transition Animation

When you click an internal link that is loaded by using AJAX, jQuery Mobile provides a transition animation. By default, you see the pages slide to the left.

jQuery Mobile provides a small number of default animations from which you can choose. They are pop, `slidefade`, `slide`, `slideup`, `slidedown`, `fade`, and `flip`. Listing 9.8 demonstrates how to change the animation on a link.

Listing 9.8   Navigating to the Second Page with an Animation

```
00 <!DOCTYPE html>
01 <html>
02   <head>
03   <title>Transition</title>
04     <meta name="viewport"
05       content="width=device-width, initial-scale=1">
06     <link rel="stylesheet" href=
07       "http://code.jquery.com/mobile/1.1.0/jquery.mobile-1.1.0.min.css">
08     <script type="text/javascript"
09       src="http://code.jquery.com/jquery-1.7.1.min.js">
10     </script>
11     <script type="text/javascript" src=
12       "http://code.jquery.com/mobile/1.1.0/jquery.mobile-1.1.0.min.js">
13     </script>
14   </head>
15 <body>
16
```

(Continues)

Listing 9.8   Navigating to the Second Page with an Animation (Continued)

```
17 <div data-role="page">
18
19   <div data-role="header">
20     <h1>First</h1>
21   </div>
22
23   <div data-role="content">
24     <p>Hello world <a href="#second" data-transition="pop">and go
25         to the second</a></p>
26         <!-- or slide, slideup, slidedown, fade, or flip
27         (support for flip is limited on Android) -->
28   </div>
29
30 </div>
31
32 <div data-role="page" id="second">
33
34   <div data-role="header">
35     <h1>Second</h1>
36   </div>
37   <div data-role="content">
38     Hello again!
39   </div>
40
41 </div>
42
43 </body>
44 </html>
```

Line 24 introduces the data-transition attribute. This attribute can also be used on form elements. The framework handles the animation under the hood.

Recipe: Specifying Custom Transition Animations

In case you need a different animation than the set of default animations provided in the previous example, you can introduce your own. You can use CSS3 transitions to create smooth hardware accelerated animations, both 2D and 3D.

Listing 9.9 provides an example animation that rotates the page as the new page is opened.

Listing 9.9   Switching Pages with a Custom CSS3 Transition

```
00 <!DOCTYPE html>
01 <html>
```

Listing 9.9   **Switching Pages with a Custom CSS3 Transition (Continued)**

```
02   <head>
03     <title>Custom Transition</title>
04     <meta name="viewport"
05       content="width=device-width, initial-scale=1">
06     <link rel="stylesheet" href=
07       "http://code.jquery.com/mobile/1.1.0/jquery.mobile-1.1.0.min.css">
08     <style>
09       .mine.in {
10           -webkit-animation-name: myslidein;
11       }
12
13       .mine.out {
14           -webkit-animation-name: myslideout;
15       }
16
17       @-webkit-keyframes myslidein {
18           from { -webkit-transform:   rotateZ(0deg) scale(0);}
19           to { -webkit-transform:   rotateZ(360deg) scale(1); }
20       }
21       @-webkit-keyframes myslideout {
22           from { -webkit-transform:  rotateZ(360deg) scale(1); }
23           to { -webkit-transform:   rotateZ(0deg) scale(0); }
24       }
25     </style>
26     <script type="text/javascript"
27       src="http://code.jquery.com/jquery-1.7.1.min.js">
28     </script>
29     <script type="text/javascript" src=
30       "http://code.jquery.com/mobile/1.1.0/jquery.mobile-1.1.0.min.js">
31     </script>
32   </head>
33 <body>
34
35 <div data-role="page">
36
37   <div data-role="header">
38     <h1>First</h1>
39   </div>
40
41   <div data-role="content">
42
43     <p>Hello world <a href="#second" data-transition="mine">and go
44       to the second</a></p>
45
46   </div>
```

(Continues)

Listing 9.9   **Switching Pages with a Custom CSS3 Transition (Continued)**

```
47
48 </div>
49
50 <div data-role="page" id="second">
51
52   <div data-role="header">
53     <h1>Second</h1>
54   </div>
55   <div data-role="content">
56     Hello again!
57   </div>
58
59 </div>
60
61 </body>
62 </html>
```

In Listing 9.9, you still do not find any custom JavaScript code. You do find a
`data-transition` attribute on line 43 that refers to a custom value: `mine`. jQuery
Mobile uses this value to add `class` attributes when the transition animation is required.

In the CSS specification, on lines 9–15, you find two definitions: the `mine` class
combined with the `in` class, and the `mine` class combined with the `out` class. Both CSS
implementations refer to a CSS3 animation specified on lines 17–24.

On lines 17–24, you find a CSS specification that makes the page rotate during the
transition. With the `-webkit-` prefix, these animations only work on iOS, Safari, and
Chrome. To make this animation work on other browsers, you can add `-moz-`, `-ms-`, or,
at some point in future when the standard has evolved sufficiently, leave the prefixes out.
The example provided here is targeted at iPhone and iPad. To learn more about CSS3
and animations visit http://www.html5rocks.com/en/features/presentation.

If you are using jQuery Mobile and using a browser that does not support 3D
transforms then the transition will fall back to a simple fade transition. You can also
choose to overwrite the default behavior of some transitions to something else. This can
be done by changing the global configuration like so:

```
$.mobile.transitionFallbacks.slideout = "none";
```

Another time that you might wish to override page transitions is on large screens
where the effect can appear to stutter. This can be changed by supplying a value to the
`maxTransitionWidth` options, as shown here:

```
$.mobile.maxTransitionWidth = 640;
```

This sets the transition to `none` whenever the device width is greater than 640.

Recipe: Listening to Mobile Events

Chapter 4, Listening and Responding to Events, explained how to catch the standard events in Web browsers. Mobile devices work with touch gestures rather than mouse moves. The way events are handled might be different between mobile devices. jQuery Mobile abstracts away from this. Listing 9.10 demonstrates how to catch a selection of typical mobile events: tapping, swiping, orientation changes, and page changes. Other mobile events are discussed next.

Listing 9.10　Catching Swipes, Orientation Changes, and More

```
00 <!DOCTYPE html>
01 <html>
02 <head>
03   <title>Events</title>
04   <meta name="viewport"
05     content="width=device-width, initial-scale=1">
06   <link rel="stylesheet" href=
07     "http://code.jquery.com/mobile/1.1.0/jquery.mobile-1.1.0.min.css">
08   <script type="text/javascript"
09     src="http://code.jquery.com/jquery-1.7.1.min.js">
10   </script>
11   <script type="text/javascript" src=
12     "http://code.jquery.com/mobile/1.1.0/jquery.mobile-1.1.0.min.js">
13   </script>
14   <script>
15   $(document).ready(function() {
16
17   $.each(('tap taphold swipe swipeleft swiperight ' +
18     'orientationchange scrollstart scrollstop pageshow ' +
19     'pagehide').split(' '),
20      function( i, name ) {
21
22      $(document).on(name, function(event) {
23        $('#status').append('target = ' + event.target + ' ' +
24                            'type = ' + event.type + ' <br>');
25      });
26    });
27   });
28   </script>
29
30 </head>
31 <body>
32
33 <div data-role="page">
34
35   <div data-role="header">
```

(Continues)

Listing 9.10   **Catching Swipes, Orientation Changes, and More (Continued)**

```
36    <h1>Events</h1>
37    </div>
38
39    <div data-role="content">
40
41    <p><a href="04b-link.html">Link to an external file</a></p>
42    <p id="status"></p>
43
44    </div>
45
46 </div>
47
48 </body>
49 </html>
```

When you run this example, you can see the behavior of events and their handlers. Rotate your device, tap it, rotate it, and swipe over the screen in all directions to see what happens.

Table 9.1 lists the events that can be used with jQuery Mobile.

Table 9.1   **Event Types Specific to jQuery Mobile**

Event Type	Description
tap	The visitor touches the device quickly on a single point
taphold	The visitor touches the device for a longer time
swipe	The visitor moves his finger over the device
swipeleft	The visitor moves his finger to the left
swiperight	The visitor moves his finger to the right
orientationchange	The device is rotated from portrait to landscape view or the other way around
scrollstart	The visitor starts scrolling the screen
scrollstop	The visitor stops scrolling the screen
pageshow	A new page is shown
pagehide	The previous page is hidden
vmouseover	Emulation of a `mouseover` event that normalizes touch events

Table 9.1   **Event Types Specific to jQuery Mobile (Continued)**

Event Type	Description
`vmousedown`	Emulation of a `mousedown` event that normalizes touch events
`vmousemove`	Emulation of a `mousemove` event that normalizes touch events
`vmouseup`	Emulation of a `mouseup` event that normalizes touch events
`vclick`	Emulation of a `click` event that normalizes touch events
`vmousecancel`	This is called when a previously emitted mouse-emulation-related event turns out to be a different event, for example a `swipe`.
`pagebeforeload`	This is called before a new page is loaded. When this event is called, in addition to the event object, a second parameter is passed, which can be one of the following: `url`, `absUrl`, `dataUrl`, `deferred`, `options`. These are three notations of the URL to be loaded, a `deferred` object with which you can override the page loading mechanism and an `options` object containing the parameters passed to the `loadPage()` function.
`pageload`	This is called after the page has successfully loaded into the DOM tree. With the event, a second parameter is passed, similar to `pagebeforeload`; however, instead of a `deferred`, it contains an `xhr` and `textStatus`. These are references to the `XmlHttpRequest` object and the result of the request in the form of a string.
`pageloadfailed`	This is called when a page load request fails. A second parameter is passed with all the values of `pagebeforeload` and `pageload`. In addition, there is an `errorThrown` property.

(Continues)

Table 9.1   **Event Types Specific to jQuery Mobile (Continued)**

Event Type	Description
`pagebeforechange`	This is called as early as possible before a page changes. So this is before the new page is loaded. With `pagebeforechange`, you can prevent the page from changing with the `event.preventDefault()` function. A second parameter is passed to this function containing a `toPage` property and an `options` property.
`pagechange`	This is called after a page change. Again, a second parameter is passed containing a `toPage` and `options` property.
`pagechangefailed`	This is when changing the page fails. Again, a second parameter is passed containing a `toPage` and `options` property.
`pagebeforeshow`	This is on the new page just before it is displayed. The transition animation did not yet start. A second parameter is passed containing a `prevPage` property.
`pagebeforehide`	This is on the current page just before it is hidden. The transition animation did not yet start. A second parameter is passed containing a `nextPage` property.
`pageshow`	This is called on the new page just after the transition animation finished. Otherwise it is similar to the `pagebeforeshow` event.
`pagehide`	This is called on the old page just after the transition animation finished. Otherwise it is similar to the `pagebeforehide` event.
`pagebeforecreate`	This is called when a new page is created, before jQuery Mobile processes the HTML and initializes widgets. Tip: Use this to keep your HTML clean and set attributes such as `data-role` from JavaScript code.
`pagecreate`	This is after a page is created, but before widgets have changed the HTML. Attach your own plugins here.

Table 9.1   **Event Types Specific to jQuery Mobile (Continued)**

Event Type	Description
pageinit	This is after the page is loaded. This serves well as a jQuery Mobile specific replacement for the document `ready` event in case you have code that needs to be executed for new pages that are loaded by using an AJAX request. It is recommended to bind this to a page `div` rather than the full document.
pageremove	This is just before a page is removed.
updatelayout	This is when a component is shown or hidden. This gives a hint to other components that they should recalculate their size and position.

Lines 16–19 contain only a selection of all these events. The events demonstrated are targeted at typical mobile user interaction. You can replace the events with others from the list to study other parts of the jQuery Event mechanism (for example, the page-loading cycle). By using the virtual mouse events, you can fine tune the control of your application for both touch and mouse-driven devices. When a device with a mouse is used, jQuery Mobile automatically sets up the correct listeners to handle the device. When a touch device is used, the events are transposed into the touch events that will follow the same order as the mouse-driven events. Information is also standardized between both touch and click events so that coordinates that would be touched or clicked report back the same numbers. While using the virtual mouse events, you might want to avoid the use of the `vclick` event. On WebKit-based mobile browsers, this can cause a 300-millisecond delay that will not only be sluggish to users, but can actually be the cause of a double-click–like behavior.

Recipe: Generating Back Buttons

When a visitor navigates through pages, sometimes he wants to go back to the previous page. Obviously, a Web browser offers a standard back button for this purpose.

There are good reasons to also provide back buttons within your Web application, though. One reason is that when your Web application runs full screen, the browser's back button might be unavailable. More important, jQuery Mobile applications mimic the look and feel of native applications. In native applications, back buttons are placed in the upper-left corner of the screen.

Listing 9.11 demonstrates how jQuery Mobile makes it easy to add back buttons when necessary.

Listing 9.11   **Navigating to a Second Page with Back Buttons Enabled**

```
00 <!DOCTYPE html>
01 <html>
02 <head>
03   <title>Back Buttons</title>
04   <meta name="viewport"
05     content="width=device-width, initial-scale=1">
06   <link rel="stylesheet" href=
07     "http://code.jquery.com/mobile/1.1.0/jquery.mobile-1.1.0.min.css">
08   <script type="text/javascript"
09     src="http://code.jquery.com/jquery-1.7.1.min.js">
10   </script>
11   <script type="text/javascript" src=
12     "http://code.jquery.com/mobile/1.1.0/jquery.mobile-1.1.0.min.js">
13   </script>
14
15 </head>
16 <body>
17   <div data-role="page">
18
19     <div data-role="header">
20       <h1>First</h1>
21     </div>
22
23     <div data-role="content">
24       <p>Go to the <a href="#second">second page</a> to see a
25         back button</p>
26     </div>
27
28   </div>
29 <div data-role="page" data-add-back-btn="true" id="second">
30
31   <div data-role="header">
32     <h1>Second</h1>
33   </div>
34
35   <div data-role="content">
36     <p>Content</p>
37   </div>
38
39 </div>
40
41 </body>
42 </html>
```

When you open up this code example, the first thing you notice is that there is *no* back button. This makes sense, because you are still on the first page and there is no history to go back to. It also makes sense because the `data-add-back-button="true"` attribute is not defined on the first page. You can try to see what happens when you do add this attribute to the first page.

When you navigate to the second page, a back button appears in the upper-left corner. Lines 33–35 do not contain a reference to a button, however.

You can also use the `data-rel="back"` attribute on an anchor tag, and that will transition the page one page back in your history. When doing this, ensure that you provide the actual link in the `href` property so that older browsers and devices are still able to get to the page to which you want them to go.

Recipe: Adding Footers to the Bottom of the Page

In the examples so far, you have seen headers and content `div`s. In a similar way, you can also define footer `div`s. When working with footers, you need to consider two things: what is the position of the footer on the screen, and what do you display inside the footer? Listing 9.12 adds a footer that contains several buttons to the bottom of the page.

Listing 9.12   Displaying a Footer with Buttons Below the Page

```
00 <!DOCTYPE html>
01 <html>
02 <head>
03   <title>Footer</title>
04   <meta name="viewport"
05     content="width=device-width, initial-scale=1">
06   <link rel="stylesheet" href=
07     "http://code.jquery.com/mobile/1.1.0/jquery.mobile-1.1.0.min.css">
08   <script type="text/javascript"
09     src="http://code.jquery.com/jquery-1.7.1.min.js">
10   </script>
11   <script type="text/javascript" src=
12     "http://code.jquery.com/mobile/1.1.0/jquery.mobile-1.1.0.min.js">
13   </script>
14
15 </head>
16 <body>
17
18 <div data-role="page">
19
20   <div data-role="header">
21     <h1>Footer</h1>
22   </div>
23
24   <div data-role="content">
25     <p>Content</p>
26   </div>
```

(Continues)

Listing 9.12   **Displaying a Footer with Buttons Below the Page (Continued)**

```
27
28    <div data-role="footer">
29        <h1>Footer</h1>
30        <a href="#">Button?</a>
31        <a href="#" data-role="button" data-icon="delete">
32          Remove
33        </a>
34        <a href="#" data-role="button" data-icon="plus">
35          Add
36        </a>
37    </div>
38 </div>
39
40
41 </body>
42 </html>
```

This first button is set up on line 30. Adding a simple link is sufficient to create a new button. Inside the footer, links are transformed into buttons by default. Lines 31–36 add two buttons in the conventional way, each button with a custom icon. The current list of available icons can be found by visiting http://jquerymobile.com/demos/1.1.0/docs/buttons/buttons-icons.html.

The content `div` in this example is almost empty. You can add more content and see what happens to the position of the footer when you scroll up and down. The footer will be below the content you add and stay at the bottom of the page.

Instead of the separate buttons, you can also create a button group. By default, the buttons in a button group are stacked vertically. By adding `data-type="horizontal"`, you can display the buttons in a single horizontal rectangle, with rounded corners on the right-most and left-most buttons. Listing 9.13 demonstrates the result.

Listing 9.13   **Displaying a Button Set Within the Footer**

```
00 <!DOCTYPE html>
01 <html>
02 <head>
03    <title>Footer Button Set</title>
04    <meta name="viewport"
05      content="width=device-width, initial-scale=1">
06    <link rel="stylesheet" href=
07      "http://code.jquery.com/mobile/1.1.0/jquery.mobile-1.1.0.min.css">
08    <script type="text/javascript"
09      src="http://code.jquery.com/jquery-1.7.1.min.js">
10    </script>
11    <script type="text/javascript" src=
```

Listing 9.13   Displaying a Button Set Within the Footer (Continued)

```
12      "http://code.jquery.com/mobile/1.1.0/jquery.mobile-1.1.0.min.js">
13   </script>
14
15 </head>
16 <body>
17
18 <div data-role="page">
19
20   <div data-role="header">
21     <h1>Footer Button Set</h1>
22   </div>
23
24   <div data-role="content">
25       <p>Content</p>
26     </div>
27
28
29   <div data-role="footer">
30     <div data-role="controlgroup" data-type="horizontal">
31       <a href="#" data-role="button">First</a>
32       <a href="#" data-role="button">Second</a>
33       <a href="#" data-role="button">Third</a>
34       <a href="#" data-role="button">Fourth</a>
35     </div>
36   </div>
37
38 </div>
39
40
41 </body>
42 </html>
```

Lines 30–35 add a `div` with `data-role="controlgroup"` and
`data-type="horizontal"` around the separate buttons.

Recipe: Fixing the Footer Across Pages

Clicking a link triggers an animation during the page change. There might be situations
for which you want the footer not to be part of the animation. Listing 9.14 demonstrates
how to keep the footer in the same place while linking to another page.

Listing 9.14   Fixing the Footer When the Page Changes

```
00 <!DOCTYPE html>
01 <html>
```

(Continues)

Listing 9.14   Fixing the Footer When the Page Changes (Continued)

```
02 <head>
03   <title>Fixed Footer</title>
04   <meta name="viewport"
05     content="width=device-width, initial-scale=1">
06   <link rel="stylesheet" href=
07     "http://code.jquery.com/mobile/1.1.0/jquery.mobile-1.1.0.min.css">
08   <script type="text/javascript"
09     src="http://code.jquery.com/jquery-1.7.1.min.js">
10   </script>
11   <script type="text/javascript" src=
12     "http://code.jquery.com/mobile/1.1.0/jquery.mobile-1.1.0.min.js">
13   </script>
14
15 </head>
16 <body>
17 <div data-role="page">
18
19   <div data-role="header">
20       <h1>First</h1>
21   </div>
22
23   <div data-role="content">
24       <p>Go to the <a href="#second">second page</a></p>
25   </div>
26
27   <div data-role="footer" data-id="myfooter" data-position="fixed">
28       <p>First page</p>
29   </div>
30
31 </div>
32 <div data-role="page" data-add-back-btn="true" id="second">
33
34   <div data-role="header">
35     <h1>Second</h1>
36   </div>
37
38   <div data-role="content">
39       <p>Content</p>
40       <p>More text</p>
41
42   </div>
43   <div data-role="footer" data-id="myfooter" data-position="fixed">
44       <p>Second page</p>
45   </div>
46
47 </div>
```

Listing 9.14   **Fixing the Footer When the Page Changes (Continued)**

```
48
49 </body>
50 </html>
```

Lines 27 and 43 both contain the `data-position="fixed"` attribute. When you click the link, you see an animation on the content and the header, but the footer remains fixed. You do see a change in the content of the footer, though.

Recipe: Keeping the Footer in a Fixed Position

In versions of jQuery Mobile prior to 1.1, when you scroll the page, the footer temporarily disappears and reappears after you stop scrolling. After version 1.1 was introduced, the header and footer stayed at the top and bottom of the page. However, it would be more elegant if the header and footer would remain on the same location and only the content scrolls. This is where fixed toolbars come into use. Listing 9.15 demonstrates how to use fixed toolbars.

Listing 9.15   **Scrolling Text Without Moving the Footer Position**

```
00 <!DOCTYPE html>
01 <html>
02 <head>
03    <title>Fixed Position</title>
04    <meta name="viewport"
05      content="width=device-width, initial-scale=1">
06    <link rel="stylesheet" href=
07      "http://code.jquery.com/mobile/1.1.0/jquery.mobile-1.1.0.min.css">
08    <script type="text/javascript"
09      src="http://code.jquery.com/jquery-1.7.1.min.js">
10    </script>
11    <script type="text/javascript" src=
12      "http://code.jquery.com/mobile/1.1.0/jquery.mobile-1.1.0.min.js">
13    </script>
14 <script>
15 $.mobile.fixedToolbars
16    .show(true);
17 $.mobile.touchOverflowEnabled = true;
18 </script>
19
20 </head>
21 <body>
22
23 <div data-role="page">
24
```

(Continues)

Listing 9.15   **Scrolling Text Without Moving the Footer Position (Continued)**

```
25   <div data-role="header" data-position="fixed">
26     <h1>Fixed Position</h1>
27   </div>
28
29   <div data-role="content" >
30     <p>
31     Lorem ipsum dolor sit amet, consectetur adipiscing elit. Cras
32     metus tellus, iaculis vestibulum ornare sit amet, semper ac
33     nisi. Suspendisse convallis, libero ut sodales interdum,
34     turpis ligula lacinia justo, a accumsan tellus est at lacus.
35     Morbi ultricies posuere enim, sit amet luctus massa faucibus
36     ut. Maecenas vel mi quis massa volutpat consequat ac non mi.
37     Nam et ornare sapien. Donec vitae magna sed neque lacinia
38     imperdiet. Vivamus tellus velit, molestie in interdum vel,
39     gravida vel mauris. Vivamus justo augue, ultrices ut viverra
40     ut, sollicitudin id lacus. Integer ornare massa ut risus
41     tempus lobortis. Donec ac nisi eu nunc volutpat posuere
42     dapibus ut nisi. Nam sit amet mauris a ante vehicula mattis.
43     Phasellus rutrum rutrum enim, at convallis neque convallis eu.
44     Duis dictum justo venenatis mauris feugiat quis aliquam enim
45     egestas. Integer et ante metus, ut faucibus libero.
46     </p>
47
48     <p>
49     Sed lobortis nunc nec ligula dictum dignissim pellentesque
50     lorem semper. Vivamus dui felis, pulvinar non accumsan ac,
51     facilisis a lectus. In blandit aliquet sapien sed eleifend.
52     Mauris ut arcu nisl. Morbi eget sapien vulputate lectus
53     dapibus congue. Cras id odio nulla, quis viverra massa. Mauris
54     tortor nisl, tincidunt et vestibulum nec, blandit ut purus. In
55     vel massa a erat tristique lacinia. Vestibulum malesuada
56     tristique nunc, in dictum quam faucibus a. Etiam sed enim
57     ante, et aliquam quam. Donec velit velit, cursus at sodales
58     id, accumsan at sapien.
59     </p>
60   </div>
61   <div data-role="footer" data-position="fixed">
62       <p>Fixed footer</p>
63   </div>
64
65 </div>
66
67
68 </body>
69 </html>
```

Lines 16 and 17 ensure that the headers and footers are on the top and bottom of the screen instead of at the top and bottom of only the content. Line 19 sets touchOverflowEnabled to true. This line limits the scrollable area to the content of the page.

Recipe: Hiding and Showing the Footer

When you return to normal footers that are shown and hidden when the user scrolls, you can also trigger whether the footer is hidden or shown from JavaScript code. Listing 9.16 demonstrates how this works.

Listing 9.16   Adding Buttons Triggering a Hide or Show of the Footer

```
00 <!DOCTYPE html>
01 <html>
02 <head>
03   <title>Fixed Footer</title>
04   <meta name="viewport"
05     content="width=device-width, initial-scale=1">
06   <link rel="stylesheet" href=
07     "http://code.jquery.com/mobile/1.1.0/jquery.mobile-1.1.0.min.css">
08   <script type="text/javascript"
09     src="http://code.jquery.com/jquery-1.7.1.min.js">
10   </script>
11   <script type="text/javascript" src=
12     "http://code.jquery.com/mobile/1.1.0/jquery.mobile-1.1.0.min.js">
13   </script>
14   <script>
15   $(document).ready(function() {
16     $.mobile.fixedToolbars
17       .setTouchToggleEnabled(false);
18     $.mobile.fixedToolbars
19       .show(true);
20     $.mobile.touchOverflowEnabled = true;
21     $('#show').on('click', function() {
22       $.mobile.fixedToolbars.show();
23     });
24     $('#hide').on('click', function() {
25       $.mobile.fixedToolbars.hide();
26     });
27   });
28   </script>
29 </head>
30 <body>
31
32   <div data-role="page">
33
34     <div data-role="header" data-position="fixed">
```

(Continues)

Listing 9.16   Adding Buttons Triggering a Hide or Show of the Footer (Continued)

```
35        <h1>Fixed Footer</h1>
36     </div>
37
38     <div data-role="content" >
39         <p>Go to the <a href="#second">second page</a></p>
40         <a href="#" id="show" data-role="button">Show Footer</a>
41         <a href="#" id="hide" data-role="button">Hide Footer</a>
42
43         <p> Lorem ipsum dolor sit amet, consectetur adipiscing elit.
44         Cras metus tellus, iaculis vestibulum ornare sit amet,
45         semper ac nisi. Suspendisse convallis, libero ut sodales
46         interdum, turpis ligula lacinia justo, a accumsan tellus est
47         at lacus. Morbi ultricies posuere enim, sit amet luctus
48         massa faucibus ut. Maecenas vel mi quis massa volutpat
49         consequat ac non mi. Nam et ornare sapien. Donec vitae magna
50         sed neque lacinia imperdiet. Vivamus tellus velit, molestie
51         in interdum vel, gravida vel mauris. Vivamus justo augue,
52         ultrices ut viverra ut, sollicitudin id lacus. Integer
53         ornare massa ut risus tempus lobortis. Donec ac nisi eu nunc
54         volutpat posuere dapibus ut nisi. Nam sit amet mauris a ante
55         vehicula mattis. Phasellus rutrum rutrum enim, at convallis
56         neque convallis eu. Duis dictum justo venenatis mauris
57         feugiat quis aliquam enim egestas. Integer et ante metus, ut
58         faucibus libero. </p>
59
60         <p> Sed lobortis nunc nec ligula dictum dignissim
61         pellentesque lorem semper. Vivamus dui felis, pulvinar non
62         accumsan ac, facilisis a lectus. In blandit aliquet sapien
63         sed eleifend. Mauris ut arcu nisl. Morbi eget sapien
64         vulputate lectus dapibus congue. Cras id odio nulla, quis
65         viverra massa. Mauris tortor nisl, tincidunt et vestibulum
66         nec, blandit ut purus. In vel massa a erat tristique
67         lacinia. Vestibulum malesuada tristique nunc, in dictum quam
68         faucibus a. Etiam sed enim ante, et aliquam quam. Donec
69         velit velit, cursus at sodales id, accumsan at sapien. </p>
70
71     </div>
72     <div data-role="footer" data-position="fixed">
73         <p>Second page</p>
74     </div>
75
76   </div>
77
78
79 </body>
80 </html>
```

Lines 16–26 contain the code that shows and hides the header and footer. When the footer is "hidden," it is still visible at the bottom of the page. It just is not at the bottom of the screen anymore. The same holds for the header.

Recipe: Optimizing Headers and Footers for Fullscreen View

jQuery Mobile offers a feature called fullscreen mode. It means that the header and footer overlap the content by default, and when you click the content, the header and footer disappear. If you install a Web application on your phone with a bookmark icon between your applications or when you integrate your Web application with a native Web application framework such as Phonegap, your application can be displayed fullscreen, without browser address bar, tool bar or status bar. To make optimal use of this fullscreen mode, it is useful if you can hide your own headers and footers completely—unlike the previous example, in which hiding only meant showing the footer at the bottom of the page. Listing 9.17 enables fullscreen mode.

Listing 9.17   Displaying Headers and Footers over Content for Fullscreen View

```
00 <!DOCTYPE html>
01 <html>
02 <head>
03   <title>Fullscreen</title>
04   <meta name="viewport"
05     content="width=device-width, initial-scale=1">
06   <link rel="stylesheet" href=
07     "http://code.jquery.com/mobile/1.1.0/jquery.mobile-1.1.0.min.css">
08   <script type="text/javascript"
09     src="http://code.jquery.com/jquery-1.7.1.min.js">
10   </script>
11   <script type="text/javascript" src=
12     "http://code.jquery.com/mobile/1.1.0/jquery.mobile-1.1.0.min.js">
13   </script>
14 </head>
15 <body>
16
17 <div data-role="page" data-fullscreen="true">
18
19   <div data-role="header" data-position="fixed">
20     <h1>This is drawn <em>over</em> the content section</h1>
21   </div>
22
23   <div data-role="content">
24     <h1>Header</h1>
25     <p>Click to hide the header and footer</p>
26     <p>Click again to get them back</p>
27   </div>
```

(Continues)

Listing 9.17   Displaying Headers and Footers over Content for Fullscreen View (Continued)

```
28
29    <div data-role="footer" data-position="fixed">
30       <p>In a long page, this footer would also be drawn over
31          the content section.</p>
32    </div>
33
34  </div>
35
36  </body>
37  </html>
```

Line 17 provides the option to enable fullscreen mode. To make optimal use of the rest of the page in fullscreen mode, it is useful to introduce some custom CSS styling.

Recipe: Changing Color Schemes with Themes

Chapter 8, Changing the Look and Feel, introduced the *theme roller* to change the look and feel of jQuery UI. jQuery Mobile offers a similar feature that you can obtain at http://jquerymobile.com/themeroller/.

Once you define your own color scheme, you can use it by setting themes inside the HTML. And even if you did not define a custom color scheme, you can still apply the default color schemes, as demonstrated in Listing 9.18.

Listing 9.18   Using Multiple Themes in a Single Page

```
00  <!DOCTYPE html>
01  <html>
02  <head>
03    <title>Themes 1</title>
04    <meta name="viewport"
05      content="width=device-width, initial-scale=1">
06    <link rel="stylesheet" href=
07      "http://code.jquery.com/mobile/1.1.0/jquery.mobile-1.1.0.min.css">
08    <script type="text/javascript"
09      src="http://code.jquery.com/jquery-1.7.1.min.js">
10    </script>
11    <script type="text/javascript" src=
12      "http://code.jquery.com/mobile/1.1.0/jquery.mobile-1.1.0.min.js">
13    </script>
14
15  </head>
16  <body>
17
18  <div data-role="page">
```

Listing 9.18   **Using Multiple Themes in a Single Page (Continued)**

```
19
20    <div data-role="header" data-theme="b">
21      <h1>Themes 1</h1>
22
23      <a href="#first" data-icon="arrow-l">First</a>
24      <a href="#second" data-icon="arrow-r" data-theme="a">Second</a>
25
26    </div>
27    <div data-role="content">
28      <p>Content</p>
29      <a href="#third" data-role="button" data-icon="arrow-u"
30        data-theme="c">Third</a>
31      <a href="#third" data-role="button" data-icon="delete"
32        data-theme="d">Fourth</a>
33      <a href="#third" data-role="button" data-icon="arrow-d"
34        data-theme="e">Fifth</a>
35    </div>
36
37    <div data-role="footer" data-position="fixed" data-theme="c">
38      <div data-role="controlgroup" data-type="horizontal">
39        <a href="#" data-role="button" data-theme="a">First</a>
40        <a href="#" data-role="button" data-theme="b">Second</a>
41        <a href="#" data-role="button" data-theme="c">Third</a>
42        <a href="#" data-role="button" data-theme="d">Fourth</a>
43        <a href="#" data-role="button" data-theme="e">Fifth</a>
44      </div>
45    </div>
46  </div>
47
48
49  </body>
50  </html>
```

Line 20 changes the theme of the header. However, within this header, the button on line 24 can get a different theme. Similarly, in the content section, which has a default theme, all buttons on lines 29–34 can all have different themes. Even buttons grouped together can all have different themes, as demonstrated in lines 39–43.

Instead of placing themes on many different elements, you can also choose a single theme for a complete page. Listing 9.19 demonstrates how to change the theme.

Listing 9.19   **Changing the Theme of a Complete Page**

```
00  <!DOCTYPE html>
01  <html>
02  <head>
```

(Continues)

Listing 9.19   **Changing the Theme of a Complete Page (Continued)**

```
03    <title>Themes 2</title>
04    <meta name="viewport"
05      content="width=device-width, initial-scale=1">
06    <link rel="stylesheet" href=
07      "http://code.jquery.com/mobile/1.0/jquery.mobile-1.0.min.css">
08    <script type="text/javascript"
09      src="http://code.jquery.com/jquery-1.7.1.min.js">
10    </script>
11    <script type="text/javascript" src=
12      "http://code.jquery.com/mobile/1.0/jquery.mobile-1.0.min.js">
13    </script>
14
15 </head>
16 <body>
17
18 <div data-role="page" data-theme="a">
19
20    <div data-role="header" >
21      <h1>Themes 2</h1>
22    </div>
23
24    <div data-role="content">
25      <h1>Heading</h1>
26      <p>Themes can also <a href="#">set the theme</a> for regular
27        content.</p>
28      <ul>
29        <li>Test</li>
30      </ul>
31    </div>
32
33 </div>
34
35
36 </body>
37 </html>
```

Line 18 sets the theme on the complete page. Looking at the resulting screen, you can see that even the background of the content is rendered in a dark colored background with light colored fonts on top.

Recipe: Using Multiple Columns

So far, you have seen pages, headers, footers, and themes. Within a page, sometimes you need to use multiple columns. Particularly when you are working on tablet devices, you might have space left for a more efficient division of the screen. jQuery Mobile offers you default classes that signify separate columns. Listing 9.20 uses them to make rows with multiple buttons.

Listing 9.20 **Demonstrating Columns by Using Buttons**

```
00 <!DOCTYPE html>
01 <html>
02 <head>
03   <title>Layout</title>
04   <meta name="viewport"
05     content="width=device-width, initial-scale=1">
06   <link rel="stylesheet" href=
07     "http://code.jquery.com/mobile/1.1.0/jquery.mobile-1.1.0.min.css">
08   <script type="text/javascript"
09     src="http://code.jquery.com/jquery-1.7.1.min.js">
10   </script>
11   <script type="text/javascript" src=
12     "http://code.jquery.com/mobile/1.1.0/jquery.mobile-1.1.0.min.js">
13   </script>
14
15 </head>
16 <body>
17
18 <div data-role="page">
19
20   <div data-role="header">
21     <h1>Layouts</h1>
22   </div>
23
24   <div data-role="content">
25
26     <div class="ui-grid-a">
27       <div class="ui-block-a">
28         <a href="#" data-role="button">Left</a>
29       </div>
30       <div class="ui-block-b">
31         <a href="#" data-role="button">Right</a>
32       </div>
33     </div>
34
35     <div class="ui-grid-b">
36       <div class="ui-block-a">
37         <a href="#" data-role="button">Left</a>
38       </div>
39       <div class="ui-block-b">
40         <a href="#" data-role="button">Middle</a>
```

(Continues)

Listing 9.20   Demonstrating Columns by Using Buttons (Continued)

```
41        </div>
42        <div class="ui-block-c">
43          <a href="#" data-role="button">Right</a>
44        </div>
45      </div>
46
47      <div class="ui-grid-c">
48        <div class="ui-block-a">
49          <a href="#" data-role="button">Left</a>
50        </div>
51        <div class="ui-block-b">
52          <a href="#" data-role="button">Leftish</a>
53        </div>
54        <div class="ui-block-c">
55          <a href="#" data-role="button">Rightish</a>
56        </div>
57        <div class="ui-block-d">
58          <a href="#" data-role="button">Right</a>
59        </div>
60      </div>
61    </div>
62
63 </body>
64 </html>
```

First, look at lines 26, 35, and 47. These `div`s contain the classes `ui-grid-a`, `ui-grid-b` and `ui-grid-c`. These classes transform the `div`s into containers for multiple columns. The classes indicate 2, 3, and 4 columns, respectively.

Within these `div`s, you find nested `div`s with classes `ui-block-a`, `-b`, `-c`, and `-d`. These are the columns. The column names can be used regardless of which container they are in. Obviously, it is better to avoid a `ui-block-c` inside a `ui-grid-a`, because `ui-grid-a` expects only two columns.

Recipe: Changing Pages by Using JavaScript Calls

At the beginning of this chapter, you have seen recipes that link between different pages with HTML links (`<a href=" ... ">`). jQuery Mobile is a JavaScript framework. And even though you need little custom JavaScript inside jQuery Mobile, you still need the option to change pages from JavaScript. Listing 9.21 demonstrates how to change to a different page by using JavaScript.

Listing 9.21   **Triggering JavaScript to Change a Page**

```
00 <!DOCTYPE html>
01 <html>
02 <head>
03   <title>Change Page</title>
04   <meta name="viewport"
05     content="width=device-width, initial-scale=1">
06   <link rel="stylesheet" href=
07     "http://code.jquery.com/mobile/1.1.0/jquery.mobile-1.1.0.min.css">
08   <script type="text/javascript"
09     src="http://code.jquery.com/jquery-1.7.1.min.js">
10   </script>
11   <script type="text/javascript" src=
12     "http://code.jquery.com/mobile/1.1.0/jquery.mobile-1.1.0.min.js">
13   </script>
14   <script>
15   $(document).ready(function() {
16
17     $('#change').on('click', function(event) {
18       $.mobile.changePage('43b-change-page.html',
19         {transition: 'fade'});
20     });
21
22   });
23   </script>
24 </head>
25 <body>
26
27 <div data-role="page">
28
29   <div data-role="header">
30     <h1>Change page</h1>
31   </div>
32
33   <div data-role="content">
34     <a href="#" id="change" data-role="button">Change Page</a>
35   </div>
36
37 </body>
38 </html>
```

Lines 18 and 19 contain the call to changePage. While changing the page to the specified URL, the code asks to use the fade transition animation instead of the default animation. Similar to the transition animation option, you can use jQuery Mobile to specify other parameters.

Other options are listed in Table 9.2.

Table 9.2   **Additional Options for the changePage() Function**

Option Name	Description
allowSamePageTransition	Set to `true` to change from the current page to the current page with a transition animation
changeHash	Set to `false` to prevent the URL from changing to different hashes
Data	Adds additional URL parameters for an AJAX request
dataUrl	Specifies what to change the window location URL to after changing the page
pageContainer	Changes the location where pages are stored inside the DOM
reloadPage	Set to `true` to reload the page after a page change
reverse	Set to `true` to let the transition go in the opposite direction
showLoadMsg	Set to `false` to prevent the loading message from showing during the page change
role	Changes the role. Similar to setting the `data-role` attribute on a link. You can use this to create a dialog, for example.
transition	Similar to the previous code example: changes the transition animation
type	Sets the HTTP method to get or post

Listing 9.22 provides the content to be loaded into the page.

Listing 9.22   **Providing Content to Load with JavaScript**

```
00 <!DOCTYPE html>
01 <html>
02 <head>
03   <title>Linked Page</title>
04 </head>
```

Listing 9.22 Providing Content to Load with JavaScript (Continued)

```
05 <body>
06
07 <div data-role="page">
08
09   <div data-role="header">
10     <h1>Linked File</h1>
11   </div>
12
13   <div data-role="content">
14     <p><a href="43-change-page.html">Link to an original
15       file</a></p>
16   </div>
17
18 </div>
19
20 </body>
21 </html>
```

Similar to earlier examples, the scripts and styles are intentionally left out of the example to demonstrate that the page is loaded by using an AJAX request. In a real-world example, there are good arguments to provide scripts and styles, because the URL of this page might be requested directly. Any scripts in the header are ignored when the code is loaded from another jQuery Mobile page.

Recipe: Loading Pages by Using JavaScript Calls

When you change to a different page, it will first be loaded into the DOM, before the mobile browser switches to the new page. Using the `data-prefetch` attribute on a link makes jQuery Mobile preload the page before the user clicks the link.

Similar behavior can be achieved even without making links inside the HTML. Listing 9.23 demonstrates how to prefetch data from JavaScript code.

Listing 9.23 Triggering JavaScript to Load a Page

```
00 <!DOCTYPE html>
01 <html>
02 <head>
03   <title>Load Page</title>
04   <meta name="viewport"
05     content="width=device-width, initial-scale=1">
06   <link rel="stylesheet" href=
07     "http://code.jquery.com/mobile/1.1.0/jquery.mobile-1.1.0.min.css">
08   <script type="text/javascript"
09     src="http://code.jquery.com/jquery-1.7.1.min.js">
10   </script>
```

(Continues)

Listing 9.23   Triggering JavaScript to Load a Page (Continued)

```
11   <script type="text/javascript" src=
12     "http://code.jquery.com/mobile/1.1.0/jquery.mobile-1.1.0.min.js">
13   </script>
14   <script>
15   $(document).ready(function() {
16
17     $('#change').on('click', function(event) {
18       $.mobile.loadPage('43b-change-page.html',
19         {transition: 'fade'})
20         .done(function() {
21           alert('Done loading!');
22         });
23     });
24
25   });
26   </script>
27 </head>
28 <body>
29
30 <div data-role="page">
31
32   <div data-role="header">
33     <h1>Load page</h1>
34   </div>
35
36   <div data-role="content">
37     <a href="#" id="change" data-role="button">Change Page</a>
38   </div>
39
40 </body>
41 </html>
```

To see the result of this load action, you need a tool such as Firebug in Firefox or similar developer tools in different browsers. Inside the DOM tree, a new page appears after clicking the button that triggers the code.

Lines 20–22 demonstrate how the `loadPage` function works with promises. The `loadPage()` method sets the page to be loaded and then uses the transition option to set the page to fade into view. For the full list of options and arguments, see http://jquerymobile.com/demos/1.1.0/docs/api/methods.html. Similar to Chapter 5, Communicating with the Server, after loading the page, the `done()` function is called.

Recipe: Attaching Data to DOM Nodes in jQuery Mobile

Chapter 1 introduced the `data()` function. Using this function, you can store data related to specific nodes in the DOM tree in an efficient way. Efficient in this case means without manipulating the DOM-tree itself.

jQuery mobile offers a variant on this function: `jqmData()`. Listing 9.24 demonstrates how you can use it in the same way as the `data()` function. The main difference is that it takes namespaces into account. Namespaces are important in jQuery Mobile to help protect the framework from any other plugins or external libraries you use in conjunction with jQuery Mobile. The jQuery Mobile team recommends that you use the `jqmData()` method over the jQuery core `data()` method when working with jQuery Mobile.

Listing 9.24 **Adding, Retrieving, and Removing Data Attached to a DOM Node in jQuery Mobile**

```
00  <!DOCTYPE html>
01  <html>
02  <head>
03    <title>jQuery Mobile Data Function</title>
04    <meta name="viewport"
05      content="width=device-width, initial-scale=1">
06    <link rel="stylesheet" href=
07      "http://code.jquery.com/mobile/1.1.0/jquery.mobile-1.1.0.min.css">
08    <script type="text/javascript"
09      src="http://code.jquery.com/jquery-1.7.1.min.js">
10    </script>
11    <script type="text/javascript" src=
12      "http://code.jquery.com/mobile/1.1.0/jquery.mobile-1.1.0.min.js">
13    </script>
14    <script>
15    $(document).ready(function() {
16
17      $('#setdata').on('click', function(event) {
18        $('#mydata').jqmData('mykey', 'myvalue');
19      });
20      $('#getdata').on('click', function(event) {
21        alert($('#mydata').jqmData('mykey'));
22      });
23      $('#removedata').on('click', function(event) {
24        $('#mydata').jqmRemoveData('mykey');
25      });
26      $('#select').on('click', function(event) {
27        alert('Number of buttons = ' +
```

(Continues)

Listing 9.24   Adding, Retrieving, and Removing Data Attached to a DOM Node in jQuery Mobile (Continued)

```
28          $('a:jqmData(role="button")').length);
29      });
30
31    });
32    </script>
33  </head>
34  <body>
35
36  <div data-role="page">
37
38    <div data-role="header">
39      <h1>jQuery Mobile Data Function</h1>
40    </div>
41
42    <div data-role="content">
43      <p id="mydata">This paragraph serves as the data container.</p>
44      <a href="#" id="setdata" data-role="button">Set Data</a>
45      <a href="#" id="getdata" data-role="button">Get Data</a>
46      <a href="#" id="removedata" data-role="button">Remove Data</a>
47      <a href="#" id="select" data-role="button">Select</a>
48    </div>
49
50  </body>
51  </html>
```

Lines 18, 21, and 24 demonstrate how to save data, fetch data, and remove data by using the jqmData() function. If you compare this example to the examples from Chapter 1, you will find more similarities than differences.

Similar to the data() function, the jqmData function also reads data- attributes from the HTML. This is especially useful to select certain elements from the DOM tree. Line 28 shows how to use the jqmData() function inside a CSS selector. This takes a little bit of extra code over $('a:data-role="button"'). In return, the code ensures that the namespaces are taken into account.

You can change the namespace with the $.mobile.ns configuration option. If you set the namespace to myns, you should set the button roles by using an attribute named data-myns-role.

Recipe: Utilizing jQuery Mobile Helper Functions

jQuery Mobile uses a number of utility functions under the hood for making AJAX requests. For your convenience, these utility functions are also available for reuse. Listing 9.25 demonstrates the use of the URL utility functions for your own purposes.

Listing 9.25   **Reading URLs with the parseUrl() Function**

```
00 <!DOCTYPE html>
01 <html>
02   <head>
03     <title>URL Utilities</title>
04     <meta name="viewport"
05       content="width=device-width, initial-scale=1">
06     <link rel="stylesheet" href=
07       "http://code.jquery.com/mobile/1.1.0/jquery.mobile-1.1.0.min.css">
08     <script type="text/javascript"
09       src="http://code.jquery.com/jquery-1.7.1.min.js">
10     </script>
11     <script type="text/javascript" src=
12       "http://code.jquery.com/mobile/1.1.0/jquery.mobile-1.1.0.min.js">
13     </script>
14     <script>
15     $(document).ready(function() {
16
17       $('#parse').on('click', function() {
18
19         var url = 'http://user:password@www.pearsonhighered.com' +
20                   ':80/educator/series/Developers-Library' +
21                   '/10483.page?key=value#first-id';
22
23         var parsedUrl =
24           JSON.stringify(
25             $.mobile.path.parseUrl(url)
26           )
27           .replace(/,/g, ',<br>');
28         $('#output').html(parsedUrl);
29       });
30       $('#absolutepath').on('click', function() {
31
32         $('#output').html(
33           $.mobile.path.makePathAbsolute(
34             'newfile.html',
35             '/root/path/oldfile.html'
36           )
37         );
38       });
39       $('#absoluteurl').on('click', function() {
40
41         $('#output').html(
42           $.mobile.path.makeUrlAbsolute(
43             'newfile.html',
44             'http://www.domain.com/root/path/oldfile.html'
```

(Continues)

Listing 9.25   **Reading URLs with the parseUrl() Function (Continued)**

```
45              )
46            );
47          });
48          $('#isabsolute').on('click', function() {
49
50            $('#output').html('isAbsoluteUrl=' +
51              $.mobile.path.isAbsoluteUrl(
52                'http://www.domain.com/root/path/oldfile.html'
53              )
54            );
55          });
56          $('#isrelative').on('click', function() {
57
58            $('#output').html('isRelativeUrl=' +
59              $.mobile.path.isRelativeUrl(
60                'http://www.domain.com/root/path/oldfile.html'
61              )
62            );
63          });
64          $('#samedomain').on('click', function() {
65
66            $('#output').html('isSameDomain=' +
67              $.mobile.path.isSameDomain(
68                'http://www.domain.com/root/path/oldfile.html',
69                'http://www.domain.com/root/path/newfile.html'
70              )
71            );
72          });
73        });
74      </script>
75    </head>
76  <body>
77
78  <div data-role="page">
79
80    <div data-role="header">
81        <h1>URL Utilities</h1>
82    </div>
83
84    <div data-role="content">
85      <a href="#" id="parse" data-role="button">Parse URL</a>
86      <a href="#" id="absolutepath" data-role="button">Make Path
87        Absolute</a>
88      <a href="#" id="absoluteurl" data-role="button">Make URL
89        Absolute</a>
```

Listing 9.25   **Reading URLs with the parseUrl() Function (Continued)**

```
90      <a href="#" id="isabsolute" data-role="button">Is Absolute
91       Url</a>
92      <a href="#" id="isrelative" data-role="button">Is Relative
93       Url</a>
94      <a href="#" id="samedomain" data-role="button">Is Same
95        Domain</a>
96
97      <p id="output">Placeholder for the output</p>
98    </div>
99
100 </div>
101
102 </body>
103 </html>
```

This code example is an aggregation of multiple utility functions. Let's discuss them one by one.

Line 25 demonstrates the parseUrl() function. It is a convenience function to read several parts from a URL string. The function returns an object structure. In this example, it is *stringified* to JSON, and new lines are added after each comma for readability. The parseUrl() function return the values listed in Table 9.3.

Table 9.3   **Options of the parseUrl() function**

Option Name	Description
hash	The fragment URL includes the leading hash (#)
host	Lists the host and port of the URL
hostname	The hostname including the prefix and postfix of the URL
href	The original value that was passed to the function as the URL
pathname	The path to the file or directory passed as the URL
port	The port specified for the URL, if no port was specified this will be empty
protocol	The protocol used for the URL
search	The query of the URL, includes the leading ? in the URL

(Continues)

Table 9.3   **Options of the parseUrl() function (Continued)**

Option Name	Description
authority	The username, password, and host information in the URL
directory	Similar to pathname, this will only give the directory of the URL
domain	The protocol, username/password, and port used in the URL
filename	The requested file in the URL
hrefNoHash	The original URL passed without the hash portion of the URL
hrefNoSearch	The original URL passed without the query portion of the URL
password	The password that was passed in the URL
username	The username that was passed in the URL

Lines 33–36 show the `makePathAbsolute()` function. When you have a relative path—either a filename, a pathname, a combination of both, or perhaps starting with ../—you can combine it with an absolute path and compute a new absolute path.

Lines 42–45 do the same thing, but for a URL with the `makeUrlAbsolute()` function. Similarly, lines 51–53 can check a string to determine whether it contains an absolute URL or not by using the `isAbsoluteUrl()` function. Lines 59–61 show the `isRelativeUrl()` function, which does the exact opposite.

Lines 67–70 use the `isSameDomain()` function to check whether two URLs refer to the same domain. This function is useful when you want to determine if you can use AJAX requests or not. This function compares the protocol as well as the domain name of the parameters passed to determine if they are on the same domain. This also evaluates sub-domains. This means that if you use the `isSameDomain()` function to compare http://foo.bar.com/foo and http://www.bar.com/foo, it will return `false`.

Summary

This chapter started with a basic introduction of jQuery Mobile. This part of jQuery is different from jQuery Core and jQuery UI. It asks you to change your full HTML into a structure that is easy to process by the JavaScript framework.

After this introduction, the basic page navigation mechanism was introduced, including AJAX calls under the hood and transition animations. Next, basic page elements such as the header and footer were discussed. There are several options to change the behavior of the header and footer. You can set them on a static location and even keep them there when you navigate to a different page. It is also possible to hide them on demand.

The chapter ended with a number of custom JavaScript calls that you can use to change the default behavior of jQuery Mobile.

Chapter 10

Interacting with jQuery Mobile

This chapter builds on the fundamentals of Chapter 9, Navigating Pages by Using jQuery Mobile, and adds components to interact with the user within the mobile page structures.

This chapter starts with toolbars, warning signs, and navigation bars. After that, it discusses collapsible elements to hide groups of content. There is an elaborate discussion of jQuery Mobile's support for HTML5 form elements. The chapter ends with many variants of item lists.

Recipe: Displaying Toolbars Inline in Content

The previous chapter introduced the basic page navigation framework offered by jQuery Mobile. Included in the page framework are headers, footers, and dialogs.

Similar to the headers and footers, you can also add elements that resemble toolbars inside the content. Toolbars are generally used for layout and formatting; they are a great way to introduce a break in content as well as help with content grouping. Listing 10.1 provides an example of a custom toolbar inside a content `div`.

Listing 10.1   **Adding a Toolbar Inside a Content Element**

```
00 <!DOCTYPE html>
01 <html>
02 <head>
03   <title>Bar Layout</title>
04   <meta name="viewport"
05     content="width=device-width, initial-scale=1">
06   <link rel="stylesheet" href=
07     "http://code.jquery.com/mobile/1.1.0/jquery.mobile-1.1.0.min.css">
08   <script type="text/javascript"
09     src="http://code.jquery.com/jquery-1.7.1.min.js">
10   </script>
11   <script type="text/javascript" src=
12     "http://code.jquery.com/mobile/1.1.0/jquery.mobile-1.1.0.min.js">
```

(Continues)

Listing 10.1   Adding a Toolbar Inside a Content Element (Continued)

```
13    </script>
14
15  </head>
16  <body>
17
18  <div data-role="page">
19
20    <div data-role="header">
21      <h1>Bar Layout</h1>
22    </div>
23
24    <div data-role="content">
25      <p><a href="#">Link to an external file</a></p>
26      <div class="ui-bar ui-bar-b">
27        <h3>I'm just a div with bar classes and a
28        <a href="#" data-role="button">Button</a></h3>
29      </div>
30
31    </div>
32
33  </div>
34
35  </body>
36  </html>
```

Lines 26–29 contain the inline bar. No JavaScript is needed to create this. The bar just consists of CSS classes. The `ui-bar` class takes care of the shape and font size. The `ui-bar-b` class changes the color to the b swatch of the theme roller, as discussed in Chapter 8, Changing the Look and Feel. for situations in which there is more text in the toolbar than viewable screen space, browsers either make the text and content wrap down a line or truncate it.

(Now, let's hope for the jQuery organization that toy manufacturer Mattel will not sue them for trademark infringement because of the class name that ends with `bar-b`.)

Recipe: Displaying a Warning Bar

Another way to add custom bars is to stack headers on top of the existing header. Listing 10.2 adds a warning header in the yellow theme and contains a button to remove the header.

Listing 10.2   Adding and Removing a Yellow Toolbar to Warn Visitors

```
00  <!DOCTYPE html>
01  <html>
02  <head>
```

Listing 10.2   Adding and Removing a Yellow Toolbar to Warn Visitors (Continued)

```
03   <title>Warning</title>
04   <meta name="viewport"
05     content="width=device-width, initial-scale=1">
06   <link rel="stylesheet" href=
07     "http://code.jquery.com/mobile/1.1.0/jquery.mobile-1.1.0.min.css">
08   <script type="text/javascript"
09     src="http://code.jquery.com/jquery-1.7.1.min.js">
10   </script>
11   <script type="text/javascript" src=
12     "http://code.jquery.com/mobile/1.1.0/jquery.mobile-1.1.0.min.js">
13   </script>
14 <script>
15 $(document).ready(function() {
16   $('#delete').on('click', function() {
17     $(this).parent().detach();
18   });
19 });
20 </script>
21 </head>
22 <body>
23
24 <div data-role="page">
25   <div data-theme="e" data-role="header">
26     <h3>Warning: you can click the x to dismiss </h3>
27     <a href="#" data-role="button" data-icon="delete"
28       data-iconpos="notext" class="ui-btn-right"
29       id="delete">Delete</a>
30   </div>
31   <div data-role="header">
32     <h1>Page with Warning</h1>
33   </div>
34
35   <div data-role="content">
36         <p>Content</p>
37   </div>
38
39 </div>
40
41 </body>
42 </html>
```

Lines 25–29 contain the HTML that adds an additional header on top of the page. Lines 15–19 contain the code to remove the warning bar when the user presses the delete button. On small screen devices, you might notice that the text is truncated with three periods appended to the last bit of text. This is to indicate to the user that there is more text than can currently be shown. When the device is rotated the text reflows into the available space.

Please be careful with the `document.ready()` event: If this example is not directly loaded, but included with an AJAX request from another page, this code is not executed. In such cases, it is better to add the script element inside the body of the HTML and bind the event handler to the `pageinit` event.

Recipe: Adding Menu Bars to Footer Elements

The footers included in Chapter 9 were mostly text containers, used primarily for things such as copyrights statements. With the interactive components that this chapter introduces, the footer can become a more useful element. Listing 10.3 shows how to add a menu inside a footer.

Listing 10.3   **Adding a Menu Inside a Footer**

```
00 <!DOCTYPE html>
01 <html>
02 <head>
03   <title>Footer Menu</title>
04   <meta name="viewport"
05     content="width=device-width, initial-scale=1">
06   <link rel="stylesheet" href=
07     "http://code.jquery.com/mobile/1.1.0/jquery.mobile-1.1.0.min.css">
08   <script type="text/javascript"
09     src="http://code.jquery.com/jquery-1.7.1.min.js">
10   </script>
11   <script type="text/javascript" src=
12     "http://code.jquery.com/mobile/1.1.0/jquery.mobile-1.1.0.min.js">
13   </script>
14
15 </head>
16 <body>
17
18 <div data-role="page">
19
20   <div data-role="header">
21     <h1>Footer Menu</h1>
22   </div>
23
24   <div data-role="content">
25     <p>Content</p>
26   </div>
27
28   <div data-role="footer">
```

Listing 10.3   **Adding a Menu Inside a Footer (Continued)**

```
29      <label for="myselect">Select</label>
30      <select id="myselect">
31        <option>First</option>
32        <option>Second</option>
33        <option>Third</option>
34      </select>
35    </div>
36
37 </div>
38
39
40 </body>
41 </html>
```

As lines 29–34 demonstrate, it is not actually a menu, but rather a selection element. You can attach a `change` event handler with code that triggers when the user selects a different option.

Recipe: Navigating with a Navigation Bar

Instead of struggling with form elements and custom JavaScript handlers, you can also add a navigation bar that specializes in doing this work for you. Listing 10.4 demonstrates how to add the navigation bar directly under the header. Or, to be more accurate, inside the header.

Listing 10.4   **Adding a Navigation Bar with Three Buttons**

```
00 <!DOCTYPE html>
01 <html>
02 <head>
03    <title>Navigation Bar 1</title>
04    <meta name="viewport"
05      content="width=device-width, initial-scale=1">
06    <link rel="stylesheet" href=
07      "http://code.jquery.com/mobile/1.1.0/jquery.mobile-1.1.0.min.css">
08    <script type="text/javascript"
09      src="http://code.jquery.com/jquery-1.7.1.min.js">
10    </script>
11    <script type="text/javascript" src=
12      "http://code.jquery.com/mobile/1.1.0/jquery.mobile-1.1.0.min.js">
13    </script>
14
15 </head>
```

(Continues)

Listing 10.4   **Adding a Navigation Bar with Three Buttons (Continued)**

```
16 <body>
17
18 <div data-role="page">
19
20   <div data-role="header">
21     <h1>Navigation Bar 1</h1>
22
23   <div data-role="navbar">
24     <ul>
25     <li><a href="#first" class="ui-btn-active">First</a></li>
26     <li><a href="#second">Second</a></li>
27     <li><a href="#third">Third</a></li>
28     </ul>
29   </div>
30   </div>
31   <div data-role="content">
32         <p>Content</p>
33   </div>
34
35 </div>
36
37
38 </body>
39 </html>
```

Lines 23–29 contain the div element to be transformed into a navigation bar. Inside the navigation bar, an unordered list with list elements that contain links provides the content of the navigation bar.

If you like, you can add multiple rows to the navigation bar, as demonstrated in Listing 10.5.

Listing 10.5   **Displaying Multiple Rows in the Navigation Bar**

```
00 <!DOCTYPE html>
01 <html>
02 <head>
03   <title>Navigation Bar 2</title>
04   <meta name="viewport"
05     content="width=device-width, initial-scale=1">
06   <link rel="stylesheet" href=
07     "http://code.jquery.com/mobile/1.1.0/jquery.mobile-1.1.0.min.css">
08   <script type="text/javascript"
09     src="http://code.jquery.com/jquery-1.7.1.min.js">
10   </script>
11   <script type="text/javascript" src=
```

Listing 10.5   Displaying Multiple Rows in the Navigation Bar (Continued)

```
12      "http://code.jquery.com/mobile/1.1.0/jquery.mobile-1.1.0.min.js">
13    </script>
14
15  </head>
16  <body>
17
18  <div data-role="page">
19
20    <div data-role="header">
21      <h1>Navigation Bar 2</h1>
22    </div>
23    <div data-role="content">
24      <p>Make a choice from the following options</p>
25    </div>
26    <div data-role="navbar">
27      <ul>
28        <li><a href="#first" class="ui-btn-active">First</a></li>
29        <li><a href="#second">Second</a></li>
30        <li><a href="#third">Third</a></li>
31        <li><a href="#fourth">Fourth</a></li>
32        <li><a href="#fifth">Fifth</a></li>
33        <li><a href="#sixth">Sixth</a></li>
34      </ul>
35    </div>
36
37
38  </div>
39
40
41  </body>
42  </html>
```

From lines 28–33, you cannot see that this navigation bar will be split over multiple rows. If you remove just a single item and you look at the resulting page, you will find five buttons on a single row. Adding more items forces jQuery Mobile to introduce multiple rows for you.

You can also add icons to the buttons in the navigation bar. Listing 10.6 shows you how.

Listing 10.6   Displaying Icons in the Navigation Bar

```
00  <!DOCTYPE html>
01  <html>
02  <head>
```

(Continues)

Listing 10.6   **Displaying Icons in the Navigation Bar (Continued)**

```
03    <title>Navigation Bar 3</title>
04    <meta name="viewport"
05      content="width=device-width, initial-scale=1">
06    <link rel="stylesheet" href=
07      "http://code.jquery.com/mobile/1.1.0/jquery.mobile-1.1.0.min.css">
08    <script type="text/javascript"
09      src="http://code.jquery.com/jquery-1.7.1.min.js">
10    </script>
11    <script type="text/javascript" src=
12      "http://code.jquery.com/mobile/1.1.0/jquery.mobile-1.1.0.min.js">
13    </script>
14
15 </head>
16 <body>
17
18 <div data-role="page">
19
20    <div data-role="header">
21      <h1>Navigation Bar 3</h1>
22
23    <div data-role="navbar" data-iconpos="top">
24      <ul>
25      <li><a href="#first" data-icon="arrow-l">
26        First</a></li>
27      <li><a href="#second" data-icon="arrow-u">
28        Second</a></li>
29      <li><a href="#third" data-icon="arrow-r">
30        Third</a></li>
31      </ul>
32    </div>
33    </div>
34    <div data-role="content">
35          <p>Content</p>
36    </div>
37
38 </div>
39
40
41 </body>
42 </html>
```

On line 23, the `data-iconpos` attribute specifies where all icons should be placed. The example sets them at the top. In many cases, you might prefer to place them at the left or right. By default the icon is placed to the left, but you can also use `data-iconpos="right"`, `data-iconpos="top"`, `data-iconpos="bottom"`, and `data-iconpos="notext"`. The `notext` option removes the text from the button and only shows the icon.

Lines 25, 27, and 29 specify an icon class from the default list of jQuery Mobile icons. If you want to use a custom icon, you should provide CSS classes accordingly, similar to the way jQuery Mobile does.

Recipe: Showing and Hiding Elements by Using Collapsible

jQuery Mobile offers a component to show and hide `divs` under a title. In its most basic form, this component works independent of other components on the page. If this makes you think of the `accordion` component discussed in Chapter 7, Interacting with Widgets, you should take a look at the next recipe. In Listing 10.7, the `collapsible` elements work independently.

Listing 10.7   Hiding and Showing Multiple Groups in Different Themes

```
00 <!DOCTYPE html>
01 <html>
02 <head>
03   <title>Collapsible</title>
04   <meta name="viewport"
05     content="width=device-width, initial-scale=1">
06   <link rel="stylesheet" href=
07     "http://code.jquery.com/mobile/1.1.0/jquery.mobile-1.1.0.min.css">
08   <script type="text/javascript"
09     src="http://code.jquery.com/jquery-1.7.1.min.js">
10   </script>
11   <script type="text/javascript" src=
12     "http://code.jquery.com/mobile/1.1.0/jquery.mobile-1.1.0.min.js">
13   </script>
14
15 </head>
16 <body>
17
18 <div data-role="page">
19
20   <div data-role="header">
21     <h1>Collapsible</h1>
22   </div>
23
24   <div data-role="content">
25
26     <div data-role="collapsible" data-collapsed="false">
```

(Continues)

Listing 10.7   Hiding and Showing Multiple Groups in Different Themes (Continued)

```
27          <h3>Touch to collapse and expand</h3>
28          <p>Hidden content in the collapsible</p>
29       </div>
30
31     <div data-role="collapsible" data-theme="b">
32       <h3>Touch to collapse and expand</h3>
33       <p>Hidden content in the collapsible</p>
34     </div>
35
36     <div data-role="collapsible" data-theme="e"
37       data-content-theme="c">
38       <h3>Touch to collapse and expand</h3>
39       <p>Hidden content in the collapsible</p>
40     </div>
41
42    </div>
43
44 </body>
45 </html>
```

Lines 26–29 contain the first example of a `collapsible` component, in the default styling. The `h3` element becomes the title of the component. Any content following that will be hidden when clicked.

The `collapsible` on line 31 provides a theme that refers to one of the color schemes set with the theme roller. Lines 36–37 provide two different themes: one for the title and one for the content.

Recipe: Adding Accordion Behavior by Using Collapsible Sets

The previous example already mentioned `accordions`. If you put `collapsibles` together into collapsible sets, they will make an `accordion` component. The difference is these `collapsibles` no longer work independently. When you open one, any other one that was already open is closed. Only a single `collapsible` can be opened at a time when they are part of a set. Listing 10.8 demonstrate how to group `collapsibles` into a collapsible set.

Listing 10.8   Grouping Collapsibles into a Collapsible Set

```
00 <!DOCTYPE html>
01 <html>
02 <head>
03   <title>Collapsible Set</title>
04   <meta name="viewport"
```

Listing 10.8   **Grouping Collapsibles into a Collapsible Set (Continued)**

```
05      content="width=device-width, initial-scale=1">
06    <link rel="stylesheet" href=
07      "http://code.jquery.com/mobile/1.1.0/jquery.mobile-1.1.0.min.css">
08    <script type="text/javascript"
09      src="http://code.jquery.com/jquery-1.7.1.min.js">
10    </script>
11    <script type="text/javascript" src=
12      "http://code.jquery.com/mobile/1.1.0/jquery.mobile-1.1.0.min.js">
13    </script>
14
15  </head>
16  <body>
17
18  <div data-role="page">
19
20    <div data-role="header">
21      <h1>Collapsible Set</h1>
22    </div>
23
24    <div data-role="content">
25
26      <div data-role="collapsible-set" data-theme="b"
27       data-content-theme="c">
28
29        <div data-role="collapsible" data-collapsed="false">
30          <h3>Touch to collapse and expand</h3>
31          <p>Hidden content in the collapsible</p>
32        </div>
33
34        <div data-role="collapsible">
35          <h3>Touch to collapse and expand</h3>
36          <p>Hidden content in the collapsible</p>
37        </div>
38
39        <div data-role="collapsible" data-theme="e"
40           data-content-theme="b">
41          <h3>Touch to collapse and expand</h3>
42          <p>Hidden content in the collapsible</p>
43        </div>
44
45      </div>
46
47    </div>
48
49  </body>
50  </html>
```

The `collapsibles` in the set are almost the same as the separate `collapsibles` in the previous recipe. The main difference is that they are contained in a `div` with a `data-role` attribute `collapsible-set`.

Another difference is the ability to set the theme and the content-theme for all `collapsibles` on the set, to prevent duplication. As lines 39 and 40 show, you can still override this setting.

Recipe: Acquiring Basic Text Input by Using Form Fields

HTML offers several types of input fields. jQuery Mobile selects these input fields and changes their styling. It ensures that it is easy to navigate to the input fields and that the text is sufficiently large to read on a mobile device. Listing 10.9 starts with the most basic text input fields.

Listing 10.9   **Displaying Text Input Fields**

```
00 <!DOCTYPE html>
01 <html>
02 <head>
03   <title>Input Field</title>
04   <meta name="viewport"
05     content="width=device-width, initial-scale=1">
06   <link rel="stylesheet" href=
07     "http://code.jquery.com/mobile/1.1.0/jquery.mobile-1.1.0.min.css">
08   <script type="text/javascript"
09     src="http://code.jquery.com/jquery-1.7.1.min.js">
10   </script>
11   <script type="text/javascript" src=
12     "http://code.jquery.com/mobile/1.1.0/jquery.mobile-1.1.0.min.js">
13   </script>
14
15 </head>
16 <body>
17
18 <div data-role="page">
19
20   <div data-role="header">
21     <h1>Input Field</h1>
22   </div>
23
24   <div data-role="content">
25
26     <form action="" method="post">
27
28       <h2>Basics</h2>
```

Listing 10.9   **Displaying Text Input Fields (Continued)**

```
29        <div data-role="fieldcontain">
30          <label for="myinput">Input</label>
31          <input type="text" id="myinput">
32        </div>
33        <div data-role="fieldcontain">
34          <label for="input-placeholder" class="ui-hidden-accessible">
35            Placeholder</label>
36          <input type="text" id="input-placeholder"
37            placeholder="Placeholder">
38        </div>
39        <div data-role="fieldcontain">
40          <label for="mytextarea">Textarea</label>
41          <textarea id="mytextarea"></textarea>
42        </div>
43      </form>
44    </div>
45
46 </body>
47 </html>
```

The examples on lines 29–32 and lines 33–38 are both text input fields. The main difference is in the visibility of the label. In the first example, the label is outside the input field and still readable after the input field is filled.

In the second example, the label is hidden by means of the `ui-hidden-accessible` class, and a `placeholder` attribute is specified. This placeholder text is placed inside the input element when it is empty. This way, the visitor knows what the input element is meant for. When the user types into the input field, the placeholder text disappears. In most cases, it is still clear to the user what the purpose of the input field is from the entered content. For more complex questions than a street name, city, and phone number, it might be better to avoid placeholders and instead use labels.

Lines 39–42 demonstrate how to initialize a multiline text area.

> **Note**
> Each pair of label and input fields is contained within a `div` that has an attribute of `data-role=fieldcontain`. jQuery Mobile uses these container `div`s to help with the alignment of labels and input fields.

Recipe: Acquiring Calendar-Based Input

In Chapter 7, a calendar input component was presented. In HTML 4 Web forms, inputting dates is not really user friendly. Web designers usually had the choice between offering a single input field and enforce a specific input format, offer three input fields, with or without drop-downs menus, or add a JavaScript-based calendar component.

HTML5 offers new input elements by which browsers can provide native controls to help the user input values. Date input is a good example of these new input fields. Mobile phones seem to have implemented these new input methods faster than the normal Web browsers. On many platforms, there already are date input components available in a user-friendly way. Listing 10.10 demonstrates the calendar-related input fields.

Listing 10.10   **Displaying Calendar Input Fields**

```
00 <!DOCTYPE html>
01 <html>
02 <head>
03   <title>Calendar Input</title>
04   <meta name="viewport"
05     content="width=device-width, initial-scale=1">
06   <link rel="stylesheet" href=
07     "http://code.jquery.com/mobile/1.1.0/jquery.mobile-1.1.0.min.css">
08   <script type="text/javascript"
09     src="http://code.jquery.com/jquery-1.7.1.min.js">
10   </script>
11   <script type="text/javascript" src=
12     "http://code.jquery.com/mobile/1.1.0/jquery.mobile-1.1.0.min.js">
13   </script>
14
15 </head>
16 <body>
17
18 <div data-role="page">
19
20   <div data-role="header">
21     <h1>Calendar Input</h1>
22   </div>
23
24   <div data-role="content">
25
26     <form action="" method="post">
27
28       <h2>Calendar</h2>
29       <div data-role="fieldcontain">
30         <label for="mytime">Time</label>
31         <input type="time" id="mytime">
32       </div>
33       <div data-role="fieldcontain">
34         <label for="mydate">Date</label>
35         <input type="date" id="mydate">
36       </div>
37       <div data-role="fieldcontain">
38         <label for="mymonth">Month</label>
```

Listing 10.10   **Displaying Calendar Input Fields (Continued)**

```
39            <input type="month" id="mymonth">
40          </div>
41          <div data-role="fieldcontain">
42            <label for="myweek">Week</label>
43            <input type="week" id="myweek">
44          </div>
45          <div data-role="fieldcontain">
46            <label for="mydatetime">Datetime</label>
47            <input type="datetime" id="mydatetime">
48          </div>
49          <div data-role="fieldcontain">
50            <label for="mydatetimelocal">Datetime-local</label>
51            <input type="datetime-local" id="mydatetimelocal">
52          </div>
53        </form>
54      </div>
55
56  </body>
57  </html>
```

Lines 29–32 is where you can input a time. Pay special attention to the `type="time"` attribute on line 31. This is native HTML5; it functions without jQuery Mobile. On platforms without support for HTML5, jQuery Mobile might degrade attributes like these including `color`, `date`, `datetime`, `datetime-local`, `email`, `month`, `number`, `range`, `search`, `tel`, `time`, `url`, and `week` to `type="text"` and provide JavaScript-based alternatives. Whenever possible, the native components should be preferred.

Lines 33–52 contain similar input fields for `date`, `month`, `week`, `datetime`, and `datetime-local`. Test these examples on several mobile devices to see what happens. For example, on iPhone and iPad, you will find these input fields more user friendly than on Safari running on a Mac.

Recipe: Displaying Input Fields by Using Alternative Keyboards

Calendar inputs require completely different input components. There are also fields that look like regular text input fields but with different requirements. Mobile devices with onscreen keyboards have limited screen space in which to present a full keyboard. So unlike regular keyboards, there is a selection of keys, and to access different keys you need to enter a submenu.

Especially when inputting specific structures such as phone numbers, e-mail addresses and URLs, it takes a lot of keyboard switching to complete a single input field. Luckily, mobile devices offer keyboard variants specialized in entering phone numbers, e-mail addresses, and URLs. Listing 10.11 demonstrates these keyboards.

Listing 10.11   **Using Purpose-Specific Keyboards**

```
00 <!DOCTYPE html>
01 <html>
02 <head>
03   <title>Keyboards</title>
04   <meta name="viewport"
05     content="width=device-width, initial-scale=1">
06   <link rel="stylesheet" href=
07     "http://code.jquery.com/mobile/1.1.0/jquery.mobile-1.1.0.min.css">
08   <script type="text/javascript"
09     src="http://code.jquery.com/jquery-1.7.1.min.js">
10   </script>
11   <script type="text/javascript" src=
12     "http://code.jquery.com/mobile/1.1.0/jquery.mobile-1.1.0.min.js">
13   </script>
14
15 </head>
16 <body>
17
18 <div data-role="page">
19
20   <div data-role="header">
21     <h1>Keyboards</h1>
22   </div>
23
24   <div data-role="content">
25
26     <form action="" method="post">
27
28       <div data-role="fieldcontain">
29         <label for="mynumber">Number</label>
30         <input type="number" id="mynumber">
31       </div>
32       <div data-role="fieldcontain">
33         <label for="myemail">E-Mail</label>
34         <input type="email" id="myemail">
35       </div>
36       <div data-role="fieldcontain">
37         <label for="myurl">Url</label>
38         <input type="url" id="myurl">
39       </div>
40       <div data-role="fieldcontain">
41         <label for="mytel">Phone number</label>
42         <input type="tel" id="mytel">
43       </div>
44
45     </form>
```

Listing 10.11   **Using Purpose-Specific Keyboards (Continued)**

```
46    </div>
47
48  </body>
49  </html>
```

Lines 28–31 start with the input of a number. This is still different from a phone number. It depends on the mobile device how this is implemented. In iOS, you go directly to the numeric keyboard that is usually hidden under an option button on the regular keyboard.

Lines 32–35 and 36–39 contain the input fields for e-mail and URL. Each has a variation on the normal qwerty-keyboard, with special attention for characters such as @ and /.

Finally, lines 40–43 are designed to accept the input of a phone number. In iOS, you get the same number pad as you get when you want to dial a number on your cell phone.

Again, pay attention to the `type` attributes on the `input` elements. These are all HTML5 standard input types, which jQuery Mobile makes clever use of for styling and cross-device display.

Recipe: Displaying Specialized Input Fields

In addition to special input fields that have their own keyboards, there are also a number of input fields with a specific look and feel. Listing 10.12 demonstrates the search, password, and color input fields.

Listing 10.12   **Displaying Search, Password, and Color Input Fields**

```
00  <!DOCTYPE html>
01  <html>
02  <head>
03    <title>Input Variants</title>
04    <meta name="viewport"
05      content="width=device-width, initial-scale=1">
06    <link rel="stylesheet" href=
07      "http://code.jquery.com/mobile/1.1.0/jquery.mobile-1.1.0.min.css">
08    <script type="text/javascript"
09      src="http://code.jquery.com/jquery-1.7.1.min.js">
10    </script>
11    <script type="text/javascript" src=
12      "http://code.jquery.com/mobile/1.1.0/jquery.mobile-1.1.0.min.js">
13    </script>
14
15  </head>
```

(Continues)

Listing 10.12   Displaying Search, Password, and Color Input Fields (Continued)

```
16 <body>
17
18 <div data-role="page">
19
20   <div data-role="header">
21     <h1>Input Variants</h1>
22   </div>
23
24   <div data-role="content">
25
26     <form action="" method="post">
27
28       <div data-role="fieldcontain">
29         <label for="mypassword">Password</label>
30         <input type="password" id="mypassword">
31       </div>
32       <div data-role="fieldcontain">
33         <label for="mysearch">Search</label>
34         <input type="search" id="mysearch">
35       </div>
36       <div data-role="fieldcontain">
37         <label for="mycolor">Color</label>
38         <input type="color" id="mycolor">
39       </div>
40     </form>
41   </div>
42
43 </body>
44 </html>
```

Inputting a password on lines 28–31 requires no different keyboard. It is important that the password remains hidden on the screen, so the view is different. Depending on user preferences, either the complete password remains hidden, or just a single character is shown at a time.

Search input fields like the one on lines 32–35 can look a little bit different than normal text input fields. In iOS, the corners are rounder and it contains a magnifying glass in the left corner. In addition to different appearance, a browser might select search input fields and integrate them into the browser toolbars. That is not yet standard behavior at this time.

Finally, a color input field such as in lines 36–39 can lead to a completely different input component. In iOS, it is indistinguishable from a regular text field. This might change over time if color input becomes more popular.

Recipe: Acquiring Integers by Using Sliders

Inputting integers can require a completely different kind of input element than a text field. For example, you could use a slider. Listing 10.13 demonstrates how to input an integer by using a slider.

Listing 10.13   **Displaying a Slider to Input an Integer Value**

```
00 <!DOCTYPE html>
01 <html>
02 <head>
03   <title>Range</title>
04   <meta name="viewport"
05     content="width=device-width, initial-scale=1">
06   <link rel="stylesheet" href=
07     "http://code.jquery.com/mobile/1.1.0/jquery.mobile-1.1.0.min.css">
08   <script type="text/javascript"
09     src="http://code.jquery.com/jquery-1.7.1.min.js">
10   </script>
11   <script type="text/javascript" src=
12     "http://code.jquery.com/mobile/1.1.0/jquery.mobile-1.1.0.min.js">
13   </script>
14
15 </head>
16 <body>
17
18 <div data-role="page">
19
20   <div data-role="header">
21     <h1>Range</h1>
22   </div>
23
24   <div data-role="content">
25
26     <form action="#" method="post">
27
28       <div data-role="fieldcontain">
29         <label for="myslider">Slider</label>
30         <input type="range" id="myslider"
31           min="0" max="10" value="3">
32       </div>
33
34     </form>
35   </div>
36
37 </body>
38 </html>
```

Lines 28–32 contain an input of type `range`. The fact that this is implemented on the screen using a slider, is a choice of either the mobile device or of jQuery Mobile. It could also have been implemented differently.

For sliders, it is important to set a minimum and maximum value. For values that could increase infinitely, a regular text field for inputting numbers is preferable. Users of jQuery Mobile 1.0 who use jQuery 1.7.1 might notice that the slider does not work with the mouse on desktop browsers. To remedy this, upgrade to jQuery Mobile 1.1, or downgrade the included jQuery library to 1.6.4.

Recipe: Setting Binaries with Flip Switches

Many forms contain input fields that ask the visitor to make a choice between two values. Something is either yes or no, on or off, male or female, and so on. You can choose to use either two radio buttons, a single check box, or a select box with two options.

In some cases, a more user-friendly choice is to provide a slider-like switch that can be switched on and off. In iOS, this switch is similar to the switches you can find in the phone's settings menu. Listing 10.14 shows how to create these by using jQuery Mobile.

Listing 10.14   Displaying a Select as a Flip Switch

```
00 <!DOCTYPE html>
01 <html>
02 <head>
03   <title>Flip</title>
04   <meta name="viewport"
05     content="width=device-width, initial-scale=1">
06   <link rel="stylesheet" href=
07     "http://code.jquery.com/mobile/1.1.0/jquery.mobile-1.1.0.min.css">
08   <script type="text/javascript"
09     src="http://code.jquery.com/jquery-1.7.1.min.js">
10   </script>
11   <script type="text/javascript" src=
12     "http://code.jquery.com/mobile/1.1.0/jquery.mobile-1.1.0.min.js">
13   </script>
14
15 </head>
16 <body>
17
18 <div data-role="page">
19
20   <div data-role="header">
21     <h1>Flip</h1>
22   </div>
23
24   <div data-role="content">
```

Listing 10.14   **Displaying a Select as a Flip Switch (Continued)**

```
25
26      <form action="" method="post">
27
28        <div data-role="fieldcontain">
29          <label for="myflip">Flip</label>
30          <select id="myflip" data-role="slider">
31            <option>Off</option>
32            <option>On</option>
33          </select>
34        </div>
35
36      </form>
37    </div>
38
39 </body>
40 </html>
```

Lines 28–34 show that creating a flip-switch with jQuery Mobile uses HTML that is a `select` element. After jQuery Mobile initialized its widgets, there is almost nothing left from the old `select` element. But in case jQuery Mobile is unavailable, the select element provides a clean degradation scenario.

Recipe: Selecting a Single Element by Using Radio Buttons

You're probably familiar with regular radio buttons in Web forms. You can also use these on mobile devices. When combined with jQuery Mobile, you can make them look nice and user friendly. Listing 10.15 demonstrates both a vertical and a horizontal set of radio buttons.

Listing 10.15   **Displaying Vertical and Horizontal Radio Button Groups**

```
00 <!DOCTYPE html>
01 <html>
02 <head>
03   <title>Radio</title>
04   <meta name="viewport"
05     content="width=device-width, initial-scale=1">
06   <link rel="stylesheet" href=
07     "http://code.jquery.com/mobile/1.1.0/jquery.mobile-1.1.0.min.css">
08   <script type="text/javascript"
09     src="http://code.jquery.com/jquery-1.7.1.min.js">
10   </script>
```

(Continues)

Listing 10.15   **Displaying Vertical and Horizontal Radio Button Groups (Continued)**

```
11    <script type="text/javascript" src=
12      "http://code.jquery.com/mobile/1.1.0/jquery.mobile-1.1.0.min.js">
13    </script>
14
15 </head>
16 <body>
17
18 <div data-role="page">
19
20    <div data-role="header">
21      <h1>Radio</h1>
22    </div>
23
24    <div data-role="content">
25
26      <form action="" method="post">
27
28        <div data-role="fieldcontain">
29          <fieldset data-role="controlgroup">
30
31            <legend>Select from Radio:</legend>
32
33              <input type="radio" name="myradio" id="myradio1"
34                value="1" checked="checked">
35              <label for="myradio1">First</label>
36
37              <input type="radio" name="myradio" id="myradio2"
38                value="2">
39              <label for="myradio2">Second</label>
40
41              <input type="radio" name="myradio" id="myradio3"
42                value="3">
43              <label for="myradio3">Third</label>
44
45          </fieldset>
46
47          <fieldset data-role="controlgroup" data-type="horizontal">
48
49            <legend>Select from Horizontal:</legend>
50
51              <input type="radio" name="myhoriz" id="myhoriz1"
52                value="1" checked="checked">
53              <label for="myhoriz1">First</label>
54
55              <input type="radio" name="myhoriz" id="myhoriz2"
```

```
56              value="2">
57          <label for="myhoriz2">Second</label>
58
59          <input type="radio" name="myhoriz" id="myhoriz3"
60              value="3">
61          <label for="myhoriz3">Third</label>
62
63        </fieldset>
64
65      </div>
66
67    </form>
68  </div>
69
70 </body>
71 </html>
```

Lines 28–45 contain the vertical set of radio buttons. These look similar to regular radio buttons but with more styling added to them. The radio buttons are contained within a `fieldset`. This is also a good HTML practice outside jQuery Mobile. By adding a `data-role="controlgroup"`, the set of radio buttons is displayed as a single group with rounded corners on the top and bottom.

Starting on line 47 is the exact same group of radio buttons with an attribute `data-type="horizontal"` added to it. The result is completely different though. On the screen, this group of radio buttons appears like regular buttons. When you start clicking them, you see that they behave similar to a radio button; only one of the buttons can be selected at a time.

Recipe: Selecting Multiple Elements by Using Check Boxes

The previous recipe demonstrated how to style a group of radio buttons by using jQuery Mobile. You can do the exact same thing with a group of check boxes. Listing 10.16 shows how to do this.

Listing 10.16   **Displaying Vertical and Horizontal Check Box Groups**

```
00 <!DOCTYPE html>
01 <html>
02 <head>
03   <title>Checkboxes</title>
04   <meta name="viewport"
```

(Continues)

Listing 10.16   Displaying Vertical and Horizontal Check Box Groups (Continued)

```
05      content="width=device-width, initial-scale=1">
06    <link rel="stylesheet" href=
07      "http://code.jquery.com/mobile/1.1.0/jquery.mobile-1.1.0.min.css">
08    <script type="text/javascript"
09      src="http://code.jquery.com/jquery-1.7.1.min.js">
10    </script>
11    <script type="text/javascript" src=
12      "http://code.jquery.com/mobile/1.1.0/jquery.mobile-1.1.0.min.js">
13    </script>
14
15 </head>
16 <body>
17
18 <div data-role="page">
19
20   <div data-role="header">
21     <h1>Checkboxes</h1>
22   </div>
23
24   <div data-role="content">
25
26     <form action="" method="post">
27
28       <div data-role="fieldcontain">
29         <fieldset data-role="controlgroup">
30
31           <legend>Select from Checkbox:</legend>
32
33             <input type="checkbox" name="mycheck" id="mycheck1"
34               value="1" checked="checked">
35             <label for="mycheck1">First</label>
36
37             <input type="checkbox" name="mycheck" id="mycheck2"
38               value="2">
39             <label for="mycheck2">Second</label>
40
41             <input type="checkbox" name="mycheck" id="mycheck3"
42               value="3">
43             <label for="mycheck3">Third</label>
44
45         </fieldset>
46
47         <fieldset data-role="controlgroup" data-type="horizontal">
```

Listing 10.16   **Displaying Vertical and Horizontal Check Box Groups (Continued)**

```
48
49          <legend>Select from Horizontal:</legend>
50
51          <input type="checkbox" name="myhoriz" id="myhoriz1"
52            value="1" checked="checked">
53          <label for="myhoriz1">First</label>
54
55          <input type="checkbox" name="myhoriz" id="myhoriz2"
56            value="2">
57          <label for="myhoriz2">Second</label>
58
59          <input type="checkbox" name="myhoriz" id="myhoriz3"
60            value="3">
61          <label for="myhoriz3">Third</label>
62
63        </fieldset>
64
65      </div>
66
67    </form>
68  </div>
69
70 </body>
71 </html>
```

Lines 29–45 are similar to the previous recipe, but they define check boxes instead of radio buttons. The check boxes are styled and placed together into a group by using the `data-role="controlgroup"` attribute.

Line 47 provides the exact same structure with a `data-type="horizontal"` attribute. The result is a set of buttons that look like regular buttons but behave like check boxes when you start clicking them; you can check as many buttons in the group as you like.

Recipe: Selecting Elements from Drop-Down Lists

The last native form element that deserves attention is the `select` element. You have already seen a `select` element being added to a footer with the intention of creating a menu-like structure. Of course, you can also use `select` elements within the regular content. jQuery Mobile provides nice styling and a user-friendly drop-down list when no user-friendly native component is available. Listing 10.17 shows a `select` element on its own and two examples of select elements in control groups.

Listing 10.17   **Displaying Drop-Down Variants**

```
00 <!DOCTYPE html>
01 <html>
02 <head>
03   <title>Select</title>
04   <meta name="viewport"
05     content="width=device-width, initial-scale=1">
06   <link rel="stylesheet" href=
07     "http://code.jquery.com/mobile/1.1.0/jquery.mobile-1.1.0.min.css">
08   <script type="text/javascript"
09     src="http://code.jquery.com/jquery-1.7.1.min.js">
10   </script>
11   <script type="text/javascript" src=
12     "http://code.jquery.com/mobile/1.1.0/jquery.mobile-1.1.0.min.js">
13   </script>
14
15 </head>
16 <body>
17
18 <div data-role="page">
19
20   <div data-role="header">
21     <h1>Select</h1>
22   </div>
23
24   <div data-role="content">
25
26     <form action="" method="post">
27
28       <div data-role="fieldcontain">
29
30         <label for="myselect">Select</label>
31         <select>
32           <option value="1">First</option>
33           <option value="2">Second</option>
34           <option value="3">Third</option>
35         </select>
36
37       </div>
38
39       <fieldset data-role="controlgroup">
40
41         <select data-theme="e" data-native-menu="false">
42           <option value="1">First</option>
43           <option value="2">Second</option>
44           <option value="3">Third</option>
45         </select>
```

Listing 10.17   **Displaying Drop-Down Variants (Continued)**

```
46            <select>
47              <option value="1">First</option>
48              <option value="2">Second</option>
49              <option value="3">Third</option>
50            </select>
51            <select>
52              <option value="1">First</option>
53              <option value="2">Second</option>
54              <option value="3">Third</option>
55            </select>
56          </fieldset>
57
58          <fieldset data-type="horizontal" data-role="controlgroup">
59
60            <select>
61              <option value="1">First</option>
62              <option value="2">Second</option>
63              <option value="3">Third</option>
64            </select>
65            <select>
66              <option value="1">First</option>
67              <option value="2">Second</option>
68              <option value="3">Third</option>
69            </select>
70            <select>
71              <option value="1">First</option>
72              <option value="2">Second</option>
73              <option value="3">Third</option>
74            </select>
75          </fieldset>
76
77
78        </form>
79      </div>
80
81  </body>
82  </html>
```

The first single select element on lines 28–35 is relatively straightforward. It is a regular select element with a label, contained within a div with an attribute of data-role=fieldcontain. The fieldcontain helps jQuery Mobile position the input elements and labels on the screen.

Next, line 39 surrounds a set of simple select elements with a fieldset element by using data-role="controlgroup". The result is a vertical stack with rounded corners.

Similarly, line 58 creates a `controlgroup` with `data-type="horizontal"`. If you have tried the previous recipes for groups of check boxes and radio buttons, you will recognize the result. It is a horizontal line with three select elements placed in a row with rounded corners.

When using iOS devices, jQuery Mobile 1.0 did not account for the zooming that the devices do when select boxes are used. In the 1.1 release, this has been accounted for and, while a slight zoom does occur, it should not leave you zoomed in when you are finished using the select box.

Recipe: Displaying Native Forms by Using jQuery Mobile Off

There might be cases for which you need form components that are not modified by jQuery Mobile. In such cases, you can turn jQuery Mobile off. Or, at least the processing of form elements, because the rest of jQuery Mobile might still be useful. Listing 10.18 demonstrates how to turn off jQuery Mobile on specific form elements.

Listing 10.18   Turning Off jQuery Mobile

```
00 <!DOCTYPE html>
01 <html>
02 <head>
03   <title>jQuery Mobile Off</title>
04   <meta name="viewport"
05     content="width=device-width, initial-scale=1">
06   <link rel="stylesheet" href=
07     "http://code.jquery.com/mobile/1.1.0/jquery.mobile-1.1.0.min.css">
08   <script type="text/javascript"
09     src="http://code.jquery.com/jquery-1.7.1.min.js">
10   </script>
11   <script type="text/javascript" src=
12     "http://code.jquery.com/mobile/1.1.0/jquery.mobile-1.1.0.min.js">
13   </script>
14
15 </head>
16 <body>
17
18 <div data-role="page">
19
20   <div data-role="header">
21     <h1>jQuery Mobile Off</h1>
22   </div>
23
```

Listing 10.18 **Turning Off jQuery Mobile (Continued)**

```
24    <div data-role="content">
25
26      <form action="" method="post" data-ajax="false">
27
28        <h2>Basics</h2>
29        <div data-role="fieldcontain">
30          <label for="myinput">Input</label>
31          <input type="text" id="myinput" data-role="none">
32        </div>
33        <div data-role="fieldcontain">
34          <label for="myselect">Select</label>
35          <select data-role="none">
36            <option value="1">First</option>
37            <option value="2">Second</option>
38            <option value="3">Third</option>
39          </select>
40        </div>
41        <fieldset data-role="controlgroup">
42
43          <legend>Select from Checkbox:</legend>
44
45          <input type="checkbox" name="mycheck" id="mycheck1"
46            value="1" checked="checked" data-role="none">
47          <label for="mycheck1">First</label>
48
49          <input type="checkbox" name="mycheck" id="mycheck2"
50            value="2" data-role="none">
51          <label for="mycheck2">Second</label>
52
53          <input type="checkbox" name="mycheck" id="mycheck3"
54            value="3" data-role="none">
55          <label for="mycheck3">Third</label>
56
57        </fieldset>
58      </form>
59    </div>
60
61 </body>
62 </html>
```

Lines 31, 35, 46, 50, and 54 all contain a `data-role="none"` attribute. The result is a form with standard HTML form components, unmodified by jQuery.

Recipe: Displaying Lists of Elements

jQuery Mobile provides a uniform look and feel for elements in pages. From a user's perspective, it might be difficult to see whether you are interacting with a form or a different component. jQuery Mobile offers several variations to present a list on a mobile device in a user-friendly way. Listing 10.19 shows a list in its simplest form.

Listing 10.19   **Displaying Simple List Items**

```
00 <!DOCTYPE html>
01 <html>
02 <head>
03   <title>List</title>
04   <meta name="viewport"
05     content="width=device-width, initial-scale=1">
06   <link rel="stylesheet" href=
07     "http://code.jquery.com/mobile/1.1.0/jquery.mobile-1.1.0.min.css">
08   <script type="text/javascript"
09     src="http://code.jquery.com/jquery-1.7.1.min.js">
10   </script>
11   <script type="text/javascript" src=
12     "http://code.jquery.com/mobile/1.1.0/jquery.mobile-1.1.0.min.js">
13   </script>
14
15 </head>
16 <body>
17
18 <div data-role="page">
19
20   <div data-role="header">
21     <h1>Lists</h1>
22   </div>
23
24   <div data-role="content">
25     <h2>Unordered List</h2>
26     <ul data-role="listview" data-inset="true">
27       <li>One</li>
28       <li>Two</li>
29       <li>Three</li>
30     </ul>
31
32     <h2>Ordered List</h2>
33     <ol data-role="listview">
34       <li>One</li>
35       <li>Two</li>
36       <li>Three</li>
37     </ol>
```

Listing 10.19   **Displaying Simple List Items (Continued)**

```
38    </div>
39
40  </body>
41  </html>
```

Lines 26–30 contain an unordered list, the most common form of a list. The content is just text, so this list component is not interactive at all. Finally, on line 26, there is a `data-inset="true"` attribute. This adds a margin around the list and gives the list rounded corners. You can compare this with the ordered list to see the difference.

Lines 33–37 contain an ordered list. In addition to the lack of a `data-inset="true"` attribute, any items in an ordered list are assigned a number. This numbering behavior is no different than using an ordered list in standard HTML.

In all Web pages, you can nest both ordered lists and unordered list to create a tree-like structure. Only the way these nested lists are handled is different in jQuery Mobile. Listing 10.20 demonstrates what happens with a simple nested structure.

Listing 10.20   **Nesting Lists**

```
00  <!DOCTYPE html>
01  <html>
02  <head>
03    <title>Nested Lists</title>
04    <meta name="viewport"
05      content="width=device-width, initial-scale=1">
06    <link rel="stylesheet" href=
07      "http://code.jquery.com/mobile/1.1.0/jquery.mobile-1.1.0.min.css">
08    <script type="text/javascript"
09      src="http://code.jquery.com/jquery-1.7.1.min.js">
10    </script>
11    <script type="text/javascript" src=
12      "http://code.jquery.com/mobile/1.1.0/jquery.mobile-1.1.0.min.js">
13    </script>
14
15  </head>
16  <body>
17
18  <div data-role="page">
19
20    <div data-role="header">
21      <h1>Nested Lists</h1>
22    </div>
23
```

(Continues)

Listing 10.20   **Nesting Lists (Continued)**

```
24   <div data-role="content">
25     <ul data-role="listview">
26       <li>One</li>
27       <li>Two</li>
28       <li>Three
29         <ol data-role="listview">
30           <li>One</li>
31           <li>Two</li>
32           <li>Three</li>
33         </ol>
34       </li>
35     </ul>
36
37   </div>
38
39 </body>
40 </html>
```

Lines 25–35 set up an ordered list inside an unordered list. It might just as well have been an unordered list inside an ordered or unordered list. What you expect is a tree with six elements on the screen. What you get, is a single unordered list with three elements. The third element contains an arrow on the right side. When you click the third element, it seems like you navigate to a new page. Technically, this is exactly what jQuery Mobile does with nested lists. It generates new pages to show them.

You can still do more with a single list without nesting or navigating to new pages. For example, if you want lists to have an extra button for each list item, you can follow the example in Listing 10.21.

Listing 10.21   **Splitting Lists into Columns**

```
00 <!DOCTYPE html>
01 <html>
02 <head>
03   <title>Split Lists</title>
04   <meta name="viewport"
05     content="width=device-width, initial-scale=1">
06   <link rel="stylesheet" href=
07     "http://code.jquery.com/mobile/1.1.0/jquery.mobile-1.1.0.min.css">
08   <script type="text/javascript"
09     src="http://code.jquery.com/jquery-1.7.1.min.js">
10   </script>
11   <script type="text/javascript" src=
12     "http://code.jquery.com/mobile/1.1.0/jquery.mobile-1.1.0.min.js">
13   </script>
```

Listing 10.21   **Splitting Lists into Columns (Continued)**

```
14
15 </head>
16 <body>
17
18 <div data-role="page">
19
20   <div data-role="header">
21     <h1>Split Lists</h1>
22   </div>
23
24   <div data-role="content">
25     <h2>Unordered List</h2>
26     <ul data-role="listview" data-split-icon="gear">
27       <li><a href="#">One</a><a href="#">Button</a></li>
28       <li><a href="#">Two</a><a href="#">Button</a></li>
29       <li><a href="#">Three</a><a href="#">Button</a></li>
30     </ul>
31
32   </div>
33
34 </body>
35 </html>
```

There are two differences between Listing 10.21 and Listing 10.20. First, the elements are no longer static text, but buttons. Second, there is an additional button on the right. Inside the HTML, it seems like two links in a single list item. To transform the second link into an icon, the ul item on line 26 contains an attribute data-split-icon="gear". The value gear could be any other icon from the available icon set.

When lists become a little bit longer, it can become more difficult to find your way inside the list. To help visitors navigate the list, you can add headers between the line items. You can decide yourself what headers you choose. The alphabet can be a good default, but it might just as well be music genres or different groups. Listing 10.22 shows an alphabetical grouping of numbers.

Listing 10.22   **Displaying Headers Between List Items**

```
00 <!DOCTYPE html>
01 <html>
02 <head>
03   <title>List Divider</title>
04   <meta name="viewport"
05     content="width=device-width, initial-scale=1">
```

(Continues)

Listing 10.22   **Displaying Headers Between List Items (Continued)**

```
06    <link rel="stylesheet" href=
07      "http://code.jquery.com/mobile/1.1.0/jquery.mobile-1.1.0.min.css">
08    <script type="text/javascript"
09      src="http://code.jquery.com/jquery-1.7.1.min.js">
10    </script>
11    <script type="text/javascript" src=
12      "http://code.jquery.com/mobile/1.1.0/jquery.mobile-1.1.0.min.js">
13    </script>
14
15  </head>
16  <body>
17
18  <div data-role="page">
19
20    <div data-role="header">
21      <h1>List with Dividers</h1>
22    </div>
23
24    <div data-role="content">
25      <ul data-role="listview">
26        <li data-role="list-divider">E</li>
27        <li>Eleven</li>
28        <li>Eight</li>
29        <li>Eighty</li>
30        <li data-role="list-divider">I</li>
31        <li>Infinity</li>
32        <li>Imaginary</li>
33        <li data-role="list-divider">N</li>
34        <li>Nine</li>
35        <li>Ninety</li>
36        <li data-role="list-divider">O</li>
37        <li>One</li>
38        <li>One Thousand</li>
39        <li>One Million</li>
40        <li data-role="list-divider">T</li> ·
41        <li>Thirty</li>
42        <li>Three</li>
43        <li>Twenty</li>
44        <li>Two</li>
45      </ul>
46    </div>
47
48  </body>
49  </html>
```

There are many reasons why this example is not as practical as it could be in a real-world situation. First and foremost, in a list this short, you might not use any grouping at all. It does demonstrate the concept though.

Line 26 contains a special `li` element with `data-role="listdivider"`. The styling makes these headers easy to recognize after rendering.

In many Web applications, you have tree-like structures or folders containing large numbers of elements. On the root level, it is useful if you can see how many items you can expect for each entrance or how many unread items, perhaps. Listing 10.23 shows how to add a number like this to items in a list.

Listing 10.23   Displaying Count Items with Lists

```
00 <!DOCTYPE html>
01 <html>
02 <head>
03   <title>Counted Lists</title>
04   <meta name="viewport"
05     content="width=device-width, initial-scale=1">
06   <link rel="stylesheet" href=
07     "http://code.jquery.com/mobile/1.1.0/jquery.mobile-1.1.0.min.css">
08   <script type="text/javascript"
09     src="http://code.jquery.com/jquery-1.7.1.min.js">
10   </script>
11   <script type="text/javascript" src=
12     "http://code.jquery.com/mobile/1.1.0/jquery.mobile-1.1.0.min.js">
13   </script>
14
15 </head>
16 <body>
17
18 <div data-role="page">
19
20   <div data-role="header">
21     <h1>Counted Lists</h1>
22   </div>
23
24   <div data-role="content">
25     <ul data-role="listview">
26       <li>One <span class="ui-li-count">238</span></li>
27       <li>Two <span class="ui-li-count">23</span></li>
28       <li>Three <span class="ui-li-count">38</span></li>
29     </ul>
30 </body>
31 </html>
```

Lines 26–28 all contain a span element with `class="ui-li-count"`. There is no JavaScript involved here. You might as well add text instead of a number. It is better to avoid that, though. In small extra items like this, visitors expect a number.

On mobile Web sites with a visual nature, you can add small images to list items. These are called thumbnails, and they are demonstrated in Listing 10.24.

Listing 10.24   **Displaying Thumbnails in List Items**

```
00 <!DOCTYPE html>
01 <html>
02 <head>
03   <title>List Thumb</title>
04   <meta name="viewport"
05     content="width=device-width, initial-scale=1">
06   <link rel="stylesheet" href=
07     "http://code.jquery.com/mobile/1.1.0/jquery.mobile-1.1.0.min.css">
08   <script type="text/javascript"
09     src="http://code.jquery.com/jquery-1.7.1.min.js">
10   </script>
11   <script type="text/javascript" src=
12     "http://code.jquery.com/mobile/1.1.0/jquery.mobile-1.1.0.min.js">
13   </script>
14
15 </head>
16 <body>
17
18 <div data-role="page">
19
20   <div data-role="header">
21     <h1>List Thumb</h1>
22   </div>
23
24   <div data-role="content">
25     <ul data-role="listview" data-theme="d">
26       <li>
27         <img src="images/1.png">
28         <!--<img src="images/1.png" class="ui-li-icon">-->
29         <h3>One</h3>
30         <p>The first</p>
31       </li>
32       <li>
33         <img src="images/2.png">
34         <h3>Two</h3>
35         <p>The second</p>
36       </li>
```

Listing 10.24   Displaying Thumbnails in List Items (Continued)

```
37        <li>
38          <img src="images/3.png">
39          <h3>Three</h3>
40          <p>The third</p>
41        </li>
42      </ul>
43 </body>
44 </html>
```

As long as images are 80×80 pixels, you can simply add an `img` element inside the list item. Line 28 is an alternative notation that you can use to provide smaller images; for example, icons of 16×16 pixels. Just add the class `ui-li-icon`.

If this is not enough styling, you can add even more HTML inside the list items, as demonstrated in Listing 10.25. This is especially useful to provide preview snippets of the content that can be expected under each list item.

Listing 10.25   Applying Text Formatting to List Items

```
00 <!DOCTYPE html>
01 <html>
02 <head>
03   <title>Formatting in Lists</title>
04   <meta name="viewport"
05     content="width=device-width, initial-scale=1">
06   <link rel="stylesheet" href=
07     "http://code.jquery.com/mobile/1.1.0/jquery.mobile-1.1.0.min.css">
08   <script type="text/javascript"
09     src="http://code.jquery.com/jquery-1.7.1.min.js">
10   </script>
11   <script type="text/javascript" src=
12     "http://code.jquery.com/mobile/1.1.0/jquery.mobile-1.1.0.min.js">
13   </script>
14
15 </head>
16 <body>
17
18 <div data-role="page">
19
20   <div data-role="header">
21     <h1>Formatting in Lists</h1>
22   </div>
```

(Continues)

Listing 10.25   **Applying Text Formatting to List Items (Continued)**

```
23
24    <div data-role="content">
25      <ul data-role="listview" data-theme="d">
26        <li>
27          <a href="#">
28          <h3>One</h3>
29          <p><strong>The first</strong></p>
30          <p>And more information</p>
31          <p class="ui-li-aside"><strong>23</strong> views</p>
32          </a>
33        </li>
34        <li>
35          <a href="#">
36          <h3>Two</h3>
37          <p><strong>The second</strong></p>
38          <p>And more information</p>
39          <p class="ui-li-aside"><strong>2</strong> views</p>
40          </a>
41        </li>
42        <li>
43          <a href="#">
44          <h3>Three</h3>
45          <p><strong>The third</strong></p>
46          <p>And more information</p>
47          <p class="ui-li-aside"><strong>3</strong> views</p>
48          </a>
49        </li>
50      </ul>
51 </body>
52 </html>
```

Lines 26–33 give an example of a styled item. It contains a title, in the form of an h3, a subtitle in strong, and a regular paragraph. Finally, there is an item with the class ui-li-aside. You can put anything in there as long as it is small. In this example, it is a number, but it can also be a time, a date, or a read status.

Recipe: Filtering List Elements

As the number of list items grows, it becomes more difficult for visitors to find the element they are looking for. In the previous recipe, there was an example that added header names inside the list. This helps until you attain a certain size list. For larger lists, jQuery Mobile comes to the rescue with a filter element. Listing 10.26 demonstrates how easy it is to add this filter.

Listing 10.26   **Filtering Lists by Using a Search Box**

```
00 <!DOCTYPE html>
01 <html>
02 <head>
03   <title>Data Filter</title>
04   <meta name="viewport"
05     content="width=device-width, initial-scale=1">
06   <link rel="stylesheet" href=
07     "http://code.jquery.com/mobile/1.1.0/jquery.mobile-1.1.0.min.css">
08   <script type="text/javascript"
09     src="http://code.jquery.com/jquery-1.7.1.min.js">
10   </script>
11   <script type="text/javascript" src=
12     "http://code.jquery.com/mobile/1.1.0/jquery.mobile-1.1.0.min.js">
13   </script>
14
15 </head>
16 <body>
17
18 <div data-role="page">
19
20   <div data-role="header">
21    <h1>Data Filter</h1>
22   </div>
23
24   <div data-role="content">
25     <ul data-role="listview" data-filter="true">
26       <li>One</li>
27       <li>Two</li>
28       <li>Three</li>
29       <li>Four</li>
30       <li>Five</li>
31       <li>Six</li>
32       <li>Seven</li>
33       <li>Eight</li>
34       <li>Nine</li>
35       <li>Ten</li>
36     </ul>
37   </div>
38
39 </body>
40 </html>
```

On line 25, there is an extra attribute data-filter="true". When you add this, jQuery Mobile adds an input box on top of the list. When the visitor starts typing, you see the list of elements shrinking quickly.

Recipe: Grouping Form Elements in Lists

So far, this chapter discussed both form elements and item lists. It is also possible to combine the two and use an item list as a container for form elements. This allows you to group multiple input types into recognizable groups with a recognizable look and feel. Listing 10.27 provides a simple example with three form elements.

Listing 10.27   **Displaying Form Elements Inside a List**

```
00 <!DOCTYPE html>
01 <html>
02 <head>
03    <title>Form Lists</title>
04    <meta name="viewport"
05      content="width=device-width, initial-scale=1">
06    <link rel="stylesheet" href=
07      "http://code.jquery.com/mobile/1.1.0/jquery.mobile-1.1.0.min.css">
08    <script type="text/javascript"
09      src="http://code.jquery.com/jquery-1.7.1.min.js">
10    </script>
11    <script type="text/javascript" src=
12      "http://code.jquery.com/mobile/1.1.0/jquery.mobile-1.1.0.min.js">
13    </script>
14
15 </head>
16 <body>
17
18 <div data-role="page">
19
20    <div data-role="header"> .
21      <h1>Form Lists</h1>
22    </div>
23
24    <div data-role="content">
25
26      <form action="" method="post">
27        <ul data-role="listview" data-inset="true">
28          <li data-role="fieldcontain">
29            <label for="myinput">Input</label>
30            <input type="text" id="myinput">
31          </li>
32          <li data-role="fieldcontain">
33            <label for="myselect">Select</label>
34            <select id="myselect">
35              <option value="1">First</option>
36              <option value="2">Second</option>
37              <option value="3">Third</option>
```

Listing 10.27   **Displaying Form Elements Inside a List (Continued)**

```
38              </select>
39          </li>
40          <li data-role="fieldcontain">
41            <label for="mytextarea">Textarea</label>
42            <textarea id="mytextarea"></textarea>
43          </li>
44        </ul>
45      </form>
46    </div>
47
48 </body>
49 </html>
```

The code in this example is a perfect combination of many snippets discussed earlier in this chapter. In plain form examples, labels and input elements were contained inside a `div` with `data-role="fieldcontain"`. In this example, the `data-role="fieldcontain"` is placed on the list items. And both the label and the input element are placed inside the list item. jQuery Mobile takes care of the proper styling. For example, on wide screens, the labels are placed on the left of the input elements. On small screens, the labels are on top of the input elements.

Summary

Both HTML 4 and HTML5 offer many possibilities to interact with users. To interact with users on mobile devices requires an interface that is easy to control on a touch device. jQuery Mobile makes it easy to provide touch-friendly user controls.

This chapter started with toolbars, navigation bars and collapsible items. Next, it provided examples for the most common form elements and how to use them on touch devices.

The chapter ended with a number of variants of item lists, both ordered and unordered. It included nested lists, lists with special markup, and larger lists containing an additional search element by which to filter the content.

PART IV

Plugins

Chapter 11

Creating Plugins

This chapter explains how to create your own plugins for jQuery. It starts with very basic recipes that can be used for small plugins. These simple recipes also demonstrate the basics of plugin development. In small steps, options, defaults, and methods are added.

When the plugin becomes too large, with superfluous copy and paste boilerplate code, the Plugin plugin is introduced. This generic plugin helps you to create your own plugins without copying boilerplate.

The second half of this chapter covers utility functions that help you to implement more advanced use cases inside your plugins. These utilities are called Callback and Deferred. jQuery uses these internally for functionality such as AJAX handling.

Recipe: Setting Up a Simple Static Plugin

When you search the Internet for how to create a jQuery plugin, it might seem like a difficult task. The examples you typically find contain a lot of boilerplate code that helps you solve problems that you probably do not have, particularly if you only need to offer a small chunk of functionality.

Actually, to add a plugin to jQuery is quite simple—deceivingly simple, to be precise. Listing 11.1 shows the simplest way to add your own function to the jQuery object in such a way that it can be called anywhere else. Note that this simplicity comes at a price. The next recipes will add functionality in small steps.

Listing 11.1   **Attaching Functions to the jQuery Object**

```
00 <!DOCTYPE html>
01
02 <html lang="en">
03 <head>
04   <title>Very basic static plugin</title>
05 </head>
06 <body>
07
08 <h2>Very basic static plugin</h2>
```

(Continues)

Listing 11.1   **Attaching Functions to the jQuery Object (Continued)**

```
09
10 <button>Click here</button>
11
12 <script src="http://code.jquery.com/jquery-1.7.1.min.js"></script>
13
14 <script>
15 // please externalize this code to an external .js file
16
17 // DEFINE PLUGIN
18
19 (function( $ ){
20
21    $.doSomething = function() {
22
23      alert('Here is something!');
24
25    };
26 })( jQuery );
27
28 // USE PLUGIN
29
30 $(document).ready(function() {
31
32    $('button').click(function() {
33
34      $.doSomething();
35
36    });
37
38 });
39 </script>
40 </body>
41 </html>
```

Lines 19–26 define the plugin. Take a look at the notation that starts on line 19 and
ends on line 26. There is a function that takes $ as a parameter and it is directly invoked
on line 26 with the jQuery object. This makes it safe to use the $ sign inside the
function. Thus, your plugin is safe to use with other libraries or plugins that might have
the $ already mapped.

Next, the most important line in this example is line 21. Here, the doSomething()
function is added to the jQuery object directly. It will stay there for as long as the jQuery
object exists.

Line 34 demonstrates how to call the plugin. Here, the plugin works directly on the
jQuery object as a static function. It is not aware of any context, even if you added
$('anything') in front of it.

Recipe: Creating Simple Context-Aware Plugins

The basics of writing a context-aware plugin are still relatively simple. In a default JavaScript object, to gain access to the context, you need to add the function to the `Object.prototype`. To improve your code readability, jQuery offers you a shorthand notation for this: `$.fn`. Listing 11.2 demonstrates how to create a context-aware plugin this way.

Listing 11.2   **Attaching a Plugin to the jQuery Prototype Object**

```
00 <!DOCTYPE html>
01
02 <html lang="en">
03 <head>
04   <title>Basic context-aware plugin</title>
05 </head>
06 <body>
07
08 <h2>See blue paragraphs below</h2>
09
10 <p>This one is blue</p>
11
12 <span>This is not blue</span>
13
14 <p>And this one is blue again</p>
15
16
17 <script src="http://code.jquery.com/jquery-1.7.1.min.js"></script>
18
19 <script>
20 // please externalize this code to an external .js file
21
22 // DEFINE PLUGIN
23
24 (function( $ ){
25
26   $.fn.makeItBlue = function() {
27
28     this.css('background-color', 'blue');
29
30   };
31 })( jQuery );
32
33 // USE PLUGIN
34
35 $(document).ready(function() {
36
37   $('p').makeItBlue();
```

(Continues)

Listing 11.2   **Attaching a Plugin to the jQuery Prototype Object (Continued)**

```
38
39 });
40 </script>
41 </body>
42 </html>
```

The most important code can be found at line 26. Similar to the first example, a function is added to the jQuery object, only in this case it is bound to `$.fn`, which is the jQuery shorthand for `jQuery.prototype`.

You can see on line 37 how this plugin can be used on a jQuery selector. The selected elements will serve as the context for your jQuery plugin. In other words, any operation you perform on the `this` keyword in your plugin will work on the elements selected in the jQuery function call before your plugin is called.

Recipe: Chaining jQuery Functions and Plugins

In earlier chapters, you learned to chain jQuery functions for readability and maintainability. Most common jQuery functions that work on selected elements will return the set of selected elements for other (chained) functions to work on, unless your function is a selector itself. In that case, obviously, it will return the elements it has selected.

Listing 11.3 demonstrates a simple instance of function chaining on top of a plugin.

Listing 11.3   **Returning the Context to Ensure Chainablity**

```
00 <!DOCTYPE html>
01
02 <html lang="en">
03 <head>
04   <title>Making the plugin chainable</title>
05 </head>
06 <body>
07
08 <h2>See blue paragraphs below</h2>
09
10 <p>This one is blue</p>
11
12 <span>This is not blue</span>
13
14 <p>And this one is blue again</p>
15
16
17 <script src="http://code.jquery.com/jquery-1.7.1.min.js"></script>
18
```

Listing 11.3   **Returning the Context to Ensure Chainablity (Continued)**

```
19 <script>
20 // please externalize this code to an external .js file
21
22 // DEFINE PLUGIN
23
24 (function( $ ){
25
26   $.fn.makeItBlue = function() {
27
28    return this.css('background-color', 'blue');
29
30   };
31 })( jQuery );
32
33 // USE PLUGIN
34
35 $(document).ready(function() {
36
37   $('p').makeItBlue().css('color', 'white');
38
39 });
40 </script>
41 </body>
42 </html>
```

Making functions chainable is relatively straightforward. On line 28, the only real change is the `return` keyword. If your plugins call other helper functions internally, it is important to have these helper functions return the selected elements, as well. In case you use default jQuery helper functions, this mostly happens automatically. For example, you can write the following:

```
return this.each(function(index) {/* ... */});
```

On line 37, the chainability is proven by adding another `css()` call at the end. With this knowledge, you can imagine how easy it is to create your own selector in the form of a plugin.

Recipe: Parameterizing Plugins

A default plugin that always performs exactly the same action is only useful in a limited number of use cases. As you have seen in Chapter 6, Interacting with the User, with jQuery UI, you can specify many options to customize the plugin behavior.

Listing 11.4 demonstrates a first naïve implementation of passing parameters to a plugin.

Listing 11.4   Adding an Options Object as a Parameter

```
00 <!DOCTYPE html>
01
02 <html lang="en">
03 <head>
04   <title>Providing options</title>
05 </head>
06 <body>
07
08 <h2>See green paragraphs below</h2>
09
10 <p>This one is green</p>
11
12 <span>This is not green</span>
13
14 <p>And this one is green again</p>
15
16
17 <script src="http://code.jquery.com/jquery-1.7.1.min.js"></script>
18
19 <script>
20 // please externalize this code to an external .js file
21
22 // DEFINE PLUGIN
23
24 (function( $ ){
25
26   $.fn.makeIt = function(options) {
27
28     return this.css('background-color', options.color);
29
30   };
31 })( jQuery );
32
33 // USE PLUGIN
34
35 $(document).ready(function() {
36
37   $('p').makeIt({color: 'green'});
38
39 });
40 </script>
41 </body>
42 </html>
```

In previous examples, the plugin was named `makeItBlue()`. To make it less specific, the plugin is renamed to `makeIt()` on line 26 and takes an options object specifying the color.

Line 28 uses the specified color from the options object. This color is passed on line 37.

This example is more flexible than the previous one. The only downside is that it takes more knowledge of the API to use this function. There is no reasonable default value for the color anymore.

Recipe: Providing Default Parameters

By making clever use of a helper function introduced in Chapter 1, Getting Started with jQuery, called `extend()`, you can invoke `extend()` on two objects, and the function will copy the attributes from the second object into the first.

Listing 11.5 shows how this function extension is used by the plugin to merge the provided options into a default object.

Listing 11.5   **Extending Default Parameters with Optional Parameters**

```
00 <!DOCTYPE html>
01
02 <html lang="en">
03 <head>
04   <title>Offering a default fallback for options</title>
05 </head>
06 <body>
07
08 <h2>See red paragraphs below</h2>
09
10 <p>This one is red</p>
11
12 <span>This is green</span>
13
14 <p>And this one is red again</p>
15
16
17 <script src="http://code.jquery.com/jquery-1.7.1.min.js"></script>
18
19 <script>
20 // please externalize this code to an external .js file
21
22 // DEFINE PLUGIN
23
24 (function( $ ){
```

(Continues)

Listing 11.5   Extending Default Parameters with Optional Parameters (Continued)

```
25
26   $.fn.makeIt = function(options) {
27
28     var settings = $.extend(
29       { color: 'red' },
30       options
31     );
32
33     this.css('background-color', settings.color);
34
35   };
36 })( jQuery );
37
38 // USE PLUGIN
39
40 $(document).ready(function() {
41
42   $('p').makeIt(); // default is red
43   $('span').makeIt({ color: 'green' });
44
45 });
46 </script>
47 </body>
48 </html>
```

In this example, lines 28–31 perform the merge between defaults and provided options. The defaults are inline on line 29. In a larger plugin, you could also define these defaults as a separate variable earlier in the code. This would even allow you to expose the defaults through public functions (or variables) to let your users override them. Because you already override the defaults with the options you provide, exposing the defaults only makes sense for use cases in which the plugin is invoked in many different places.

Recipe: Operating the Plugin by Using Methods

It is bad practice to jam the jQuery object with many functions. The jQuery documentation recommends you to add only a single function to the jQuery object for one plugin. Attaching functions sparingly avoids the risk of collisions between plugins.

For larger plugins, it is likely that you need to add multiple functions. There are several ways to do that. If you search the Internet, you will find a handful of posts with code examples. The problem is that they are somewhat contradictory. On some blogs, you find subsequent versions that are not consistent with each other.

From this, you can draw two conclusions: First, it seems that the advice on jQuery's Web site is not appreciated by the entire community; and second, it seems that there is no universal agreement on a better way yet.

This book stays close to the original jQuery recommendations. However, it also fixes the need to copy and paste some code by introducing the Plugin plugin. That will be the next recipe. First, let's start with the basics of calling functions on a plugin, as demonstrated in Listing 11.6.

Listing 11.6   Calling Methods Based on Function Parameters

```
00 <!DOCTYPE html>
01
02 <html lang="en">
03 <head>
04   <title>Adding method calls to your plugin</title>
05 </head>
06 <body>
07
08 <h2>Change the background color of this header</h2>
09
10 <button id="blue">Blue</button>
11 <button id="green">Green</button>
12 <button id="light">Light</button>
13 <button id="dark">Dark</button>
14
15 <script src="http://code.jquery.com/jquery-1.7.1.min.js"></script>
16
17 <script>
18 // please externalize this code to an external .js file
19
20 // DEFINE PLUGIN
21
22 (function( $ ){
23
24    var helper = function( options, prefix ) {
25        var settings = $.extend(
26          { color: 'gray' },
27          this.data('settings'),
28          options
29        );
30        this.data('settings', settings);
31        this.css('background-color',
32            (prefix != undefined ? prefix : '')
33            + settings.color);
34    };
35
36    var methods = {
37      init : helper,
38      dark : function( options ) {
39        helper.apply(this, [options, 'dark']);
40      },
```

Listing 11.6   Calling Methods Based on Function Parameters (Continued)

```
41        light : function( options ) {
42          helper.apply(this, [options, 'light']);
43        }
44      };
45
46      $.fn.makeIt = function( method ) {
47
48        // Method calling logic
49        if ( methods[method] ) {
50          return methods[ method ].apply( this,
51              Array.prototype.slice.call( arguments, 1 ));
52        } else if ( typeof method === 'object' || ! method ) {
53          return methods.init.apply( this, arguments );
54        } else {
55          $.error( 'Method ' +  method + ' does not exist' );
56        }
57
58      };
59
60 })( jQuery );
61
62 // USE PLUGIN
63
64 $(document).ready(function() {
65
66    $('#green').click(function() {
67      $('h2').makeIt({ color: 'green' });
68    });
69    $('#blue').click(function() {
70      $('h2').makeIt({ color: 'blue' });
71    });
72    $('#dark').click(function() {
73      $('h2').makeIt('dark'); // default is gray
74    });
75    $('#light').click(function() {
76      $('h2').makeIt('light'); // default is gray
77    });
78
79 });
80 </script>
81 </body>
82 </html>
```

Before diving into the details, it must be mentioned that the methods in this example could also have been implemented as option parameters. In an actual application, the best practice is to use methods for code that can be characterized as an action that works on the plugin, such as `enable`, `disable`, `collapse`, `expand`, `submit`, and so on.

The reason to implement light and dark as methods in this plugin is so that you can switch them with a button, without knowing the currently selected color; as long as it is a color name that has a light and a dark variant, of course.

In this example, making it light and making it dark is implemented by using actions. Under the hood, the settings from the plugin instantiation are stored by using the `data()` method.

As you can see, the `extend` function can integrate more than two objects. If there are no options and no previous settings, the default values will be used. If there are settings and no options, the settings will be preferred over the default values. However, if there are current settings and new options, the new options will be used.

Lines 36–44 rely on the `helper()` function defined on lines 24–34. This helper function prevents duplication. It is called by using `apply()` to pass the context along.

Lines 48–56 read the method name provided to the plugin and execute the appropriate method with the arguments provided. In case no method name is supplied, the function defaults to `init`.

Recipe: Creating a Plugin that Creates Plugins

Creating a larger plugin that handles methods and passes along options to these methods implies boilerplate code. Boilerplate code is another word for duplication, and duplication is evil.

The general recipe to eliminate duplication is to separate the code that stays the same from the code that changes every time. The most notable part of the code that remains unchanged is the logic to read method arguments and invoke the right method. What if you could create a plugin that contains this logic for you so that you can focus on the code that is specific to your use case? Can you imagine a plugin that creates plugins?

Listing 11.7 shows an example plugin to create plugins to isolate the method handling logic and allow you to focus on your own code. Let's call this the Plugin plugin.

Listing 11.7 **Extracting the Boilerplate into a Separate Static Plugin**

```
00 <!DOCTYPE html>
01
02 <html lang="en">
03 <head>
04   <title>A plugin to create plugins</title>
05 </head>
06 <body>
07
08 <h2>Change the background color of this header</h2>
09
10 <button id="blue">Blue</button>
11 <button id="green">Green</button>
12 <button id="light">Light</button>
13 <button id="dark">Dark</button>
14
```

(Continues)

Listing 11.7   Extracting the Boilerplate into a Separate Static Plugin (Continued)

```
15 <script src="http://code.jquery.com/jquery-1.7.1.min.js"></script>
16
17 <script>
18 // please externalize this code to an external .js file
19
20 // DEFINE PLUGIN PLUGIN
21
22 (function( $ ){
23
24     $.pluginPlugin = function(methods) {
25         return function( method ) {
26           if ( methods[method] ) {
27             return methods[ method ].apply( this,
28                 Array.prototype.slice.call( arguments, 1 ));
29           } else if ( typeof method === 'object' || ! method ) {
30             return methods.init.apply( this, arguments );
31           } else {
32             $.error( 'Method ' +  method + ' does not exist' );
33           }
34         };
35     };
36
37 })( jQuery );
38
39 // DEFINE PLUGIN (using the plugin plugin)
40
41 (function( $ ){
42
43     $.fn.makeIt = $.pluginPlugin(function() {
44         // private functions and variables
45         var helper = function( options, prefix ) {
46             var settings = $.extend(
47               { color: 'gray' },
48               this.data('settings'),
49               options
50             );
51             this.data('settings', settings);
52             this.css('background-color',
53                 (prefix != undefined ? prefix : '')
54                 + settings.color);
55         };
56         // publicly available functions
57         return {
```

Listing 11.7   Extracting the Boilerplate into a Separate Static Plugin (Continued)

```
58              init : helper,
59              dark : function( options ) {
60                 return helper.apply(this, [options, 'dark']);
61              },
62              light : function( options ) {
63                 return helper.apply(this, [options, 'light']);
64              }
65           }}());
66
67 })( jQuery );
68
69 // USE PLUGIN
70
71 $(document).ready(function() {
72
73    $('#green').click(function() {
74       $('h2').makeIt({ color: 'green' });
75    });
76    $('#blue').click(function() {
77       $('h2').makeIt({ color: 'blue' });
78    });
79    $('#dark').click(function() {
80       $('h2').makeIt('dark'); // default is gray
81    });
82    $('#light').click(function() {
83       $('h2').makeIt('light'); // default is gray
84    });
85
86 });
87 </script>
88 </body>
89 </html>
```

Lines 22–37 contain the Plugin plugin. You could save this code to a separate .js file and reuse it every time you define a plugin. This is especially helpful if you define more than one custom plugin on a Web site.

The Plugin plugin is defined as a static method on the jQuery object. It does not take any context. It expects a dictionary of methods as parameters. Best practice is to pass at least one method under the key init. This will serve as the default method.

You might think that this setup prevents you from using private methods, or that there is a risk that the scope of the private methods will be larger than desirable. There are several ways around this. First of all, the containing function on line 41 should prevent this from happening. But in case you want an even more local helper function, consider the construction on lines 43–65. This code sets up a function that returns a dictionary of functions and executes it directly. As a result, the dictionary of functions is passed to the Plugin plugin and the helper function is not accessible anywhere else.

In case you really need to, you can repeat this principle recursively within the method array being returned.

Finally, on lines 73–84, there is a demonstration that the Plugin plugin works. Now compare this plugin with the previous recipe. All plugin code is on lines 41–67. There is almost no copy-paste code anymore.

Yes, if you have a background in the Scala programming language, you might think that the light and dark functions look too much alike. In Scala you could provide an even cleaner construction for this. Welcome to the world of functional programming.

Recipe: Registering and Invoking Callback Functions

When you create more sophisticated plugins, some of the internals of jQuery can help you achieve results. An example of this is the `Callback()` object. jQuery relies on this object to implement its `Deferred()` object—which will be introduced later on in this chapter.

The idea of a callback is that the user of the plugin passes along functions and these functions are all called at a certain time. For example, they can be called when a certain event arises, when a state changes, or when an amount of time has passed.

Listing 11.8 demonstrates how to add functions to a callback handler and sets a timer to call them after three seconds.

Listing 11.8   **Using the jQuery Callback() Object to Handle Sets of Callback Functions**

```
00 <!DOCTYPE html>
01
02 <html lang="en">
03 <head>
04   <title>Testing the Callback utility</title>
05 </head>
06 <body>
07
08 <h2>Callbacks will add content below</h2>
09
10 <p>This is a first attach point</p>
11
12 <span>This element is ignored</span>
13
14 <p>This is a second attach point</p>
15
16 <script src="http://code.jquery.com/jquery-1.7.1.min.js"></script>
17
18 <script>
```

Listing 11.8   Using the jQuery Callback() Object to Handle Sets of Callback Functions (Continued)

```
19 // please externalize this code to an external .js file
20
21 // DEFINE PLUGIN
22
23 (function( $ ){
24
25   $.fn.testCallbacks = function() {
26
27     var hello = function(jqEl, to) {
28       jqEl.append('<br>hello ' + to);
29       //callbacks.lock();
30       //callbacks.disable();
31     }
32     var bye = function(jqEl, to) {
33       jqEl.append('<br>bye ' + to);
34       }
35
36     var callbacks = $.Callbacks();
37
38     window.setTimeout(callbacks.fire, 3000, this, 'world');
39
40     callbacks.add(hello);
41     callbacks.add(bye);
42     //callbacks.remove(bye);
43     //callbacks.empty();
44
45   };
46 })( jQuery );
47
48 // USE PLUGIN
49
50 $(document).ready(function() {
51
52   $('p').testCallbacks();
53
54 });
55 </script>
56 </body>
57 </html>
```

First, look at the callback functions themselves, `hello` and `bye`. Noteworthy is the first parameter, the HTML element to work on. Next, within the hello function, notice the disabled lines `lock()` and `disable()`. You can uncomment these to see the effect. Both functions are new in jQuery 1.7 and prevent further callback functions from being executed. The `lock()` function locks the callback in its current state; the `disable()` function stops the callback list from doing anything else.

Similarly, on lines 42 and 43, there are commented lines removing a callback and making the stack empty. Again, uncomment these to see the effect.

Finally, try adding more functions after firing or try firing again. With callback, you can call the registered functions multiple times.

The Callback object can take a lot of work off your hands when it comes to managing sets of callback functions to be called.

Recipe: Passing Context to Callback Functions

In the previous example, a parameter is passed with the elements that the function works on. This seems a bit awkward and superfluous and, in fact, it is.

If you pass a context to the callback functions, they only need a single argument, or in your use case, perhaps none at all. You can achieve this effect by calling the `fireWith()` function instead of `fire()`. Listing 11.9 shows the changes you should make in your code to make this work.

Listing 11.9   **Using fireWith() to Pass Context to a Callback**

```
00 <!DOCTYPE html>
01
02 <html lang="en">
03 <head>
04   <title>The timeout property</title>
05 </head>
06 <body>
07
08 <h2>Callbacks will add content below</h2>
09
10 <p>This is a first attach point</p>
11
12 <span>This element is ignored</span>
13
14 <p>This is a second attach point</p>
15
16 <script src="http://code.jquery.com/jquery-1.7.1.min.js"></script>
17
18 <script>
19 // please externalize this code to an external .js file
20
21 // DEFINE PLUGIN
22
23 (function( $ ){
24
25   $.fn.testCallbacks = function() {
```

Listing 11.9 **Using fireWith() to Pass Context to a Callback (Continued)**

```
26
27    var hello = function(to) {
28      this.append('<br>hello ' + to);
29    }
30    var bye = function(to) {
31      this.append('<br>bye ' + to);
32      }
33
34    var callbacks = $.Callbacks();
35
36    window.setTimeout(callbacks.fireWith, 3000, this, ['world']);
37
38    callbacks.add(hello);
39    callbacks.add(bye);  ·
40    //callbacks.lock();
41
42    };
43 })( jQuery );
44
45 // USE PLUGIN
46
47 $(document).ready(function() {
48
49   $('p').testCallbacks();
50
51 });
52 </script>
53 </body>
54 </html>
```

First, notice lines 27 and 30. The `hello` and `bye` functions only take a single parameter. Instead of passing elements, a context is passed to them, so they can work on `this`.

Next, investigate line 36. There are two changes on this line compared to the previous recipe. First, the function name changed from `fire` to `fireWith`. Second, the `world` parameter is now inside an array. This is because the `fireWith` function expects an array of arguments instead of a variable number of arguments. The reason for this is that `fireWith` performs a call to the `apply` function under the hood.

Recipe: Returning Deferred Objects to Call Separate Callbacks on Success and on Error

On top of Callback, jQuery offers an object called *Deferred*. Actually, Deferred existed before Callback. It seems the creators of jQuery have extracted the Callback object while cleaning up the internal implementation of Deferred.

For fast understanding of the Deferred object, you should consider that you probably already used it. Consciously or not, you are likely to have used a Deferred construct when making an AJAX request with the jQuery library.

If your plugin performs actions that either succeed or fail after a certain amount of time, the Deferred object helps you offer a similar interface to the users of your plugin. Listing 11.10 illustrates how to create your own Deferred object, register callbacks, and call all registered functions in the end. Please be aware that the usage of Deferred in this first example is still flawed; the recipes that follow will fix this.

Listing 11.10   Returning the Deferred() Object As Is

```
00 <!DOCTYPE html>
01
02 <html lang="en">
03 <head>
04   <title>Deferred - basic usage</title>
05 </head>
06 <body>
07
08 <h2>Please wait 5 sec for a popup</h2>
09
10 <script src="http://code.jquery.com/jquery-1.7.1.min.js"></script>
11
12 <script>
13 // please externalize this code to an external .js file
14
15 // DEFINE PLUGIN
16
17 (function( $ ){
18
19   $.myStaticPlugin = function() {
20     return $.Deferred();
21   };
22 })( jQuery );
23
24   // USE PLUGIN
25
26 $(document).ready(function() {
27
28   var deferred = $.myStaticPlugin().done(function(msg) {
29       alert('Plugin came back with ' + msg);
30   });
31
32   window.setTimeout(
33       function () {
34           deferred.resolve('Ready...');
```

Listing 11.10   **Returning the Deferred() Object As Is (Continued)**

```
35        }, 5000
36    );
37 });
38 </script>
39 </body>
40 </html>
```

Lines 19–22 show a plugin that simply returns the Deferred object directly, as is. This plugin is instantiated on line 28, directly followed by the registration of a done callback function.

To show how the Deferred object resolves registered callback functions, lines 32–36 invoke all registered callback handlers after five seconds. However, the location of this code is problematic. This code resides outside the plugin. This means that the internals of the plugin are exposed. Other JavaScripts could hack the plugin and add undesired behavior.

Recipe: Returning a Promise to Protect Internals

The Deferred object offers a separate, smaller interface to the outside world. This interface is called a Promise. The returned object only exposes methods that are safe to call from outside the plugin, which are mostly the methods used to register additional callback handlers. Listing 11.11 returns a Promise object and integrates the resolving code into the plugin.

Listing 11.11   **Calling promise() to Return a Protected Version of the Deferred Object**

```
00 <!DOCTYPE html>
01
02 <html lang="en">
03 <head>
04    <title>Deferred - promises</title>
05 </head>
06 <body>
07
08 <h2>Please wait 5 sec for a popup</h2>
09
10 <script src="http://code.jquery.com/jquery-1.7.1.min.js"></script>
11
12 <script>
13 // please externalize this code to an external .js file
14
15 // DEFINE PLUGIN
```

(Continues)

Listing 11.11   Calling promise() to Return a Protected Version of the Deferred Object (Continued)

```
16
17 (function( $ ){
18
19   $.myStaticPlugin = function() {
20     var deferred = $.Deferred();
21     window.setTimeout(
22        function () {
23            deferred.resolve('Ready!');
24        }, 5000
25     );
26     return deferred.promise();
27   };
28
29 })( jQuery );
30
31 // USE PLUGIN
32
33 $(document).ready(function() {
34
35   $.myStaticPlugin().done(function(msg) {
36       alert('Plugin came back with ' + msg);
37   });
38
39 });
40 </script>
41 </body>
42 </html>
```

Consider lines 19–21. You see the same Deferred object and the same setTimeout function invoking all registered callback handlers with the resolve function. The difference is that the setTimeout function is now integrated within the plugin and at the end, the promise() method is called.

From the perspective of the plugin user, it seems like nothing has changed. Lines 35–37 registering the callback function remain unchanged.

Recipe: Demonstrating the Promise(d) Protection

To see the difference between an uncensored Deferred object and a Promise, let's try to violate the restrictions. Listing 11.12 clearly contains an error to demonstrate that the internals of the Deferred can no longer be manipulated outside the plugin when only a Promise is returned.

Listing 11.12   Generating an Intentional JavaScript Error to Show that a Promise Does not Reveal Internals

```
00 <!DOCTYPE html>
01
02 <html lang="en">
03 <head>
04   <title>Deferred - promise - ERROR!</title>
05 </head>
06 <body>
07
08 <h2>Error on purpose to demonstrate the use of promise()</h2>
09
10 <script src="http://code.jquery.com/jquery-1.7.1.min.js"></script>
11
12 <script>
13 // please externalize this code to an external .js file
14
15 // DEFINE PLUGIN
16
17 (function( $ ){
18
19   $.myStaticPlugin = function() {
20     return $.Deferred().promise();
21   };
22
23 })( jQuery );
24
25 // USE PLUGIN
26
27 $(document).ready(function() {
28
29   var deferred = $.myStaticPlugin().done(function(msg) {
30     alert('Plugin came back with ' + msg);
31   });
32
33   window.setTimeout(
34     function () {
35         // ERROR! (on purpose)
36         deferred.resolve('This is impossible!');
37     }, 5000
38   );
39
40 });
41 </script>
42 </body>
43 </html>
```

This code example is a mixture of the previous two code examples. Within the plugin the `resolve()` function is not called. The `promise()` function is called, however.

The code written to call the `resolve()` function is outside the plugin again. You can try this code example to see what happens. Open an error console in your browser and see what errors occur.

Recipe: Using Promise to Control Flow Structures

So far, the Promise interface has only been called with the `done()` function. In case the plugin fails, no callback functions would be invoked.

The Promise object also exposes functions like `fail()`, `always()`, and `then()`. Listing 11.13 provides examples of their usage to indicate subtle difference between these functions.

Listing 11.13   **Adding fail(), then(), and always() to the Example Code**

```
00 <!DOCTYPE html>
01
02 <html lang="en">
03 <head>
04   <title>Deferred - promise - other outcomes</title>
05 </head>
06 <body>
07
08 <h2>Please wait 5 sec for a popup</h2>
09
10 <script src="http://code.jquery.com/jquery-1.7.1.min.js"></script>
11
12 <script>
13 // please externalize this code to an external .js file
14
15 // DEFINE PLUGIN
16
17 (function( $ ){
18
19   $.myStaticPlugin = function() {
20     var deferred = $.Deferred();
21     window.setTimeout(
22         function () {
23             deferred.resolve('Ready!');
24             //or:
25             //deferred.reject('Fail!');
26         }, 5000
27     );
28     return deferred.promise();
29   };
```

Listing 11.13   Adding fail(), then(), and always() to the Example Code (Continued)

```
30
31 })( jQuery );
32
33 // USE PLUGIN
34
35 $(document).ready(function() {
36
37   $.myStaticPlugin()
38   .done(function(msg) {
39       alert('Done ' + msg);
40   })
41   .fail(function(msg) {
42          alert('Fail ' + msg);
43   })
44   .then(
45     function(msg) {
46          alert('Then-Success ' + msg);
47     },
48     function(msg) {
49          alert('Then-Error ' + msg);
50   })
51   .always(function(msg) {
52       alert('Always ' + msg);
53   });
54
55 });
56 </script>
57 </body>
58 </html>
```

When you play around with this example, notice that on lines 23–25 you can switch from resolving to rejecting. Resolve is equal to success and reject is equal to failure.

On lines 37–53, functions are registered for all possible outcomes of the plugin. Actually, there are only two possible outcomes: success (`done`) and failure (`fail`). The `then()` function provides a shorthand notation to register both a success and a failure function and is compatible with the CommonJS *Promises/A* specification. The `always()` function can be used to register callbacks that will be invoked regardless of the outcome.

Recipe: Visualizing Progress Before the Final Callback

Once you call either `resolve()` or `reject()` on a Deferred object, you cannot use that Deferred object again. The callbacks are registered for one-time use only. Otherwise, it would not be a Deferred object, but an Observer object.

For some long-running actions, you might want to visualize progress before the final callback functions are invoked. The Deferred object exposes a mechanism to communicate progress. Listing 11.14 demonstrates progress notifications.

Listing 11.14   Adding Callbacks to progress() and Calling notify() to Invoke Them

```
00 <!DOCTYPE html>
01
02 <html lang="en">
03 <head>
04   <title>Deferred - promise - progress</title>
05 </head>
06 <body>
07
08 <h2>Please wait 2.5 sec for an update and 5 sec for a popup</h2>
09      .
10 <script src="http://code.jquery.com/jquery-1.7.1.min.js"></script>
11
12 <script>
13 // please externalize this code to an external .js file
14
15 // DEFINE PLUGIN
16
17 (function( $ ){
18
19   $.myStaticPlugin = function() {
20     var deferred = $.Deferred();
21     window.setTimeout(
22         function () {
23             deferred.resolve('Ready!');
24             //or:
25             //deferred.reject('Fail!');
26         }, 5000
27     );
28     window.setTimeout(
29         function () {
30             deferred.notify('Halfway there!');
31         }, 2500
32     );
33     return deferred.promise();
34   };
35
36 })( jQuery );
37
38 // USE PLUGIN
39
40 $(document).ready(function() {
```

Listing 11.14   Adding Callbacks to progress() and Calling notify() to Invoke Them (Continued)

```
41
42    $.myStaticPlugin()
43    .progress(function(msg) {
44         alert('Progress ' + msg);
45    })
46    .always(function(msg) {
47        alert('Always ' + msg);
48    });
49
50 });
51 </script>
52 </body>
53 </html>
```

The process of registering a callback handler for the final result, remains unchanged. In this example, lines 46–48 provide an `always()` handler.

On lines 43–45, however, a progress handler is registered. To demonstrate how this works, lines 28–32 add an extra timeout after 2.5 seconds indicating 50 percent progress. This indication is handled by the `notify()` function. Although the example only calls this function a single time, it can be invoked as many times as you like.

Recipe: Providing Context to Callback Functions

Up until this point, callback handlers were unaware of any context. For many plugins, to do something useful inside a callback handler, some context is required. For this purpose, the Deferred object exposes alternatives to `resolve()` and `reject()`: `resolveWith()` and `rejectWith()`.

Listing 11.15 calls the `resolveWith()` function and illustrates a subtle difference in the way function parameters need to be passed.

Listing 11.15   Using resolveWith() to Provide a Context to a Callback

```
00 <!DOCTYPE html>
01
02 <html lang="en">
03 <head>
04   <title>Deferred - resolve with</title>
05 </head>
06 <body>
07
08 <h2>Please wait 5 sec for a popup and a green background</h2>
09
```

(Continues)

Listing 11.15   **Using resolveWith() to Provide a Context to a Callback (Continued)**

```
10 <script src="http://code.jquery.com/jquery-1.7.1.min.js"></script>
11
12 <script>
13 // please externalize this code to an external .js file
14
15 // DEFINE PLUGIN
16
17 (function( $ ){
18
19   $.myStaticPlugin = function() {
20     var deferred = $.Deferred();
21     window.setTimeout(
22         function () {
23             deferred.resolveWith($('h2'), ['Ready!']);
24             //or:
25             //deferred.rejectWith($('h2'), ['Fail!']);
26         }, 5000
27     );
28     return deferred.promise();
29   };
30
31 })( jQuery );
32
33 // USE PLUGIN
34
35 $(document).ready(function() {
36
37   $.myStaticPlugin()
38   .done(function(msg) {
39       this.css('background-color', 'green');
40       alert('Done ' + msg);
41   })
42   .fail(function(msg) {
43       alert('Fail ' + msg);
44   });
45
46 });
47 </script>
48 </body>
49 </html>
```

First, focus on line 23. Not only is resolve() replaced by resolvedWith(), the parameter Ready! is now inside an array: ['Ready!']. You might recognize this difference from earlier recipes in this chapter. The Callback object has a similar difference between the fire() and fireWith() functions.

Functions like `resolveWith()` and `rejectWith()` pass context. Under the hood, they use the generic `apply()` function, which expects function parameters to be passed in the form of an array.

Recipe: Providing a Context to Progress Functions

Similar to `resolveWith()` and `rejectWith()`, you can also pass a context to the progress indication functions. Listing 11.16 shows how to use the `progressWith()` function to indicate progress while providing context from the plugin.

Listing 11.16   **Invoking notifyWith() to Add Context to a Progress Callback**

```
00 <!DOCTYPE html>
01
02 <html lang="en">
03 <head>
04    <title>Deferred - notify with</title>
05 </head>
06 <body>
07
08 <h2>Watch the background go red, orange, and green</h2>
09
10 <script src="http://code.jquery.com/jquery-1.7.1.min.js"></script>
11
12 <script>
13 // please externalize this code to an external .js file
14
15 // DEFINE PLUGIN
16
17 (function( $ ){
18
19   $.myStaticPlugin = function() {
20     var deferred = $.Deferred();
21     var context = $('h2').css('background-color', 'red');
22     window.setTimeout(
23         function () {
24             deferred.resolveWith(context, ['100%']);
25         }, 5000
26     );
27     window.setTimeout(
28         function () {
29             deferred.notifyWith(context, ['50%']);
30         }, 2500
31     );
32     return deferred.promise();
```

(Continues)

Listing 11.16   **Invoking notifyWith() to Add Context to a Progress Callback (Continued)**

```
33   };
34
35 })( jQuery );
36
37 // USE PLUGIN
38
39 $(document).ready(function() {
40
41   $.myStaticPlugin()
42   .progress(function(msg) {
43     this.css('background-color', 'orange');
44     // ignore message
45   })
46   .always(function(msg) {
47     this.css('background-color', 'green');
48     // ignore message
49   });
50
51 });
52 </script>
53 </body>
54 </html>
```

You might be wondering when you would want to have context in a progress function. The example uses the context for output. You might consider the output a concern that should not be controlled from the plugin. This depends on your use case, however.

An obvious use case for which you need context in your progress indicators is when you have multiple instances of your plugin simultaneously performing work for you. In case of a progress notification, you might want to know from which instance it was called.

The example code uses the context for its output. It gives the provided context different background colors depending on the progress.

Summary

If you search for your information on the Internet, it can seem that creating jQuery plugins is a difficult task. Most of the examples available are meant to facilitate relatively large plugins. And if you have to decide on the implementation method, it will be difficult to make the right choice.

This chapter showed that the implementation of a small plugin can actually be quite simple. And as your plugin grows, you can add more sophisticated handling methods.

To avoid duplication of code, this chapter showed you how to write a Plugin plugin. This is a generic plugin that helps you with the development of more specific plugins. This one is suitable for the larger use cases.

As jQuery evolved, the jQuery team extracted some design patterns from the code and evolved them into generic libraries that can be reused. For example, an AJAX call could either succeed or fail and for each of these actions a list of callback functions can be registered and called.

The Callback object is extracted from this to help you register and invoke callback functions. The Deferred object is available to help you register and invoke callbacks, depending on the outcome of an action which can either succeed or fail.

On top of these helper functions, this chapter demonstrated how to provide context and how to notify the user interface of any progress before the final result.

Chapter 12

Working with Third-Party Plugins

Y ou already learned how to develop your own plugins, but depending on your project and timeline, you might want to incorporate a plugin written by someone else. Thousands of jQuery plugins are available on the Internet, and many have been tracked and updated at http://plugins.jquery.com/. Although this started out as a good idea, there were architectural problems with the site, and hundreds of plugins were submitted that have long since been abandoned or have not received an update to newer versions of jQuery.

Currently, the site is undergoing a major overhaul. In fact, you are greeted with a warning when you visit it. Even though this site will eventually be recreated and help you locate plugins to use, you might want to use some plugins that are a little more stable or come from a company or person whom you can trust. So, for this chapter, we look into some jQuery plugins that are available from a very popular and recognized name in the development, design, and social networking business. The Twitter Bootstrap framework (http://twitter.github.com/bootstrap/) is a fantastic set of plugins and styles that helped developers do everything from responsive site layout to incorporating widgets and plugins that help make the Web not only look better, but work, regardless of the device used. For these recipes, we will be using Bootstrap version 2.0.4.

Recipe: Displaying a Modal

A few years back, there were a couple of ways that a Web site or application could get the attention of a user. One was to pop up another smaller window over or under the current window; the other way was to use the JavaScript `alert()` function. Now, when you want to display important information, you can use a *modal window*. A modal (as it's commonly referred) works in similar fashion to the window that is displayed by `alert()`. However, instead of relying on the browser to create and show the window and information, the modal is injected into the DOM; thus, you can control its style.

The modal plugin from Bootstrap gives you the ability to listen for events on the modal and trigger other functions based on them. Listing 12.1 demonstrates creating and calling a modal window as well as using the `hidden` event to trigger another function.

Listing 12.1   **Modal with an Event Trigger**

```
00 <!DOCTYPE html>
01 <html lang="en">
02   <head>
03     <meta charset="utf-8">
04     <title>Bootstrap - Modal</title>
05     <meta name="viewport"
06       content="width=device-width, initial-scale=1.0">
07
08     <link href="css/bootstrap.css" rel="stylesheet">
09     <style>
10       body {
11         padding-top: 60px;
12       }
13     </style>
14     <link href="css/bootstrap-responsive.css" rel="stylesheet">
15
16   </head>
17
18   <body>
19
20     <div class="navbar navbar-fixed-top">
21       <div class="navbar-inner">
22         <div class="container">
23           <a class="brand" href="#">Using a Modal</a>
24         </div>
25       </div>
26     </div>
27
28     <div class="container">
29
30       <p>Click the link below to launch a modal</p>
31       <a class="btn" data-toggle="modal" href="#modal">Launch!</a>
32       <div class="modal hide" id="modal">
33         <div class="modal-header">
34           <h3>Modal plugin by Bootstrap</h3>
35         </div>
36         <div class="modal-body">
37           <p>
38             Modals are great alternative to using ye olde alert()
39           </p>
40           <p>
```

Listing 12.1   **Modal with an Event Trigger (Continued)**

```
41              When you close this modal, an alert will appear
42          </p>
43        </div>
44        <div class="modal-footer">
45          <a href="#" class="btn" data-dismiss="modal">
46            Close the Modal
47          </a>
48        </div>
49      </div>
50
51    </div> <!-- /.container -->
52
53    <script src=
54      "http://code.jquery.com/jquery-1.7.1.min.js">
55    </script>
56    <!--[if lt IE 9]>
57      <script src="js/respond.min.js"></script>
58    <![endif]-->
59    <script src="js/bootstrap-modal.js"></script>
60    <script>
61      $(document).ready(function() {
62        $('#modal').on('hidden', function() {
63          alert("This was triggered from the modal 'hidden' event.");
64        });
65      });
66    </script>
67  </body>
68 </html>
```

This recipe shows the basic outline of a page using Bootstrap that is used throughout the rest of the recipes. I'll walk through and explain some of the layout here so that you are familiar with it.

Lines 8 and 14 show the addition of the Bootstrap suggested styles, and the lines in between show a style element that adds some padding to the body to display the navigation bar without overlapping content in the rest of the page.

Lines 20–26 contain the navbar that is used as a title and/or navigation section for the page. Line 28 shows the div element that is used as a container to house the bulk of the displayed site.

Unlike jQuery Mobile, bootstrap does not require scripts to be loaded in the head, so to help with performance, the included JavaScript files have been moved to the bottom of the document, just before the closing body tag.

Lines 53–66 show the included and inline code that is being used. You can see that jQuery 1.7.1 is being included as well as respond.min.js, which is used to add responsive media query support in Internet Explorer 7 and 8.

The modal plugin works by looking for some key classes and data-attributes. On line 31, you can see that `data-toggle="modal"` has been added to the a element. This will turn the link into a trigger that will launch the modal. The link should then be pointed to the container that will be displayed as the modal. In this instance you can see the target defined as `href="#modal"`. The other key to this is the class `hide` that has been applied to the target `div` element as shown on line 32.

To demonstrate using events with the modal, lines 62–64 show some jQuery script that is attaching a function to run on the hidden event of the modal. When the modal is closed, the hidden event runs and a browser alert is displayed.

Recipe: Using a Drop-Down Menu

Drop-down menus are perfect for use in navigation systems or when you need to give the user options but you don't want to display them all of the time. In Listing 12.2, we build a quick drop-down navigation system for site links.

Listing 12.2   **Creating a Navigation System**

```
00  <!DOCTYPE html>
01  <html lang="en">
02    <head>
03      <meta charset="utf-8">
04      <title>Bootstrap - Dropdown</title>
05      <meta name="viewport"
06        content="width=device-width, initial-scale=1.0">
07
08      <link href="css/bootstrap.css" rel="stylesheet">
09      <style>
10        body {
11          padding-top: 60px;
12        }
13      </style>
14      <link href="css/bootstrap-responsive.css" rel="stylesheet">
15
16    </head>
17
18    <body>
19
20      <div class="navbar navbar-fixed-top">
21        <div class="navbar-inner">
22          <div class="container">
23            <a class="brand" href="#">Using Dropdown</a>
24            <ul class="nav nav-pills">
25              <li class="active"><a href="#">Home</a></li>
26              <li class="dropdown" id="internal">
27                <a class="dropdown-toggle" data-toggle=
```

Listing 12.2   Creating a Navigation System (Continued)

```
28              "dropdown" href="#internal">
29              Internal
30              <b class="caret"></b>
31            </a>
32            <ul class="dropdown-menu">
33              <li><a href="01-modal.html">Modal</a></li>
34              <li><a href="04-tab.html">Tab</a></li>
35              <li><a href="05-tooltip.html">Tooltip</a></li>
36            </ul>
37          </li>
38          <li class="dropdown" id="external">
39            <a class="dropdown-toggle" data-toggle=
40              "dropdown" href="#external">
41              External
42              <b class="caret"></b>
43            </a>
44            <ul class="dropdown-menu">
45              <li>
46                <a href="http://twitter.github.com/bootstrap/">
47                  Bootstrap
48                </a>
49              </li>
50              <li><a href="http://jquery.com/">jQuery</a></li>
51            </ul>
52          </li>
53        </ul>
54      </div>
55    </div>
56  </div>
57
58  <div class="container">
59
60    <p>The menu above is created through the dropdown plugin.</p>
61    <p>
62      The internal menu will point to local html files while
63      the external menu will link to other sites.
64    </p>
65
66  </div> <!-- /.container -->
67
68  <script src=
69    "http://code.jquery.com/jquery-1.7.1.min.js">
70  </script>
71  <!--[if lt IE 9]>
```

(Continues)

```
72        <script src="js/respond.min.js"></script>
73     <![endif]-->
74     <script src="js/bootstrap-dropdown.js"></script>
75   </body>
76 </html>
```

The key to setting up a drop-down menu with Bootstrap is shown on lines 24–53. Here, you can see that a `ul` element has been created that contains several `li` elements. The `active` class is used to change the visual styles applied to the menu item, and in this instance will designate to the user where he is.

Lines 26 and 38 show list elements with `class="dropdown"` elements applied to them. This will apply the appropriate styles to the elements. Lines 27 and 29 show some links that contain `class="dropdown-toggle"` and `data-toggle="dropdown"` which are used for both styling and by the plugin to create the drop-down menus. Each of these links also contains a link that points back to the containing list element, which can be used to target a specific drop-down menu. That means if you really wanted to, you could replace `#internal` on line 28 with `#external`, and when clicked, the external drop-down menu would be triggered.

Line 74 shows the reference to the bootstrap-dropdown.js file. Because this is the plugin responsible for making the drop-down menus work, it must be included.

Recipe: Using ScrollSpy

A feature that you might have seen on some Web sites is a floating or fixed navigation that changes styles based on the location of the page you are currently on. The ScrollSpy plugin handles this and can be easily added to your page to impart this behavior.

The plugin works on the DOM that is visible when the plugin is called. This means that if you modify the DOM, then you will need to refresh the plugin in order to pick up the changes. Listing 12.3 gives an example of adding an extra navigation item and refreshing the plugin.

Listing 12.3   **Adding a Dynamic Navigation Item**

```
00 <!DOCTYPE html>
01 <html lang="en">
02   <head>
03     <meta charset="utf-8">
04     <title>Bootstrap - Scrollspy</title>
05     <meta name="viewport"
06       content="width=device-width, initial-scale=1.0">
07
08     <link href="css/bootstrap.css" rel="stylesheet">
09     <style>
```

Listing 12.3   **Adding a Dynamic Navigation Item (Continued)**

```
10        body {padding-top: 60px;}
11          #one {height: 600px;padding-top: 60px;}
12          #two {height: 500px;padding-top: 60px;}
13          #three {height: 800px;padding-top: 60px;}
14          #four {height: 500px;padding-top: 60px;}
15      </style>
16      <link href="css/bootstrap-responsive.css" rel="stylesheet">
17
18    </head>
19
20    <body data-spy="scroll">
21
22      <div id="navbar" class="navbar navbar-fixed-top">
23        <div class="navbar-inner">
24          <div class="container">
25            <a class="brand" href="#">Using Scrollspy</a>
26            <ul class="nav">
27              <li><a href="#one">One</a></li>
28              <li><a href="#two">Two</a></li>
29              <li><a href="#three">Three</a></li>
30            </ul>
31          </div>
32        </div>
33      </div>
34
35      <div id="content" class="container">
36        <p>The nav will update the active nav.</p>
37        <p><button id="addButton">Add another</button></p>
38        <div id="one">
39          <p>
40            Section one
41          </p>
42        </div>
43        <div id="two">
44          <p>
45            Section two
46          </p>
47        </div>
48        <div id="three">
49          <p>
50            Section three
51          </p>
52        </div>
53
```

(Continues)

Listing 12.3   **Adding a Dynamic Navigation Item (Continued)**

```
54    </div> <!-- /.container -->
55
56    <script src=
57      "http://code.jquery.com/jquery-1.7.1.min.js">
58    </script>
59    <!--[if lt IE 9]>
60      <script src="js/respond.min.js"></script>
61    <![endif]-->
62    <script src="js/bootstrap-scrollspy.js"></script>
63    <script>
64      $(document).ready(function() {
65        $('#navbar').scrollspy();
66        $("#addButton").click(function() {
67          $('#navbar .nav')
68            .append('<li><a href="#four">Four</a></li>');
69          $('#content')
70            .append('<div id="four"><p>Section four</p></div>');
71          $('[data-spy="scroll"]').each(function () {
72            var $spy = $(this).scrollspy('refresh')
73          });
74        });
75      });
76    </script>
77  </body>
78 </html>
```

Line 20 shows the body element containing an attribute of data-spy="scroll". This attribute must be applied to the area to which the ScrollSpy is going to be applied.

Lines 26–29 show the additional navigation items that are visible in the navigation bar. These are the items that will have styles applied to them based on scrolling location. Each of these items targets an element that is within the main content section of the page. For ScrollSpy to work, these links must be set up.

Lines 35–54 show the content area. These elements have been styled to be large so that you will be able to scroll around and see the nav section change. On line 27 is button that when clicked appends a new navigation item as well as inserts a new div element and refreshes the ScrollSpy plugin.

Line 62 shows the inclusion of the bootstrap-scrollspy.js file that is required for the plugin to work.

Lines 64–75 show the jQuery script that is responsible for adding the button as well as refreshing the plugin. This is done through some simple append() functions as well as a check of the DOM for all elements that contain a data-spy="scroll" attribute, that when found are refreshed.

Something that you might have noticed when you load this example up is a bug that will be fixed in the 2.1 release of Bootstrap: The last navigation item is selected as the active item on page load, but then will change as soon as the page is scrolled past the initial padding added for the menu. You can fix this by adding some jQuery script that removes the active class from the last element and re-applies it to the first, or you can wait for the next release of Bootstrap.

Recipe: Toggling Tabs

Tabs have been in use for several years and are almost a staple on e-commerce sites. These tabs often contain figures, statistics, reviews, features, benefits, pricing, plans, and all sorts of data that is better served when the user requests it rather than just thrown on the page in a jumble.

Listing 12.4 shows the set up for a simple tab group and content area.

Listing 12.4   **Toggle the Active Tab and Content**

```
00  <!DOCTYPE html>
01  <html lang="en">
02    <head>
03      <meta charset="utf-8">
04      <title>Bootstrap - Tab</title>
05      <meta name="viewport"
06        content="width=device-width, initial-scale=1.0">
07
08      <link href="css/bootstrap.css" rel="stylesheet">
09      <style>
10        body {padding-top: 60px;}
11      </style>
12      <link href="css/bootstrap-responsive.css" rel="stylesheet">
13
14    </head>
15
16    <body>
17
18      <div id="navbar" class="navbar navbar-fixed-top">
19        <div class="navbar-inner">
20          <div class="container">
21            <a class="brand" href="#">Using Tab</a>
22          </div>
23        </div>
24      </div>
25
26      <div id="content" class="container">
27        <p>Use the tabs below to switch displayed content</p>
28        <ul class="nav nav-tabs">
29          <li class="active">
30            <a href="#features" data-toggle="tab">Features</a>
```

(Continues)

Listing 12.4   **Toggle the Active Tab and Content (Continued)**

```
31          </li>
32          <li>
33            <a href="#specs" data-toggle="tab">Specifications</a>
34          </li>
35          <li>
36            <a href="#reviews" data-toggle="tab">Reviews</a>
37          </li>
38        </ul>
39
40        <div class="tab-content">
41          <div class="tab-pane active" id="features">
42            Featured content is shown here
43          </div>
44          <div class="tab-pane" id="specs">
45            Specification content is shown here
46          </div>
47          <div class="tab-pane" id="reviews">
48            Review content is shown here
49          </div>
50        </div>
51
52      </div> <!-- /.container -->
53
54      <script src=
55        "http://code.jquery.com/jquery-1.7.1.min.js">
56      </script>
57      <!--[if lt IE 9]>
58        <script src="js/respond.min.js"></script>
59      <![endif]-->
60      <script src="js/bootstrap-tab.js"></script>
61    </body>
62 </html>
```

Lines 28–38 show the tabs section which is created by using a `ul` element as the container, with `li` elements as the individual tabs. The `data-toggle="tab"` attribute that is inside of the link elements informs the plugin that these will be used as the tabs. The `href` attribute is then used to point to what will be used as the content area.

Lines 40–50 show the container for all of the tab content. Each one of the content areas is wrapped in a separate `div` with an id. The `tab-pane` class is applied for styling; the `active` class is the one responsible for allowing the `div` to be visible.

Line 60 shows the reference to the required bootstrap-tab.js file that makes the tab magic happen.

Recipe: Adding Tooltips

Occasionally, you might need to define a term on your Web site, pack a little extra description into some keywords, or add some text to an image-only navigation section. This is a perfect time to use the tooltip plugin.

Listing 12.5 demonstrates a paragraph of text with some links that are being used to display tooltips.

Listing 12.5   **Displaying Information by Using a Tooltip**

```
00 <!DOCTYPE html>
01 <html lang="en">
02   <head>
03     <meta charset="utf-8">
04     <title>Bootstrap - Tooltip</title>
05     <meta name="viewport"
06       content="width=device-width, initial-scale=1.0">
07
08     <link href="css/bootstrap.css" rel="stylesheet">
09     <style>
10       body {padding-top: 60px;}
11     </style>
12     <link href="css/bootstrap-responsive.css" rel="stylesheet">
13
14   </head>
15
16   <body>
17
18     <div id="navbar" class="navbar navbar-fixed-top">
19       <div class="navbar-inner">
20         <div class="container">
21           <a class="brand" href="#">Using Tooltip</a>
22         </div>
23       </div>
24     </div>
25
26     <div id="content" class="container">
27
28       <p>Tooltip has been applied below; hover to see it.</p>
29       <p>
30         Every once in a while you may have some text that requires
31         a little extra description.  Or perhaps a keyword that
32         needs further
33         <a href="#" rel="tooltip"
34           title="Your tooltip text goes here">
```

(Continues)

Listing 12.5   **Displaying Information by Using a Tooltip (Continued)**

```
35          explanation</a>. For more than text in a tooltip, you should
36          look at
37          <a href="#" rel="tooltip" title="We'll cover popovers soon">
38          popovers</a>. A delay has been set on these tooltips so they
39          will stay visible for 600ms after you move your mouse from
40          them.
41        </p>
42
43      </div> <!-- /.container -->
44
45      <script src=
46        "http://code.jquery.com/jquery-1.7.1.min.js">
47      </script>
48      <!--[if lt IE 9]>
49        <script src="js/respond.min.js"></script>
50      <![endif]-->
51      <script src="js/bootstrap-tooltip.js"></script>
52      <script>
53        $(document).ready(function() {
54          $("#content a").tooltip({delay:{show: 300, hide: 600}});
55        });
56      </script>
57    </body>
58  </html>
```

Tooltips are fairly straightforward: All you need to do is add `rel="tooltip"` and put the text you want to appear in the tooltip in the `title` attribute. Lines 33 and 34, as well as line 37, show an a element with the required attributes to create the tooltip.

You will need to include the bootstrap-tooltip.js file (shown on line 51) as well as initialize the tooltip by using a selector and calling the `tooltip()` function.

Line 54 shows the `tooltip()` function being called and also having some options passed to it that adjust the display timing of the tooltip. Using the `delay` option, you can pass a show and hide option that will set the timing for your tooltip. This is based on the selector, so if you wanted to make some tooltips appear faster or remain on the screen longer than others, you can do so by using a different selector and passing different options to it.

Keep in mind that tooltips are not for displaying large amounts of data or content; they are used to simply add a larger definition or description.

Recipe: Adding a Popover

A popover is kind of a mix between a modal and a tooltip. It displays on hover like a tooltip, but it can contain extra content like a modal. These are useful when you want to include extra formatting, or when you want a popover to stand out.

Listing 12.6 shows a simple example of using a popover.

Listing 12.6   **Show Data in a Popover**

```
00 <!DOCTYPE html>
01 <html lang="en">
02   <head>
03     <meta charset="utf-8">
04     <title>Bootstrap - Popover</title>
05     <meta name="viewport"
06       content="width=device-width, initial-scale=1.0">
07
08     <link href="css/bootstrap.css" rel="stylesheet">
09     <style>
10       body {padding-top: 60px;}
11     </style>
12     <link href="css/bootstrap-responsive.css" rel="stylesheet">
13
14   </head>
15
16   <body>
17
18     <div id="navbar" class="navbar navbar-fixed-top">
19       <div class="navbar-inner">
20         <div class="container">
21           <a class="brand" href="#">Using Popover</a>
22         </div>
23       </div>
24     </div>
25
26     <div id="content" class="container">
27
28       <p>
29         Although a popover is like a tooltip, it has more content.
30       </p>
31       <p>
32         Learn more about
33         <a href="#"
34           rel="popover"
35           data-content="I enjoy front-end development using jQuery"
36           data-original-title="About me">
37         me</a>
38       </p>
39
40     </div> <!-- /.container -->
41
```

(Continues)

Listing 12.6   **Show Data in a Popover (Continued)**

```
42     <script src=
43       "http://code.jquery.com/jquery-1.7.1.min.js">
44     </script>
45     <!--[if lt IE 9]>
46       <script src="js/respond.min.js"></script>
47     <![endif]-->
48     <script src="js/bootstrap-tooltip.js"></script>
49     <script src="js/bootstrap-popover.js"></script>
50     <script>
51       $(document).ready(function() {
52         $('#content a').popover({placement: 'bottom'});
53       });
54     </script>
55   </body>
56 </html>
```

Adding a popover is nearly as easy as adding a tooltip. The difference lies in the link found on lines 33–37. In this element, you can see that three attributes have been added: `rel="popover"`, `data-content`, and `data-original-title`. The `rel` attribute informs the plugin that this link should be handled as a popover. The data-attributes are used to populate the content that will be displayed in the popover. The `data-content` attribute is used to display text in the content portion of the popover, whereas the `data-original-title` is used to add a headline or title to the popover.

The last thing to note is lines 48 and 49, where you can see that both bootstrap-tooltip .js and bootstrap-popover.js have been included. The popover requires that the tooltip plugin be included.

Recipe: Alerting the User

Usually, when I hear about an alert, I think of a browser-generated window that is typically the sign of old-school debugging or of super-annoying Web sites that in reality want to install some malware. An alert, in the Bootstrap sense, is much more acceptable and useful. Alerts are used as sections of content that appear which can give information and can easily be dismissed. Another way you could think about them is a modal that is displayed on the page rather than above it and taking focus.

Listing 12.7 presents an example of displaying an alert with Bootstrap.

Listing 12.7   **Using a Button to Display an Alert**

```
00 <!DOCTYPE html>
01 <html lang="en">
02   <head>
03     <meta charset="utf-8">
```

Listing 12.7 **Using a Button to Display an Alert (Continued)**

```
04      <title>Bootstrap - alert</title>
05      <meta name="viewport"
06        content="width=device-width, initial-scale=1.0">
07
08      <link href="css/bootstrap.css" rel="stylesheet">
09      <style>
10        body {padding-top: 60px;}
11      </style>
12      <link href="css/bootstrap-responsive.css" rel="stylesheet">
13
14    </head>
15
16    <body>
17
18      <div id="navbar" class="navbar navbar-fixed-top">
19        <div class="navbar-inner">
20          <div class="container">
21            <a class="brand" href="#">Using Alert</a>
22          </div>
23        </div>
24      </div>
25
26      <div id="content" class="container">
27
28        <p>Click the button below to display an alert</p>
29        <button id="btnAlert">Display the alert!</button>
30
31      </div> <!-- /.container -->
32
33      <script src=
34        "http://code.jquery.com/jquery-1.7.1.min.js">
35      </script>
36      <!--[if lt IE 9]>
37        <script src="js/respond.min.js"></script>
38      <![endif]-->
39      <script src="js/bootstrap-alert.js"></script>
40      <script>
41        $(document).ready(function() {
42          $('#btnAlert').click(function() {
43            $('#content').prepend(
44                '<div class="alert fade in">'+
45                '<button class="close" data-dismiss="alert">'+
46                '&times;'+
47                '</button>'+
```

(Continues)

Listing 12.7   **Using a Button to Display an Alert (Continued)**

```
48                 '<h3>You triggered the alert!</h3>'+
49                 '<p>Good job, now close it</p>'+
50                 '</div>'
51             );
52           });
53         });
54     </script>
55   </body>
56 </html>
```

The alert in this example is easy to set up because the bulk of the code is contained in the jQuery script at the bottom of the page. There is a button on line 29 that, when clicked, will add an alert to the page. You can click it multiple times, and multiple alerts will be displayed on the page. This is due to the `click()` used on line 42.

Within the `click()`, you can see that code is prepended to the `div` element with an ID of `content`. The added code contains a `div` of class `alert`, `fade`, and `in`. These classes help style and give functionality to the alert. A button is also included with a class of `close` for styling, and more important, contains an attribute of `data-dismiss="alert"`, which means that it will be used to remove the alert. The `h3` and `p` elements on lines 48 and 49 are displayed in the alert container. You can use other elements if you want, but I recommend avoiding `h1` and `h2` elements unless you are using custom styles because they really throw off the visual balance of the alert container.

Recipe: Button Control

Unless you have played with Bootstrap before, you might be thinking that a button is really only great for submitting forms or triggering events. Bootstrap injects extra life and usability into buttons. You can group them, use them as *stateful* buttons, and even use them as toggles.

Listing 12.8 demonstrates using a button as a toggle and using several buttons grouped together by using check box functionality.

Listing 12.8   **Toggling Styles with Buttons**

```
00 <!DOCTYPE html>
01 <html lang="en">
02   <head>
03     <meta charset="utf-8">
04     <title>Bootstrap - button</title>
05     <meta name="viewport"
06       content="width=device-width, initial-scale=1.0">
07
08     <link href="css/bootstrap.css" rel="stylesheet">
09     <style>
```

Listing 12.8   **Toggling Styles with Buttons (Continued)**

```
10        body {padding-top: 60px;}
11        #textBox {margin: 10px 0;}
12        #textToggle {margin: 5px;}
13      </style>
14      <link href="css/bootstrap-responsive.css" rel="stylesheet">
15
16    </head>
17
18    <body>
19
20      <div id="navbar" class="navbar navbar-fixed-top">
21        <div class="navbar-inner">
22          <div class="container">
23            <a class="brand" href="#">Using Button</a>
24          </div>
25        </div>
26      </div>
27
28      <div id="content" class="container">
29        <p>Use the button below to toggle page styles</p>
30        <button id="btnToggle" class="btn btn-primary"
31            data-toggle="button">Toggle</button>
32        <div id="textBox">
33          <p>Use the buttons below to change the text</p>
34          <div id="textToggle">Sample Text</div>
35          <div class="btn-group" data-toggle="buttons-checkbox">
36            <button id="bold" class="btn btn-inverse">
37              Bold
38            </button>
39            <button id="emph" class="btn btn-inverse">
40              Emphasis
41            </button>
42            <button id="underline" class="btn btn-inverse">
43              Underline
44            </button>
45          </div>
46        </div>
47      </div> <!-- /.container -->
48
49      <script src=
50        "http://code.jquery.com/jquery-1.7.1.min.js">
51      </script>
52      <!--[if lt IE 9]>
53        <script src="js/respond.min.js"></script>
54      <![endif]-->
```

(Continues)

Listing 12.8   **Toggling Styles with Buttons (Continued)**

```
55    <script src="js/bootstrap-button.js"></script>
56    <script>
57      $(document).ready(function() {
58        $('#btnToggle').click(function() {
59          $(this).hasClass("active") ?
60            $("body").css({background:"#fff", color:"#000"}) :
61            $("body").css({background:"#000", color:"#fff"});
62        });
63        $('#bold').click(function() {
64          $(this).hasClass("active") ?
65            $("#textToggle").css("font-weight", "normal") :
66            $("#textToggle").css("font-weight", "bold");
67        });
68        $('#emph').click(function() {
69          $(this).hasClass("active") ?
70            $("#textToggle").css("font-style", "normal") :
71            $("#textToggle").css("font-style", "italic");
72        });
73        $('#underline').click(function() {
74          $(this).hasClass("active") ?
75            $("#textToggle").css("text-decoration", "none") :
76            $("#textToggle").css("text-decoration", "underline");
77        });
78      });
79    </script>
80  </body>
81 </html>
```

The first thing to look at is the button on line 30. Here, you can see that some classes have been applied for style and an attribute of `data-toggle="button"` has been added. This gives the button toggle capability.

Line 35 shows a `div` element with a class applied for styling as well as a `data-toggle="buttons-checkbox"` attribute. This attribute informs the plugin to treat the buttons contained within with check box functionality along with grouping them together. Inside of the `div` container there several buttons with IDs that will be used for selectors and classes that are used for styling them.

The button plugin will automatically add the active class to any button that is depressed. Line 55 shows the include for the bootstrap-button.js file, which is required for the plugin to work.

Lines 57–78 show the block of jQuery script that we are using to make the buttons do things when clicked. You can see in this block that we are setting up some click methods that are used to check the element they are bound to for the `active` class. Whether or not the `active` class is found, they will change various styles.

Recipe: Collapsing Content

Collapsible content is content that is originally hidden but expands when needed.
Whether this is for a FAQ page or the shopping cart of an e-commerce site for which
areas expand as you need them, you might run into a need for collapsible content.

Listing 12.9 demonstrates the use of collapsible content in a simple question and
answer style. It also gives an example of standard and accordion-style collapsible content.

Listing 12.9   **A Simple Question and Answer Page**

```
00 <!DOCTYPE html>
01 <html lang="en">
02   <head>
03     <meta charset="utf-8">
04     <title>Bootstrap - collapse</title>
05     <meta name="viewport"
06       content="width=device-width, initial-scale=1.0">
07
08     <link href="css/bootstrap.css" rel="stylesheet">
09     <style>
10       body {padding-top: 60px;}
11     </style>
12     <link href="css/bootstrap-responsive.css" rel="stylesheet">
13   </head>
14
15   <body>
16
17     <div id="navbar" class="navbar navbar-fixed-top">
18       <div class="navbar-inner">
19         <div class="container">
20           <a class="brand" href="#">Using Collapse</a>
21         </div>
22       </div>
23     </div>
24
25     <div id="content" class="container">
26
27       <p>Click on a question below to see the answer</p>
28
29       <a class="accordion-toggle"
30          data-toggle="collapse"
31          href="#faqOne">1. Where can I use this?</a>
32       <div id="faqOne" class="collapse">
33         You can use collapse anywhere you have content that you
34         want to either be shown or hidden on click.
35       </div>
```

(Continues)

Listing 12.9   **A Simple Question and Answer Page (Continued)**

```
36      <a class="accordion-toggle"
37         data-toggle="collapse"
38         href="#faqTwo">2. What if I wanted to use a button?</a>
39      <div id="faqTwo" class="collapse">
40        If you mean as the toggle, then you can absolutely use a
41        button for the toggle mechanism.
42      </div>
43      <a class="accordion-toggle"
44         data-toggle="collapse"
45         href="#faqThree">3. What about as an accordion?</a>
46      <div id="faqThree" class="collapse">
47        This section does not use an accordion, but the section
48        below does.
49      </div>
50
51      <p> </p>
52
53      <div id="accordion">
54        <div class="accordion-group">
55          <div class="accordion-heading">
56            <a class="accordion-toggle" data-toggle="collapse"
57               data-parent="#accordion" href="#aContent1">
58              Accordion Link 1
59            </a>
60          </div>
61          <div id="aContent1" class="accordion-body collapse">
62            <div class="accordion-inner">
63              Accordions are great for large amounts of
64              content or for making sure that the focus
65              stays in one area
66            </div>
67          </div>
68        </div>
69        <div class="accordion-group">
70          <div class="accordion-heading">
71            <a class="accordion-toggle" data-toggle="collapse"
72               data-parent="#accordion" href="#aContent2">
73              Accordion Link 2
74            </a>
75          </div>
76          <div id="aContent2" class="accordion-body collapse">
77            <div class="accordion-inner">
78              You are free to style the accordions however you
79              would like. In this example, we are leaning on
```

Listing 12.9   **A Simple Question and Answer Page (Continued)**

```
80                    the default Bootstrap style classes.
81              </div>
82            </div>
83          </div>
84        </div>
85
86    </div> <!-- /.container -->
87
88    <script src=
89      "http://code.jquery.com/jquery-1.7.1.min.js">
90    </script>
91    <!--[if lt IE 9]>
92      <script src="js/respond.min.js"></script>
93    <![endif]-->
94    <script src="js/bootstrap-collapse.js"></script>
95  </body>
96 </html>
```

Lines 29–49 show the markup used to build the standard collapsible sections. This is done by using an a element with a class of `accordion-toggle`, an attribute of `data-toggle="collapse"`, and then the `href` attribute with the value pointing at the container that should be expanded when clicked. The content that will be shown when the link is clicked should contain a class of `collapse`. Failure to add that class will result in odd click behavior and show/hide problems for the section.

Lines 53–85 show the code for the accordion section. This starts out with a `div` element that wraps all of the collapsible content. The `id` of the `div` is important because it will be referenced by each of the items in the accordion.

Line 54 shows another container `div` of class `accordion-group`. Inside of this `div` are two more `div` elements: One is used for the displayed heading and the other contains the content that is shown when the heading is clicked.

Line 56 shows an a element of class `accordion-toggle`, an attribute of `data-toggle="collapse"`, an attribute of `data-parent="#accordion"`, and an `href` attribute that points to the content area that should expand when clicked. The value of `data-parent` should reference the containing `div` element, which in this case is the `div` element that starts on line 53.

Line 61 shows a collapsible content `div` that has some classes applied for styling. It wraps around another `div` that contains the text that becomes visible when the accordion is active.

This structure is repeated from lines 69–83 to create a second collapsible structure that will be part of the accordion.

Line 94 contains the reference to the required bootstrap-collapse.js file.

Recipe: Putting Content in a Carousel

It seems like every site today has either an image gallery in which you can see a product from different angles, or a social image service. No matter what you are doing with images, when you need to build either a slide show or a content carousel, the Bootstrap carousel is a plugin that is here to help.

Listing 12.10 shows a simple three–image carousel, with captions for each image.

Listing 12.10   **A Simple Image Gallery with Captions**

```
00  <!DOCTYPE html>
01  <html lang="en">
02    <head>
03      <meta charset="utf-8">
04      <title>Bootstrap - carousel</title>
05      <meta name="viewport"
06        content="width=device-width, initial-scale=1.0">
07
08      <link href="css/bootstrap.css" rel="stylesheet">
09      <style>
10        body {padding-top: 60px;}
11      </style>
12      <link href="css/bootstrap-responsive.css" rel="stylesheet">
13
14    </head>
15
16    <body>
17
18      <div id="navbar" class="navbar navbar-fixed-top">
19        <div class="navbar-inner">
20          <div class="container">
21            <a class="brand" href="#">Using Carousel</a>
22          </div>
23        </div>
24      </div>
25
26      <div id="content" class="container">
27
28        <div class="row">
29
30          <div class="span3 columns">
31            <p>The carousel will pause when hovered on.</p>
32            <p>
33              If you do not include bootstrap-transition.js
34              your images will not slide and will jump from one
35              to the next.
36            </p>
```

Listing 12.10   **A Simple Image Gallery with Captions (Continued)**

```
37             <p>
38               IE users will not get the nice sliding transition,
39               they will get the image jump.
40             </p>
41           </div><!-- /.span3 -->
42
43           <div class="span9 columns">
44             <div id="myCarousel" class="carousel slide">
45               <div class="carousel-inner">
46                 <div class="active item">
47                   <img src="img/tiltshift.jpg" alt="an image" />
48                   <div class="carousel-caption">
49                     <h4>Developer Roundup!</h4>
50                     <p>
51                       Who knew that 'keynote' actually means 'corral'.
52                     </p>
53                   </div>
54                 </div>
55                 <div class="item">
56                   <img src="img/soccer.jpg" alt="Playing Soccer" />
57                   <div class="carousel-caption">
58                     <h4>Adventures in Soccer</h4>
59                     <p>
60                       Discover fresh cut grass and bunch-ball.
61                     </p>
62                   </div>
63                 </div>
64                 <div class="item">
65                   <img src="img/ducky.jpg" alt="Rubber Ducky" />
66                   <div class="carousel-caption">
67                     <h4>The Rubber Ducky</h4>
68                     <p>
69                       Never underestimate the power of a rubber duck.
70                     </p>
71                   </div>
72                 </div>
73               </div>
74               <a class="carousel-control left"
75                  href="#myCarousel" data-slide="prev">&lsaquo;</a>
76               <a class="carousel-control right"
77                  href="#myCarousel" data-slide="next">&rsaquo;</a>
78             </div><!-- /#myCarousel -->
79           </div><!-- /.span9 -->
80
```

(Continues)

Listing 12.10   **A Simple Image Gallery with Captions (Continued)**

```
81        </div><!-- /.row -->
82
83      </div> <!-- /.container -->
84
85      <script src=
86        "http://code.jquery.com/jquery-1.7.1.min.js">
87      </script>
88      <!--[if lt IE 9]>
89        <script src="js/respond.min.js"></script>
90      <![endif]-->
91      <script src="js/bootstrap-transition.js"></script>
92      <script src="js/bootstrap-carousel.js"></script>
93      <script>
94        $(document).ready(function() {
95          $('#myCarousel').carousel();
96        });
97      </script>
98    </body>
99  </html>
```

Lines 44–78 show the carousel `div` container. This will be used as a selector for the plugin to run on.

Lines 46, 55, and 64 show the container `div` elements that will hold the images and caption text for the carousel. They all have the class of `item` applied, but the first one has an additional class of `active`. Whichever `div` has the `active` class will be the one shown on page load.

Lines 48, 57, and 66 show a `div` element of class `carousel-caption`. This does exactly what you think; it styles the text to be at the bottom of the picture on a transparent background (if the browser supports this) with white text. If you are using the Bootstrap styles, you will want to use an `h4` element for the caption title or else you will need to add some custom styles to fix the text size and color.

The a elements on lines 74–77 are used to add direction arrows to the carousel. They are specified through the use of the `data-slide` attribute.

Line 91 shows the reference to bootstrap-transition.js, which is an animation library that causes the carousel to "slide." If you opt to skip this file, then your carousel will behave in all browsers like it does in any version of Internet Explorer prior to version 9; that is, it will skip directly from one image to the next (how boring!).

Line 92 shows the reference to the required bootstrap-carousel.js file. Line 95 shows the required jQuery script that enables the plugin. You can see that the container has been selected and the `carousel()` function is called on it.

Recipe: Using typeahead for Autocomplete

The last recipe for Bootstrap is for the typeahead plugin. You can use this excellent plugin to populate a data-attribute with data that can be used to help simplify text entry. You see this behavior on your favorite search engine, when it tries to guess what you are typing so that you can simply select from the list instead of typing out the entire phrase.

Listing 12.11 gives a demonstration of the typeahead plugin working with a text input field.

Listing 12.11   **Adding Autocomplete to a Text Input**

```
00 <!DOCTYPE html>
01 <html lang="en">
02   <head>
03     <meta charset="utf-8">
04     <title>Bootstrap - typeahead</title>
05     <meta name="viewport"
06       content="width=device-width, initial-scale=1.0">
07
08     <link href="css/bootstrap.css" rel="stylesheet">
09     <style>
10       body {padding-top: 60px;}
11     </style>
12     <link href="css/bootstrap-responsive.css" rel="stylesheet">
13
14   </head>
15
16   <body>
17
18     <div id="navbar" class="navbar navbar-fixed-top">
19       <div class="navbar-inner">
20         <div class="container">
21           <a class="brand" href="#">Using Typeahead</a>
22         </div>
23       </div>
24     </div>
25
26     <div id="content" class="container">
27
28       <p>People</p>
29       <input type="text"  id="people"
30           data-provide="typeahead"
31           data-items="5" />
32
33     </div> <!-- /.container -->
34
```

(Continues)

```
35     <script src=
36       "http://code.jquery.com/jquery-1.7.1.min.js">
37     </script>
38     <!--[if lt IE 9]>
39       <script src="js/respond.min.js"></script>
40     <![endif]-->
41     <script src="js/bootstrap-typeahead.js"></script>
42     <script>
43       $(document).ready(function() {
44         var names = ["Aaron","Adam","Adrian","Anna","Becky","Ben",
45         "Bert","Carmen","Cathrine","Cedric","Cort","Dan","Darcy",
46         "Doug","Ed","Ella","Elliot","Frank","Fred","Fiona",
47         "Gabriele","Gary","Gerard","Hayden","Holli","Homer","Jeff",
48         "Jenny","Jon","Jules","Kimberly","Kirby","Kurt","Lance",
49         "Lenny","Lindsay","Mark","Marshall","Molly","Neal","Ned",
50         "Nicki","Otis","Omar","Olive","Phil","Piper","Porter",
51         "Ray","Reagan","Rhett","Rick","Sam","Samantha","Santiago",
52         "Sid","Tamara","Tony","Tristan","Tyrell","Vanessa",
53         "Victor","Wendy","Wesley","Will","Xavier","Xuan","Yevette",
54         "Yolanda","Zack","Zoe"];
55         $('#people').data('source', names);
56       });
57     </script>
58   </body>
59 </html>
```

Starting with line 29, you can see a text input that contains attributes of `data-provide="typeahead"` and `data-items="5"`. The `data-provide` attribute is used to instruct the plugin that this input should be used. The `data-items` attribute controls how many suggestions the typeahead plugin will display. By default, this number is 8, but you can see that it has been limited to 5.

Although you could add another attribute called `data-source` and populate it with data, in this example, we are going to load the data in by using jQuery to give you an idea of loading data that could be passed in dynamically.

Lines 44–54 show the creation of a variable called `names`. This variable is a simple array that has been loaded with names. Line 55 shows a selector for the text input (from line 29 which has the attribute of `id=people`) and is then using the `data()` function to insert and populate the `data-source` attribute with the `names` variable.

Summary

This chapter showed you that there are options and plugins that are made by third parties that can be included in your projects and that they can be as simple as drag and drop, or as complex as working with dynamic data.

You saw 11 plugins from the Twitter Bootstrap framework and at least one way to implement each one. You also learned that there are many plugins available on the Internet, but you might not want to use or trust them all.

If you enjoyed working with Bootstrap, check out the official documentation and everything it brings to the table by visiting http://twitter.github.com/bootstrap/.

Index

D

Adriaan de Jonge
Phil Dutson

Covers
jQuery 1.6.4
and 1.7,
with Tips for
1.8

jQuery, jQuery UI, and jQuery Mobile

Recipes and Examples

Developer's Library

FREE
Online Edition

Safari
Books Online

Your purchase of *jQuery, jQuery UI, and jQuery Mobile: Recipes and Examples* includes access to a free online edition for 45 days through the **Safari Books Online** subscription service. Nearly every Addison-Wesley Professional book is available online through **Safari Books Online**, along with over thousands of books and videos from publishers such as Cisco Press, Exam Cram, IBM Press, O'Reilly Media, Prentice Hall, Que, Sams, and VMware Press.

Safari Books Online is a digital library providing searchable, on-demand access to thousands of technology, digital media, and professional development books and videos from leading publishers. With one monthly or yearly subscription price, you get unlimited access to learning tools and information on topics including mobile app and software development, tips and tricks on using your favorite gadgets, networking, project management, graphic design, and much more.

Activate your FREE Online Edition at
informit.com/safarifree

STEP 1: Enter the coupon code: DOIZQZG.

STEP 2: New Safari users, complete the brief registration form.
Safari subscribers, just log in.

If you have difficulty registering on Safari or accessing the online edition,
please e-mail customer-service@safaribooksonline.com